T0295938

The Green Economy Transition in Europe

The Green Economy Transition in Europe

Strategies, Regulations, and Instruments

Edited by
Altuğ Günar and Çağatay Başarır

LEXINGTON BOOKS
Lanham • Boulder • New York • London

Published by Lexington Books
An imprint of The Rowman & Littlefield Publishing Group, Inc.
4501 Forbes Boulevard, Suite 200, Lanham, Maryland 20706
www.rowman.com

86-90 Paul Street, London EC2A 4NE

British Library Cataloguing in Publication Information Available

Library of Congress Cataloging-in-Publication Data

Names: Günar, Altuğ, 1985- editor. | Basarir, Cagatay, 1980- editor.
Title: The green economy transition in Europe : strategies, regulations, and instruments / edited by Altuğ Günar and Çağatay Başarır.
Description: Lanham : Lexington Books, [2024] | Includes bibliographical references and index.
Identifiers: LCCN 2024004557 (print) | LCCN 2024004558 (ebook) | ISBN 9781666947458 (cloth) | ISBN 9781666947465 (epub)
Subjects: LCSH: Clean energy—Europe. | Europe—Economic policy—21st century. | Economic development—Environmental aspects—Europe. | Green technology—Europe.
Classification: LCC HD9502.5.C542 G734 2024 (print) | LCC HD9502.5.C542 (ebook) | DDC 333.79/4094—dc23/eng/20240205
LC record available at https://lccn.loc.gov/2024004557
LC ebook record available at https://lccn.loc.gov/2024004558

Contents

List of Figures

ILLUSTRATIONS

FIGURES

List of Tables

Introduction

The green economy and finance have gained importance in the last decade after climate change and developments. The European Union, member states and Europe closely follow the policy tools and instruments of green finance and economics, which consider preserving world biology and nature as the main objective, instead of the traditional development policies and industrial production followed in the past. Contrary to conventional production and development methods, most countries have implemented green finance and economic policies in the context of sustainability, protection of nature, and production through sustainable resources. In the European Union, green financial and economic practices have gained momentum in the last decade (remember the Lisbon Strategy in 2000). In particular, the "Green Deal" prepared by the European Commission aims to transform the European Union economy into a sustainable economic system, and resources can be used much more efficiently. It is planned that there will be no greenhouse gas emissions by 2050, and economic growth will be separated from resource use. At the same time, the actions foreseen in the Green Deal, which is accepted as a strategy for getting out of the European economy from the COVID-19 pandemic/crisis, are expected to be financed by the NextGenerationEU Recovery Plan, which has a budget of **1.8 trillion euros**. The study examines the current green economic and financial practices, strategies and regulations in Europe, the European Union and its member states. The EU's current green economic policies, instruments and procedures will be discussed and analysed in this context. The study seeks to answer the question: "Did climate change and the unsustainability of fossil resources initiate the green transformation in Europe in finance and economy, and how were the tools, policies and regulations used for this shaped?" Although the green economy has gained importance in the last two decades, few studies are specific to Europe. Existing studies have examined a few EU member states or EU policies regarding the green economy. Our study differs from other studies with an interdisciplinary approach, focusing in detail on green economic transition and transformation issues in Europe and the European Union. It has a comprehensive and divergent approach to addressing green economics, financial practices, strategies and policies. There are studies on the economic and political transformation process initiated by the European Union under the guidance of the EU Green Deal. However, most studies examine the issue through the European Union Green Deal and its financing. The point is that the European Union sees the global transformation, called green transformation, as a transition and approaches the issue differently. From this point of view, it is challenging to find a study that deals with the subject comprehensively.

After war broke out between Ukraine and Russia, the dependence of European countries on energy in terms of economy and energy has been seriously discussed, and an atmosphere of crisis has emerged. In this respect, the realisation of the green deal targets, Europe's transition plan to green and sustainable energy, is in danger. In the European Union, the energy issue, especially green energy and the economic transition, will be discussed for many years. While the European Union was hurrying to achieve green targets, its dependence on old energy sources continued. As a result of the war, the European Union wants to stick to green targets to end the reliance on Russia in terms of energy, which paves the way for green discussions. The war started a vital transformation for Europe. It revealed the necessity for transition and how the energy issue could become a robust national interest and a diplomatic coercive tool.

In the first chapter of the study, Pınar Koç evaluates the connection between environmental innovation, economic growth and environmental degradation. In the second chapter, Salih Ziya Kutlu and Tahir Anıl Güngördü investigate the vital question of energy transformation and resource sufficiency. In the next chapter, Çağatay Başarır and Altuğ Günar touch on the green transition process of the European Union regarding economy, politics and energy. In their work, they discuss the challenges the EU will face in the green transition and the tools created to overcome them. İhsan Erdem Kayral and Baki Rıza Balcı make an excellent econometric evaluation of the European Union energy market in the context of the European Energy index volatility in the shadow of the Ukraine and Russia war in chapter four.

In the fifth chapter, Samet Zenginoğlu and Ferhat Apaydın shed light on the European Green Deal in the dichotomy of nature efficiency. The sixth chapter, by Kaan Çelikok and Gülden Poyraz, highlights the role of green bonds in the EU economy and their transformational roles in sustainability. In the next chapter, Arzu Alvan highlights the importance of the digital green economy and green finance regarding the issue of sustainability. In the light of her final findings, she asserts that "organisations are encouraged to prioritise the development of ethical and environmentally friendly digital solutions."

In the eighth chapter, Seher Suluk and Serdar Öztürk present an assessment of G7 countries and analyse the relationship between environmental pollution and sustainable development for G7 countries. In their opinion, "to protect the health of all living things and the environment, it is important and necessary to seriously develop and implement policies and strategies to prevent environmental pollution. For this reason, G7 countries should attach more importance to actualising and implementing environmentally friendly policies and practices." Next, İbrahim Tanju Akyol attracts attention to global governance regarding sustainable development. In addition, Alper Çakmak and M. İnanç Özekmekçi provide a remarkable analysis of the impact of green movements and green political parties on EU/European politics. While Sina Kısacık and Arzu Alvan, in their chapter on how the European Union will implement its green policies amidst the Ukraine-Russia war and its actions towards the energy crisis, conclude that Europe now and in the future demands a rational and clear internal/external energy policy, it needs to act and speak in consensus to avoid condemnation for its "economic greatness but political dwarfism." Otherwise, the current and future goals of decarbonisation and drastically reduced energy dependence within the framework of the Green Energy Agreement cannot be achieved. In the following chapter, Kendal Deniz and Erdal Eroğlu elaborate on the green tax practices and regulations in the European Union and Türkiye. Their comparative analysis reaches a vital conclusion that underlines the differences between the two tax systems. In the next chapter, Omca Altın tries to compare and analyse the harmonisation of Türkiye's European Union Green Deal. In the next chapter, Didem Öztürk Günar analyses the green transition process of the European Investment Bank, the green instruments created by the bank and the role of the investment bank in achieving the objectives envisaged in the Green Deal and establishing a climate-friendly economic model for the European Union. She argues that transforming the investment bank into a climate bank in the EU's fight against climate change and the green transition process is a globally unique initiative. Eventually, Nahit Bek highlights the relationship between global warming, climate change, drought and forest fires.

Moreover, it is worth noting that there is an external review process in all chapters of this book. We'd like to thank all the authors and researchers who are experts in this field for their diligent work, and we hope that we can assist our readers. We would also like to thank the external reviewers for their expertise and contributions to our book. With our last phrase, we'd also like to thank everyone who inspires us and the authors with their patience and support during the conduct of these valuable works.

Our respect,

Editors
Assoc. Prof. Dr. Çağatay Başarır
Assoc. Prof. Altuğ Günar

The Analysis of the Nexus of Environmental Innovations, Economic Growth, and Environmental Degradations

Pınar Koç

INTRODUCTION

The Industrial Revolution, which accelerated with the contributions of scientific and technological developments, caused significant changes in production and consumption patterns and changed social life significantly. The production revolution, which started with the Industrial Revolution, had a positive effect on the economic development process and brought important environmental problems. With the Industrial Revolution, meeting the growing energy demand worldwide by using nonrenewable energy sources is one of the most important causes of environmental problems (Yang et al., 2021).

Fossil fuels have a large carbon component and thus intensive use of fossil fuels causes significant deterioration in the ecosystem by increasing carbon emissions. The increase in carbon emissions leads to acid rain and water pollution by rising air pollution. Second, extraction of fossil fuels leads to deterioration in soil quality and an increase in environmental pollution. Third, an increase in carbon emissions triggers global warming, disturbing the gas balance in the atmosphere (Gani, 2021). Also, climate changes that occur due to global warming have recently caused flooding and a rise in respiratory diseases. In the report titled "Limits to Growth" published in 1972, it is emphasised that if the production model based on fossil fuels continues to be implemented, environmental degradation may increase and the risk of resource depletion may be faced. This report marked the starting point of the transition process to sustainable development policies (Colombo, 2001). It was the first international activity on environmental problems. With this

Declaration, environmental problems began to be discussed at the international level. The World Conservation Strategy (WCS) was organised in 1980. The main goals of the WCS are as follows (IUCN, 1980);

• Protecting basic ecological processes and life support systems on which human survival and development depend,
• Providing the necessary breeding programs for the protection and development of genetic diversity and cultural plants, and using the necessary safe scientific and technical resources,
• Receiving the support of large industrial organisations as well as rural communities to ensure sustainable use of ecosystems.

In 1985, the Vienna Convention was signed. The main aim of the Vienna Convention is to protect the ozone layer. In 1987, the Montreal Protocol was accepted. The principal purpose of the Montreal Protocol is to restrict ozone-depleting anthropogenic substances on the basis of a multilateral agreement (Weiss, 2009).

The concept of sustainable development was described for the first time in the report titled "Our Common Future" prepared in 1987 as *"development that meets the needs of the present without compromising the ability of future generations to meet their needs"* (Bonnedahl et al., 2022). The report examines environmental problems and offers solutions. In 1989, the Multilateral Fund was organised. Its basic objective is to ensure the implementation of the Montreal Protocol. In 1992, the United Nations Conference on Environment and Development (Rio Conference–Agenda 21) was held. The Rio Declaration was accepted and the conventions on climate change, biological diversity, forest principles, and desertification were signed. In 1993, the Commission on Sustainable Development was established (Kaasa, 2007). In 1994, the International Conference on Population and Development was held. In this conference, it was stated that human health, human rights, and the empowerment of women are important for sustainable development (United Nations, 1995). In 1996, the United Nations Conference on Human Settlements: Habitat II was held. This conference addresses the importance of human settlements for sustainable development and Rio+5 was organised in 1997. The main goals of this conference are as follows (Drexhage and Murphy, 2010):

• Identify issues that are important and successful in the implementation of sustainable development,
• Support local and national sustainability against the negative consequences of economic globalisation.

Since 2000, the scope of sustainable development has been expanded. In 2000, the UN Millennium Summit was held and the new millennium's goals were determined. The principal objectives are as follows (United Nations, 2000):

- Eradicating absolute poverty and hunger,
- Ensuring everyone receives a basic education,
- Empowering women and decreasing gender inequality,
- Decreasing child mortality,
- Improving maternal health,
- Fighting infectious diseases such as HIV/AIDS,
- Providing environmental sustainability,
- Developing global partnerships for development.

With the 2002–Johannesburg Summit (Rio+10), the process of implementing the decisions taken at the Rio Conference in 1992 was evaluated. In 2005, the Kyoto Protocol started to be implemented to reduce carbon emissions that cause global warming. In addition, the UN Economic and Social Commission for Asia and the Pacific Ministerial Declaration on Green Growth was accepted. The green growth model was first presented as a new sustainable low-carbon model in Asian countries (United Nations Economic and Social Council, 2005). With the adoption of this model, new green economy policies such as the EU Environment Action Programme and six actions for green growth in China in 2006, the official presentation of green growth on international platforms in 2007, and the transition program to low-carbon green growth in South Korea in 2008 were adopted. These programs include green economy policies focusing on renewable energy.

In 2009, OECD Green Growth Declaration was adopted. The objective is to develop a Green Growth Strategy, bringing together economic, environmental, social, technological, and development aspects into a comprehensive framework (OECD–Summary, 2011a). In 2010, the World Urban Forum (WUF) was organised. The main topic for WUF is to address how to tackle rapid urbanisation and its impact on the poor (OECD–Summary, 2011a). In 2011, OECD Green Growth Indicators were determined. The principal aim is to follow the development of the green economy (OECD–Monitoring Progress, 2011b). In 2012, the Rio+20 Summit was held and a final document named "The Future We Want" was adopted as a roadmap for development (United Nations, 2012). In 2015, New York–Sustainable Development Summit was organised. Sustainable development goals replaced the Millennium Development Goals and they expanded. Sustainable development goals are as follows (United Nations, 2015):

- Eradicating poverty and hunger,
- Ensuring good health and well-being,
- Increasing the quality of education,
- Providing gender equality and decreasing inequalities,
- Meeting clean water and sanitation,
- Supporting the use of affordable and clean energy,
- Promoting decent work and economic growth,
- Developing industry, innovation and infrastructure,
- Building sustainable cities and societies,
- Strengthening institutions,
- Providing peace and justice,
- Saving life underwater and on land,
- Increasing partnerships for the goals,
- Tackling climate change.

In 2019, Social Good and SDG Summits were held. What can be done to combat the negative impacts of climate change was discussed in the Social Good Summit. The political declaration emphasising the need to accelerate activities for the achievement of sustainable development goals was adopted in the SDG Summit. In 2021, SDG Moment was organised. SDG aims to accelerate the transition process to sustainable development and to demonstrate how close we are to reaching the 2030 goals (United Nations, 2021).

Renewable energy sources are important for achieving sustainable development goals. Renewable energy investments and the use of technologies with low-carbon emissions have grown significantly in recent years worldwide. Figure 1.1 gives the change in global energy investments and fossil fuels during 2015–2023.

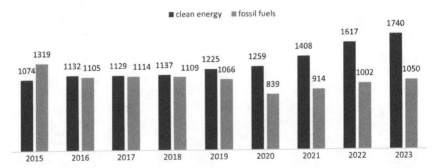

Figure 1.1   Global Energy Investment in Clean Energy and in Fossil Fuels, 2015–2023 (Billion USD 2022). *Source*: Created by authors via the dataset obtained from the IEA database.0

When figure 1.1 is examined, it is seen that clean energy investments are increasing while fossil fuels are decreasing until 2020. But it is also observed that there has been a slight increase in nonrenewable energy investments after 2015. Global clean energy investment realised as $1,740 billion with a 62.01-percentage point increase. The energy crisis that occurred after the COVID-19 pandemic has increased the rate of clean energy investment. Despite the growth in renewable energy investments, the share of nonrenewable energy consumption in total final energy consumption still exceeds 70 percent. Figure 1.2 illustrates the share of world total energy consumption by source in 1973 and 2019.

According to figure 1.2, while the share of oil in total energy consumption was 48 percent in 1973, this ratio occurred as 40 percent with an 8-percentage point decrease. Oil is still the most widely used energy source.

Environmental innovations are important to achieve the expected sustainable development goals with the green economy model based on low-carbon emissions. This study investigates the impact of environmental innovations on the validity of the EKC Hypothesis in G7 countries.

ENVIRONMENTAL KUZNETS CURVE

Kuznet (1955) examined the connection between economic development and income inequality; he concluded that the greater the economic development, the higher the income inequality in the initial stage. In later stages, as economic development improves, income inequality decreases. This finding means that there is an inverted U-shaped nexus between economic

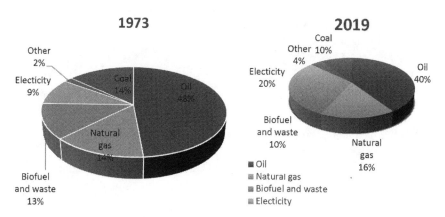

Figure 1.2   Share of World Total Energy Consumption by Source in 1973 and 2019. *Source*: Created by authors via the dataset obtained from the IEA database.

development and income inequality. Grossman and Krueger (1991) examined the connection between GDP (gross domestic product) and environmental degradation and they concluded that there is an inverted U-shaped relationship between national income and environmental degradation similar to the Kuznets Curve. This nexus between economic development and environmental degradation is referred to in the literature as the Environmental Kuznets Curve Hypothesis. The results obtained from this study can be explained by four different factors. The first of these factors is the scale effect. With economic development, production increases. Growth in production triggers environmental pollution by increasing the use of natural resources as well as carbon emissions. Another factor is called composition impact. The initial stage of economic development covers the process of the transition from agriculture to industry. The growth in the share of the industry in total production led to an increase in environmental deterioration. With the knowledge era, the economic structure shifted from industry to the services sector, and thus, environmental degradation decreased. The other impact is the income elasticity of environmental quality. As income rises, the life quality of the societies also improves and environmental sensitivity develops. Increasing environmental awareness helps to reduce environmental degradation. The last effect is the technological effect. Initially, meeting with nonrenewable energy sources energy demand caused an increase in environmental deterioration (Tsurumi and Managi, 2010).

Environmental Kuznets Curve can be formulated as follows;

$$Y_t = \beta_0 + \beta_1 X_t + \beta_2 X_t^2 + \varepsilon_t \qquad (1)$$

Where Y_t represents environmental degradation, while X_t demonstrates national income level. X_t^2 indicates the square of national income. Signs and statistically significant parameters determine whether EKC Hypothesis is valid or not.

1) $\beta_1 = \beta_2 = 0$, EKC is not valid.

2) $\beta_1 > 0$ *and* $\beta_2 = 0$, EKC is not valid. There is a positive relationship between environmental degradation and national income.

3) $\beta_1 < 0$ *and* $\beta_2 = 0$, EKC is not valid. There is a negative nexus between environmental degradation and economic development.

4) $\beta_1 > 0$ *and* $\beta_2 < 0$, EKC is valid. There is an inverted-U-shaped relationship between environmental degradation and economic growth.

5) $\beta_1 \langle 0$ *and* $\beta_2 \rangle 0$, EKC is not valid. There is a U-shaped connection between environmental degradation and economic growth.

If EKC Hypothesis is valid, the turning point of Environmental Kuznets Curve $\left(X^* \right)$ equals $-\dfrac{\beta_1}{2\beta_2}$

ECONOMETRIC MODEL

This study examines the impact of environmental innovations on the validity of the EKC in G7 countries for the period of 1990–2019. In the study, ecological footprint per capita demonstrates environmental degradation and it is the dependent variable of the model. GDP per capita, GDP per capita squared, and environmental innovations are independent variables of the model. The number of environmental patents shows environmental innovations. In the study *lnef*, *lninnov*, and *lngdp* represent environmental degradations, technological innovations and, GDP per capita, respectively.

Methodology

Westerlund and Edgerton (2008) panel cointegration test with structural breaks was applied to the effect of environmental innovations on the validity of the Environmental Kuznets Curve. In the literature, there is a large number of panel cointegration tests. Kao (1999) and Pedroni (1999, 2004) are some of these tests. Such tests do not take into account problems such as cross-section dependency and heterogeneous slope. Westerlund (2007) and Gengenbach et al. (2015) panel cointegration tests consider cross-section dependency and heterogeneous slope, but do not take into account structural breaks. Unlike these other tests, Westerlund and Edgerton (2008) panel cointegration tests take into account the heterogeneous slope parameters, cross-section dependency, and structural breaks. Test equation is formulated as follows:

$$y_{it} = A_i + \mu_i t + \alpha_i D_{it} + x_{it}' B_i + \left(D_{it} x_{it} \right)' b_i + \varepsilon_{1it} \qquad (2)$$

Where i and t represent cross-section units and time, respectively, x_{it} donates the set of independent variables. D_{it} is a dummy variable representing structural breaks and ε_{1it} is the error term. The null hypothesis indicates that there is no cointegration between variables. If it can be rejected, there is cointegration between variables.

Diagnostic Tests

In econometric analyses, diagnostic tests must be applied to select the appropriate method. Cross-section dependency and heterogeneity of coefficients decrease the power of the test. Second, nonstationary series can cause spurious regression problems. Therefore, first, cross-section dependency, heterogeneity of coefficients, and the stationarity of panel datasets must be tested. Breusch and Pagan (1980), Pesaran (2004) CD Test, and Pesaran, Ullah, and Yamagata (2008) tests are used to test cross-section dependency. Breusch and Pagan LM test can apply if the time dimension of panel data is greater than the cross-section dimension. However, Pesaran CD test can be used for panel datasets where time dimension is smaller than cross-section dimension. NLM test developed by Pesaran, Ullah, and Yamagata can be applied when time dimension and cross-section dimension are bigger.

Breusch and Pagan LM test is appropriate for this study because the cross-section dimension is smaller than the time dimension. Pesaran and Yamagata (2008) homogeneity test was employed to test the heterogeneity of coefficients. Table 1.1 illustrates the results of cross-section dependency, homogeneity, and unit root test.

According to table 1.1, panel dataset includes cross-section dependency, and slope coefficients are heterogeneous. The cointegration test can be applied if all series are I(1). Therefore, FPKPSS unit root test developed by Nazlıoğlu and Karul (2017) was employed to test the stationarity of the series. According to the results of the FPKPSS unit root test, series are stationary at first differences.

Table 1.1   Cross-Section Dependency, Homogeneity, and FPKPSS Unit Root Test

	Breusch & Pagan Test	
Variables	*LM stat*	*Prob*
lnef	274.14	0.000
lninnov	592.47	0.000
lngdp	439.99	0.000
lngdp²	498.34	0.000
	Pesaran & Yamagata Homogeneity Test	
Homogeneity Statistics	*Test stat*	*Prob*
Δ	11.758	0.000
Δ_{adj}	12.881	0.000

	FPKPSS Unit Root Test			
	Level		*First Difference*	
Variables	*Test stat (k=1)*	*Prob*	*Test stat (k=1)*	*Prob*
lnef	8.762	0.000	1.664	0.480
lngdp	4.482	0.000	1.011	0.707
lngdp²	4.459	0.000	1.09	0.161
lninnov	2.326	0.010	1.22	0.111

Source: Author's calculations

Table 1.2　Westerlund and Edgerton (2008) Panel Cointegration Test

Model	Z_τ	Prob	Z_ϕ	Prob
No Shift	1.162	0.877	1.733	0.958
Level Shift	−1.403	0.080***	−2.044	0.066***
Regime Shift	−0.552	0.291	−0.364	0.358

	Structural Break Dates	
Countries	Level Shifts	Regime Shifts
USA	1993	1993
England	2008	2007
Italy	1992	2016
France	2016	2016
Japan	1995	2010
Canada	2008	2008
Germany	2009	1993

Source: Author's calculations

ESTIMATION RESULTS

The findings indicate that Westerlund and Edgerton (2008) panel cointegration test is correct for this study. Table 1.2 illustrates the results of Westerlund and Edgerton panel cointegration test. There is a cointegration relationship between environmental degradation, national income, and national income squared.

DOLSMG estimator was employed to estimate the cointegration coefficient. Table 1.3 illustrates estimated cointegration coefficients. According to table 1.3, the findings vary from country to country.

EKC Hypothesis is valid for only Japan. There is a U-shaped relationship between environmental degradation and economic growth in France and Germany. Environmental innovation has a negative impact on environmental degradation in USA and Canada while they affect environmental degradation. According to G7 group statistics, EKC Hypothesis is not valid for G7 countries.

CONCLUSION AND POLICY IMPLICATIONS

Growing global energy demand due to traditional economic development policies and meeting global energy demand through nonrenewable energy sources led to important problems. Nonrenewable energy sources such as natural gas, oil, and coal consist of carbon elements; intensive use of them led to increased carbon emissions by disturbing the gas balance in the atmosphere. Increasing carbon emissions triggers environmental degradation. In this

Table 1.3   DOLSMG Estimators

Countries	lnGDP	lnGDP²	lninnov	EKC Hypothesis
USA	0.160	−0.049	−0.577*	Not valid
England	3.605	−0.002	1.055*	Not valid
Italy	4.525	−0.170	0.648*	Not valid
France	−53.03*	2.502*	0.277*	Not valid (U-shaped)
Japan	87.32*	−4.181*	2.828*	Valid
Canada	−12.03**	0.583**	−0.399**	Not valid (U-shaped)
Germany	45.23	−2.098	−0.932	Not valid
Panel	10.83	−0.48	0.508	Not valid

Source: Author's calculations

context, the EKC Hypothesis plays an important role in the environmental economy. Global warming and growing pollution have revealed the need for global studies to protect the environment. The green economy model that has been put forward recently is seen as a solution to reduce the negative effects of global warming. In this context, alternative solutions such as the use of energy-efficient technologies, increasing renewable energy investments, and zero-waste policies have been developed. The validity of environmental degradation can be used to measure green economy policies. The results of the study show that the EKC Hypothesis is not valid for G7 countries. Environmental degradations have a negative impact on environmental degradation in the USA and Canada. Environmental innovations are statistically insignificant in Germany. They affect environmental degradation in other G7 countries such as England, Italy, and France. There is a U-shaped connection between environmental degradation and economic development. These findings can be explained by the heavy use of nonrenewable energy sources. The share of nonrenewable energy in total final energy consumption is still over 70 percent, although renewable energy investments have increased significantly. Supporting the use of green technologies, increasing environmental sensitivity, and developing environmentally friendly new energy sources is important to decrease the negative impact of global warming.

REFERENCES

Bonnedahl, K. Johan, Pasi Heikkurinen, and Jouni Paavola. 2022. Strongly Sustainable Development Goals: Overcoming Distances Constraining Responsible Action. *Environmental Science & Policy* 129:150–158.

Breusch, Trevor, and Adrian Pagan. 1980. The Lagrange Multiplier Test and its Applications to Model Specification in Econometrics. *Review of Economic Studies* 47:239–253.

Colombo, Umberto. 2001. The Club of Rome and Sustainable Development. *Futures* 33(1):7–11.

Drexhage, John, and Deborah Murphy. 2010. Sustainable Development: From Brundtland to Rio 2012. Background Paper Prepared for Consideration by the High Level Panel on Global Sustainability at Its First Meeting, 19 September 2010, UN Headquarters, New York.

Fukuda-Parr, Sakiko. 2016. From The Millennium Development Goals to the Sustainable Development Goals: Shifts İn Purpose, Concept, and Politics of Global Goal-Setting for Development. *Gender & Development* 24:43–52.

Gani, Azmat. 2021. Fossil Fuel Energy and Environmental Performance in an Extended STIRPAT Model. *Journal of Cleaner Production* 297. https://doi.org/10.1016/j.jclepro.2021.126526

Gengenbach, Christian, Jean-Pierre Urbain, and Joakim Westerlund. 2015. Error Correction Testing in Panels with Common Stochastic Trends. *Journal of Applied Econometrics* 13(6):982–1004.

Grossman, Gene M., and Alan B. Krueger. 1991. Environmental Impacts of a North American Free Trade Agreement. National Bureau of Economic Research Working Paper No. 3194. Cambridge, MA: NBER. https://doi.org/10.3386/w3914

IUCN, 1980. World Conservation Strategy Living Resource Conservation for Sustainable Development. International Union for Conservation of Nature and Natural Resources (IUCN), with United Nations Environment Programme (UNEP) and World Wildlife Fund (WWF). https://portals.iucn.org/library/efiles/documents/WCS-004.pdf

Kaasa, Stine Madland. 2007. The UN Commission on Sustainable Development: Which Mechanisms Explain Its Accomplishments? *Global Environmental Politics* 7(3):107–129.

Kao, Chihwa. 1999. Spurious Regression and Residual-Based Tests for Cointegration in Panel Data. *Journal of Econometrics* 90:1–44.

Kuznets, Simon. 1955. Economic Growth and Income Inequality. *American Economic Review* 45(1): 1–28.

Nazlıoğlu, Şaban, and Çağin Karul. 2017. A Panel Stationarity Test with Gradual Structural Shifts: Re-Investigate the International Commodity Price Shocks. *Economic Modelling* 61(C):181–192.

OECD. 2011a. Towards Green Growth: A Summary for Policy Makers, May 2011. Paris: OECD Report.

———. 2011b. Towards Green Growth: Monitoring Progress, OECD Indicators. https://www.oecd.org/greengrowth/48224574.pdf

Pedroni, Peter. 1999. Critical Values for Cointegration Tests in Heterogeneous Panels with Multiple Regressors. *Oxford Bulletin of Economics and Statistics* 61:653–670.

———. 2004. Panel Cointegration: Asymptotic and Finite Sample Properties of Pooled Time Series Tests with an Application to Ppp Hypothesis. *Econometric Theory* 20(3):597–625.

Pesaran, M. Hashem. 2004. General Diagnostic Tests for Cross-Section Dependence in Panels. IZA Discussion Paper No. 1240, IZA Institute of Labor Economics.

https://www.iza.org/publications/dp/1240/general-diagnostic-tests-for-cross-sec-tion-dependence-in-panels

Pesaran, Mohammad, and Takashi Yamagata. 2008. Testing Slope Homogeneity in Large Panels. *Journal of Econometrics* 142:50–93.

Pesaran, Mohammad, Aman Ullah, and Takashi Yamagata. 2008. A Bias-Adjusted LM Test of Error Cross-Section Independence. *Econometrics Journal* 11(1):105–127.

Tsurumi, Tetsuya, and Shunsuke Managi. 2010. Decomposition of the Environmental Kuznets Curve: Scale, Technique, and Composition Effects. *Environmental Economics and Policy Studies* 11:19–36.

UN-Habitat. 2010. Evaluation of the Fifth Session of the World Urban Forum. Final Report. UN-Habitat For A Better Urban Future. https://unhabitat.org/evaluation-of-the-fifth-session-of-the-world-urban-forum-2010

United Nations. 1995. Report of the International Conference on Population and Development. Cairo, 5–13 September 1994. https://www.unfpa.org/sites/default/files/event-pdf/icpd_eng_2.pdf

———. 2000. Millennium Summit, 6–8 September 2000, New York. https://www.un.org/en/conferences/environment/newyork2000

———. 2012. Report of the United Nations Conference on Sustainable Development, Rio+20. Rio de Janeiro, Brazil, 20–22 June 2012. https://sustainabledevelopment.un.org/rio20 United Nations. 2021. SDG Moment 2021. https://www.un.org/sustainabledevelopment/sdg-moment-2021/

United Nations Economic and Social Council. 2005. Draft Ministerial Declaration on Environment and Development in Asia and the Pacific, 2005. https://www.unescap.org/sites/default/d8files/SOMCED5_4E_Ministerial_Declaration.pdf

Weiss, Edith Brown. 2009. The Vienna Convention for the Protection of the Ozone Layer and the Montreal Protocol on Substances that Deplete the Ozone Layer. Introductory note, Edith Brown Weiss, Francis Cabell Brown Professor of International Law, Georgetown University Law Center. https://legal.un.org/avl/pdf/ha/vcpol/vcpol_e.pdf

Westerlund, Joakim. 2007. Testing for Error Correction in Panel Data. *Oxford Bulletin of Economics and Statistics* 69(6):709–748.

Westerlund, Joakim, and David E. Edgerton. 2008. A Simple Test for Cointegration in Dependent Panels with Structural Breaks. *Oxford Bulletin of Economics and Statistics* 70(5):665–704.

Yang, Jiafeng, Yun Yu, Teng Ma, Cuiguang Zhang, and Quan Wang. 2021. Evolution of Energy and Metal Demand Driven by Industrial Revolutions and its Trend Analysis. *Chinese Journal of Population, Resources and Environment* 19(3):256–264.

2

Transformation of Energy Resources in the European Union

Salih Ziya Kutlu and Tahir Anıl Güngördü

INTRODUCTION

The concept of energy has gained increasing importance from the late eighteenth century until the present day. Particularly since the Industrial Revolution, having access to energy resources has become one of the most significant factors in enhancing a country's economic, political, and military power. In fact, wars have been waged to secure these resources. As a result, countries formulate energy policies to continuously meet their energy needs.

The unequal distribution of energy resources worldwide, the supply-related problems that emerged during the 1973 Oil Crisis, and the dependency on fossil fuels in energy production necessitate countries to develop import- and export-based policies and explore alternative ways to ensure energy security through energy policies, such as renewable sources (Şimşek et al., 2019, 25).

Contemporary worldwide issues like global warming, climate change, rapid population growth, crises in regions rich in commonly used energy resources, and the heavy financial burdens placed on economies due to the cost of acquiring energy resources have turned the concept of energy into a popular topic in international politics. These issues are being addressed through concepts such as sustainable development, energy efficiency, energy security, renewable energy, green energy, etc., and different countries adopt various tools for implementation, including legal regulations, taxation, subsidies, quota restrictions, price regulations, investment incentives, etc. (Shao and Ma, 2022, 449–450).

The purpose of this study is to identify the place and status of renewable energy sources among the energy sources used in the European Union. In this context, the research question of the study is defined as "Is the rate of preference for renewable energy sources sufficient among the energy sources used in the European Union?" The significance of the study lies in presenting the current situation after examining the environmental risks faced by Europe and the problems encountered in energy source supply in the international system.

LITERATURE REVIEW

The sources from which energy is economically obtained are defined as energy sources. These sources can be classified in various ways. Energy sources are primarily classified into nonrenewable and renewable sources based on their usage and convertibility. Nonrenewable and renewable energy sources are grouped according to their usage, and primary and secondary sources based on their convertibility (Koç & Şenel, 2013, 33).

Nonrenewable energy sources consist of fossil fuels and are energy sources that will eventually deplete over time. The most significant drawback of these energy sources is the production of toxic by-products that pollute the world (Nature's Generator, 2023, 1). Nonrenewable sources are further divided into fossil and nuclear sources. Fossil sources include coal, oil, and natural gas, while the term nuclear is used for energy derived from uranium and thorium (Koç & Şenel, 2013, 33). Renewable energy, on the other hand, refers to the energy obtained from natural resources that renew at a rate higher than their consumption (UN, 2023, 1).

Renewable energy sources include solar, wave, wind, hydraulic, biomass, geothermal, and hydrogen. In combatting environmental problems today, renewable energy sources are the most commonly used. The classification based on convertibility is designed as primary and secondary sources. Accordingly, primary sources comprise coal, oil, gas, nuclear, hydraulic, wind, solar, biomass, and wave energies. Secondary sources encompass electricity, gasoline, diesel, air gas, LPG, coke, and petcoke. The primary energy sources in the classification based on convertibility are those that have not undergone any intervention or transformation. Secondary energy sources are the result of interventions in primary sources (Koç et al., 2018, 88).

Over the last fifty years, a transformation in the use of energy sources worldwide can be observed (figure 2.1). The weight of nonrenewable sources such as coal and oil in energy and electricity production has decreased, while renewable energy sources and environmentally less harmful sources like natural gas have become more preferred.

When examining the graph figure 2.1, it is evident that the share of renewable sources in electricity production globally has steadily increased and reached 26.49 percent in 2019, despite minor fluctuations over the last two decades. During the same period, the use of nonrenewable energy sources, specifically oil, declined to 2.77 percent. However, coal remains the most

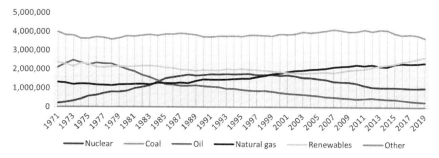

Figure 2.1 World Electricity Generation Mix by Fuel, 1971–2019. *Source*: International Energy Agency, World Energy Balances

widely used source for electricity production globally, with a share of 36.81 percent in 2019. These data indicate that though the desired progress is yet to be achieved, renewable sources are increasingly preferred due to reasons such as energy security and the environment.

PRINCIPLES OF THE EUROPEAN UNION'S ENERGY POLICY

The issue of energy security is addressed in Union texts under three different headings: measures to prevent oil crises, diversification, and transportation processes (EC, 1995, 22). Additionally, rationalising demand without compromising social and economic objectives can also be considered among the principles (Dursun, 2011, 53). Since the mid-2000s, sustainable development and competitiveness have also become fundamental tenets (Sencar et al., 2014, 117).

Another significant aspect that the European Union prioritises in organising energy policies is taxation practices. Through taxation, the focus is on improving energy efficiency and reducing greenhouse gas emissions within the scope of energy policies, aiming to ensure common energy security and protect the Union's natural environment (Türkeş and Kılıç, 2004, 9). Within this context, competitiveness and sustainability principles are among the targets of EU energy policies within the approach of taxation (Zajaczkowska, 2018, 320).

The environmental principles guiding the European Union's energy policies are identified as combatting climate change and global warming within the framework of reducing negative impacts (Vavrek and Chovancová, 2020, 2). Therefore, when it comes to EU energy policies, it is possible to mention the existence of many principles; while some revolve around preserving energy supply and reorganising it within a real-political framework, others emerge in the context of universal objectives such as environmental protection.

Energy Single Market

Establishing a common energy market is one of the European Union's most important objectives. In this context, the strategy is defined as the full integration of an internal energy market (Vanham et al., 2019, 1). The EU common market process in the field of energy, which began in the 1980s, and the liberalisation of this market has posed exceptional challenges due to differences in attitudes among member countries (Uslu, 2004, 163). In 1996, with its directive on the establishment of the "electricity internal market," the Union took the first step. According to the directive, all member states were obliged to make necessary administrative regulations by February 1999 and transfer electricity markets to the private sector to make them competitive (EC, 1996a, 29).

In 1998, the gas directive titled "Concerning Common Rules for the Internal Market in Natural Gas" declared the aim of establishing a competitive energy internal market with reference to the principle of the free movement of goods and services. The document encompasses the gradual establishment of an internal market in natural gas and the integration of all infrastructural systems so that they can be interconnected (EC, 1998, 1).

In 2003, the directive "Establishing a Scheme for Greenhouse Gas Emission Allowance Trading within the Community" designed an emission trading system, which was put into effect in 2005. This initiative, which aims to restrict greenhouse gas emissions, is considered both a move towards a common market and progress in environmental protection efforts (EC, 2003, 32). Another method that the European Union has particularly strengthened in the context of achieving a common market during the pandemic is based on a negotiation process called "ex-ante governance." According to this governance version, member states negotiate within the Union to align their regulation and commitments on energy and climate policies before accepting them in their national parliaments. In this way, the Union aligns its energy goals with national objectives (Misik and Oravcova, 2022, 9).

Energy Security

The security of energy supply is evaluated in the context of stock procurement, coordination during crisis moments, and reducing the costs associated with the measures taken. However, like many other concepts, it is also accused of being ambiguous. In the aftermath of World War II, energy security covered the supply of oil for military institutions, but over the years, the concept has evolved and been used in connection with the possibility of scarcity of fossil fuel reserves (Kovacic and Felice, 2019, 159). Therefore, the concept is broadly understood, and the possibility of an energy interruption due to EU energy dependence and the risk of sudden price changes are evaluated within the framework of energy security. Proposed solutions include reducing energy demand, utilising domestic resources, opting for renewable energy, and diversification.

The measures to prevent oil crises, which are among the first topics related to energy security, are formed by considering these crises as both short and long-term risk factors. Particular emphasis is placed on the significance of oil as a crucial input in the transportation sector (EC, 1995, 22). The European Union describes the security of energy supply as an important factor in reducing import dependence and thereby ensuring price stability within the market (Pacesila et al., 2016, 157).

Diversification, which can be considered as a subheading of energy security, involves making energy use options—such as banning the use of fuel oil for electricity production under certain conditions—more flexible through various directives (EC, 1995, 24). It is also an approach that includes the diversification of supply sources (Kovacic and Felice, 2019, 165). Therefore, diversification can play a decisive role in energy policy concerning the change of any supply source for any reason and its impact on the types of fuels used.

ENERGY POLICIES IN THE EUROPEAN UNION

The roots of the European Union's energy policies can be traced back to the 1951 Paris Treaty, which established the European Coal and Steel Community (ECSC). The emphasis on coal in the organisation's name directly relates to energy. However, the first significant step came with the 1957 Rome Treaty, which established the European Atomic Energy Community (EURATOM). EURATOM focused on joint nuclear power development and increased cooperation in the energy sector. Nuclear energy was utilised to address the energy deficit on the European continent (Cotella et al., 2016, 14). During this period, the responsibility for petroleum, natural gas, and electricity markets was assigned to EURATOM (Yorkan, 2009, 25). However, nuclear energy was treated exceptionally, and member states were encouraged, like the Community, to make various regulations (Dursun, 2011, 37). As a result, even in the late 2010s, EU energy policy was largely conducted by member states, and nongovernmental organisations were largely excluded from the system, which has been a subject of criticism (Haas, 2019, 69).

In 1962, ideas about a common energy policy and the free movement of energy within the Union were discussed in various working groups, but concrete steps to implement this vision were not taken due to the relatively low cost of petroleum as an input at that time (Sancar, 1992, 24). In the 1970s, EU energy policies were marked by oil crises. Following the first oil crisis in 1973, a policy document that emphasised environmental issues, titled "Concerning a New Energy Policy Strategy for the Community," was put into effect in 1974. The document highlighted the fundamental vision of energy policies as "secure and lasting supply under satisfactory economic conditions." Strategies to be implemented by 1985 were declared within the framework of the strategy document. These strategies mainly focused on limiting the increase rate of domestic consumption without jeopardising economic growth and ensuring secure nuclear energy production (EC, 1974, 1). Therefore, EU energy policies were largely shaped by the tendency to unite arising from the instability of fossil fuel prices (Flamos et al., 2011, 424).

Although the year 1973 saw a shift from fossil fuels towards nuclear energy, it also brought the global prominence of renewable energy sources (Toke. 2011, 65). Especially after the nuclear accident in Chernobyl in 1986, trust in atomic energy rapidly decreased, and the energy topic became inevitably associated with human and environmental health concerns (Cotella et al., 2016, 16).

Following the dissolution of the Soviet Union, the European Union aimed to establish energy cooperation with Eastern European countries through the European Energy Charter. One of the objectives of the agreement was to encompass market-oriented reforms and modernisation of the energy sectors of former Soviet Union member countries (Energy Charter Secretariat, 2016, 93). Within this framework, enhancing energy security, market governance, mutual interdependence, and rule-based market multilateralism principles were prioritised (Maltby, 2013, 438).

The first legal basis for the Union's energy policy was established with the document titled "For a European Union Energy Policy" in 1995. The document suggested competitive energy policies, reducing state economic control and seeking solutions through free market methods. Consequently, the EU approach to energy issues became more liberal after this date. Additionally, principles of supply security and environmental protection were put forward during this process (EC, 1995, 2). In 1996, the document known as "Green Paper," was published. The document criticised the low level of renewable energy use and emphasised the importance of conducting research and development within the community (EC, 1996b, 3).

In the 2000s, particularly due to the changing position of Russia, energy supply for Europe began to be counted among security threats (Maltby, 2013, 238). During this period, obligations arising from the Kyoto Protocol and the "Action Plan to Improve Energy Efficiency in the European Community" were included in EU legislation. While the emphasis on member states' responsibilities regarding energy policies, taxation, and tariff applications was maintained, local considerations such as regional and urban policy-making were integrated into the texts (EC, 2000a, 2). In addition to assigning roles to public authorities, efforts were made to involve the private sector in the process by removing existing barriers hindering the development of the energy market (EC, 2000a, 5).

Another significant energy-related EU legislation in 2000 is the document known as "Towards a European Strategy for the Security of Energy Supply." According to the document, the European Union currently does not have a unified energy policy. Changes in demand structures and environmentally focused taxation were prioritised among the main tools. Sectors that need to be controlled within this framework were highlighted as transportation and construction (EC, 2000b, 4). One of the key emphases in the document was the diversification of supply (Maltby, 2013, 438). Additionally, nuclear energy was considered one of the sources to be utilised at least in the medium term (EC, 2000b, 4).

In 2001, the regulation named "Promotion of Electricity Produced from Renewable Energy Sources in the Internal Electricity Market" emphasised the reiteration of responsibilities under the Kyoto Protocol and the creation of local employment through investments in renewable energy. Member states were assigned various responsibilities concerning renewable energy and, when setting national obligations, the collective commitments made by the Community in Kyoto were also taken into account for the member states (EC, 2001, 33).

The natural gas crisis that emerged between Ukraine and Russia in 2006 marked another turning point in EU energy policies. The impact of this crisis on policies led to a focus on diversifying energy resources (Şimşek et al., 2019, 28). The EU energy policy in the 2000s appears to be largely associated with foreign policy tendencies. Russia and OPEC members supplying energy, other major consumers such as the United States, China, Japan, India, as well as poor countries with limited access to energy at a basic level, were identified as three separate groups of independent political actors (Meritet, 2007, 4771). The political problems in Ukraine in 2014 also posed risks to energy security, and when disputes over gas prices between Russia and the European Union were added, the idea of reducing Russia's share in total gas imports began to shape EU energy policies. The Nabucco pipeline project was initiated in light of these developments (Ibrayeva, 2018, 151). Additionally, the "European Energy Security Strategy" came to the agenda due to the crisis atmosphere following the annexation of Crimea (Hasanov et al., 2020, 1).

In 2007, the document named "An Energy Policy for Europe" attempted to outline a roadmap for the Union's energy policy and emphasised that combatting climate change should also have an impact on import preferences (EC, 2007, 5). This change was interpreted as the first stage of the necessary legislative process to create an internal energy market that would bring effective competition. This was followed by the text titled "Energy Security and Solidarity Action Plan" in 2008. The plan highlights infrastructure incentives, considering the importance of the energy issue in international relations, stock increase, new efficiency practices, and the preference for domestic energy reserves (Bahgat, 2011, 41).

In 2015, the European Union declared the vision of the "Energy Union Framework Strategy." Within this vision, reducing dependence on specific fuel types, energy suppliers, and energy route corridors was emphasised (Zajaczkowska, 2018, 323). The importance of "solidarity and trust" was emphasised, implying the qualities that suppliers should possess (EC, 2015, 2). In 2016, the European Union released a new report titled "Clean Energy for All Europeans," where energy efficiency was included among the Union's strategic objectives (Petrović et al., 2018, 216). The 2019 version of the report highlighted solutions sought through the coordination of public regulatory tools and the private sector. In addition to promoting clean energy, micro-solutions such as smart meters for homes were also suggested (EC, 2019, 12).

In the 2020s, the European Union's energy security seems to be largely dependent on investments in the Mediterranean region, aiming to weaken Russia's monopoly over the energy supply (Ruble, 2017, 351). The EU goals for 2030 appear to be more focused on achieving a low-carbon social formation rather than a radical response to climate change. These goals do not seem to be fully aligned with the expectations of the Paris Agreement and the carbon-neutral efforts outlined in the "European Green Deal" for 2050 (Kulovesi and Oberthür, 2020, 151). In the European Green Deal, the European Union sets a vision of a zero-carbon industry as a target and asserts its ambition to be a leader in the production of clean energy products (EC, 2023, 1). However, there are doubts about the realisation of these ambitions, and it is noted that energy transmission networks and the increasing number of wind turbines are perceived as a risk by local communities, leading to various dissatisfactions. To address this issue, it is emphasised that various citizen participation methods need to be integrated into energy policy decision-making processes (Kamlage and Nanz, 2016, 80).

ENERGY TRANSFORMATION IN
THE EUROPEAN UNION

Due to global warming and climate change, many regions in Europe are at significant risk. Western, Central, and Eastern Europe face threats such as floods, droughts, forest fires, storms, avalanches, etc., and these hazards pose significant challenges for the energy sector in Europe (Ministry of Treasury and Finance, 2019, 6–7). In addition to the current situation, the conflict between Ukraine and the Russian Federation that began in 2022 has further exacerbated the situation for the energy sector. Russia supplied 41 percent of the total natural gas imports of the European Union in 2021. However, Russia's policies threatening the EU partnership and European energy security have prompted the Union to seek alternatives (EC, 2022, 5).

The European Union is working towards creating a common energy policy to ensure the sustainability of the energy sector by integrating member states' energy markets, diversifying energy resources to ensure energy security, and developing infrastructure and renewable energy sources for low-carbon energy (Vladimirov and Özenç, 2017, 7). The main reason for this is the different levels of economic development among EU member countries. Studies have shown that economic and technological development is crucial in transitioning to renewable energy and reducing CO_2 emission rates (Hao, 2023, 55159–55160).

In Europe, more than half of the CO_2 emissions stem from electricity generation, heat production, and road transport. Therefore, reducing CO_2 emission rates, prioritising clean energy sources, and increasing the use of electric energy in transportation are considered important objectives in Europe's energy transition (Institut Montaigne, 2021, 7). To achieve these goals, it is crucial for European countries to have access to secure, sustainable, affordable, and competitive energy. To accomplish this, efforts are being made in five main areas (Eurelectric, 2015, 1):

- Decarbonisation
- Energy efficiency
- Energy security
- Internal energy market
- Research, innovation, and competitiveness.

Energy policies implemented within the European Union encourage the greater use of renewable sources. Figure 2.2 shows the proportion of renewable sources in the total energy production of EU member countries during five-year periods between 2005 and 2020. It can be observed that the share of renewable energy sources has continuously increased in all countries. Among these countries, Sweden has the highest percentage of renewable energy usage at 60.1 percent, while Malta has the lowest at 10.7 percent. Fifteen out of the twenty-seven EU member countries have a proportion of renewable energy use below the EU average.

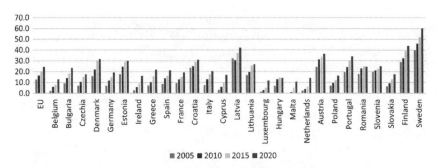

Figure 2.2   Share of Energy from Renewable Sources, 2005–2020. *Source*: Eurostat

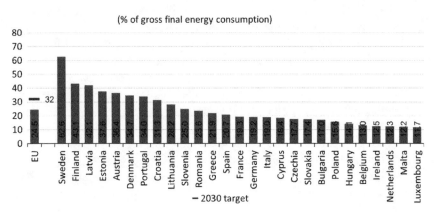

Figure 2.3   Share of Energy from Renewable Sources, 2021. *Source*: Eurostat

Figure 2.3 displays the percentage of renewable energy in the total energy production of EU member countries in 2021. Sweden had the highest rate at 62.6 percent, whereas Luxembourg had the lowest at 11.7 percent. In 2021, a total of seventeen countries fell below the EU average, and seven countries had already reached the 2030 target of 32 percent renewable energy use set by the European Union.

Figure 2.4 presents the source-based classification of EU electricity production in 2022. Fossil fuel-based sources accounted for 38.7 percent, with gas at 19.6 percent, coal at 15.8 percent, oil at 1.6 percent, and other sources at 1.7 percent. Renewable sources contributed 39.4 percent, with wind at 15.9 percent, hydro at 11.3 percent, solar at 7.6 percent, biomass at 4.4 percent, and geothermal at 0.2 percent. Nuclear fuels provided 21.9 percent of the energy production.

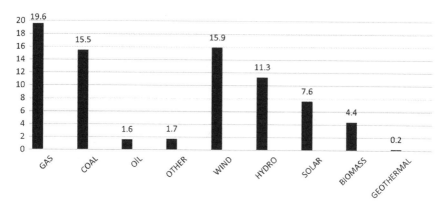

Figure 2.4   Net Electricity Generation in the EU by Fuel Type, 2022. *Source*: European Council, Infographic—How is EU Electricity Produced and Sold?

CONCLUSION

Industrialisation and urbanisation ultimately lead to significant raw material and energy shortages. Following the Second World War, especially after the 1973 Oil Crisis, the European Union had to address the energy issue seriously. Initially, the focus was on sources such as nuclear and renewable energy; however, the subsequent gas relationship it established with Russia had critical implications. The Ukraine crisis necessitated a reevaluation of all energy-related decisions within the European Union. Moreover, the energy policy, influenced by changes in the management paradigm, started to be associated with relatively new concepts such as governance.

Although EU dependence on fossil fuels has shown a decreasing trend over the years, it is challenging to claim that it has achieved sufficient results in combatting climate change. Reliance on coal and natural gas persists. In this context, while the Kyoto Protocol and the 2030 and 2050 visions hold promise for the transformation to renewable energy, the momentum towards such a shift must be increased more resolutely.

Considering the increasing costs of fossil fuels, particularly petroleum, and the awareness that they will be depleted in the long term, it appears inevitable for the European Union to invest in alternative energy production, especially renewable energy. Additionally, in light of past and potential crises with Russia, it will undoubtedly need new methods of energy production, resources, and energy transit routes.

The European Union's level of technological advancement is expected to facilitate the proper organisation of renewable energy and set a good example for other countries. Encouraging the preference for renewable energy sources and exploring the vast market opportunities presented by the twenty-seven countries should be pursued with bolder steps.

REFERENCES

Bahgat, Gawdat. 2011. *Energy Security: An Interdisciplinary Approach.* Wiley.
Cotella, Giancarlo, Silvia Crivello, and Marat Karatayev. 2016. European Union Energy Policy Evolutionary Patterns. In *Low-Carbon Energy Security from a European Perspective*, edited by P. Lombardi and M. Gruning (pp. 13–42). Academic Press.
Dursun, Suat. 2011. *Avrupa Birliği'nin Enerji Politikası ve Türkiye.* Ankara: Ankara Üniversitesi Yayınları.
EC. 1974. Concerning a New Energy Policy Strategy for the Community. *Official Journal of the European Communities.*
EC. 1995. An Energy Policy for the European Union. *Official Journal of the European Communities.*
EC. 1996a. Common Rules for the Internal Market in Electricity. *Official Journal of the European Communities*, s. 20–29.
EC. 1996b. *Energy for the Future: Renewable Sources of Energy.* European Union.
EC. 1998. Concerning Common Rules for the Internal Market in Natural Gas. *Official Journal of the European Communities*, s. 1–12.
EC. 2000a. Action Plan to Improve Energy Efficiency in the European Community. *Official Journal of the European Communities.*
EC. 2000b. Towards a European Strategy for the Security of Energy Supply. *Official Journal of the European Communities.*
EC. 2001. Promotion of Electricity Produced from Renewable Energy Sources in the Internal Electricity Market. *Official Journal of the European Communities.*
EC. 2003. Establishing a Scheme for Greenhouse Gas Emission Allowance Trading within the Community. *Official Journal of the European Union*, s. 32–46.
EC. 2007. An Energy Policy for Europe. *Official Journal of the European Communities.*
EC. 2015. *New Impetus for Coordination and Integration of Energy Policies in the EU.* European Parliamentary Research Service.
EC. 2019. *Clean Energy for All Europeans.* European Union.
EC. 2022. *State of the Energy Union 2022.* Brussels.
EC. 2023. A Green Deal Industrial Plan for the Net-Zero Age. *Official Journal of the European Communities.*
Energy Charter Secretariat. 2016. *The International Energy Charter Consolidated Energy Charter Treaty.* European Union.
Eurelectric. 2015. *A Eurelectric Report, Power Statistics and Trends: The Five Dimensions of the Energy Union*, December.
European Council: Council of the European Union. 2023. *Infographic—How is EU Electricity Produced and Sold?* Accessed July 27, 2023. https://www.consilium

.europa.eu/en/infographics/how-is-eu-electricity-produced-and-sold/#:~:text=In %202022%2C%2039.4%25%20of%20electricity,Coal%3A%2015.8%25

EUROSTAT. n.d. *Renewable Energy Statistics*, accessed July 27, 2023. https://ec .europa.eu/eurostat/statistics-explained/index.php?title=Renewable_energy_statis- tics#Share_of_renewable_energy_more_than_doubled_between_2004_and_2021

Flamos, Alexandros, Panikos Georgallis, H. Doukas, and John Psarras. 2011. Using Biomass to Achieve European Union Energy Targets—A Review of Biomass Status, Potential, and Supporting Policies. *International Journal of Green Energy* 8(4):411–428.

Haas, Tobias. 2019. Struggles in European Union Energy Politics: A Gramscian Perspective on Power in Energy Transitions. *Energy Research & Social Science* (48):66–74.

Hao, Chin Hui. 2023. Does Governance Play Any Role in Energy Transition? Novel Evidence from BRICS Economies. *Environmental Science and Pollution Research* 30(19):55158–55170.

Hasanov, Fakhri J., Ceyhun Mahmudlu, Kaushik Deb, Shamkhal Abilov, and Orkhan Hasanov. 2020. The Role of Azeri Natural Gas in Meeting European Union Energy Security Needs. *Energy Strategy Reviews* 28:100464.

Ibrayeva, Aigerim, Dmitriy V. Sannikov, Marsel A. Kadyrov, Vladimir N. Zape- valov, Elnur L. Hasanov, and Vladimir N. Zuev. 2018. Importance of the Caspian Countries for the European Union Energy Security. *International Journal of Energy Economics and Policy* 8(3):150–159.

Institut Montaigne. 2021. *Europe's Energy Transition: A Common Challenge.* Report: September 2021.

International Energy Agency. 2021. *World Electricity Generation Mix by Fuel, 1971–2019.* Accessed July 27, 2023. https://www.iea.org/data-and-statistics/charts /world-electricity-generation-mix-by-fuel-1971-2019

Kamlage, Jan-Hendrik, and Patrizia Nanz. 2016. Crisis and Participation in the Euro- pean Union: Energy Policy as a Test Bed for a New Politics of Citizen Participa- tion. *Global Society* 31(1):65–82.

Koç, Ali, Hüseyin Yağli, Yıldız Koç, and İrem Uğurlu. 2018. Dünyada ve Türkiye'de Enerji Görünümünün Genel Değerlendirilmesi. *Mühendis ve Makine* 59(692):86–114.

Koç, Erdem, and Mahmut Can Şenel. 2013. Dünyada ve Türkiye'de Enerji Durumu— Genel Değerlendirme. *Mühendis ve Makine* 54(639):32–44.

Kovacic, Zora, and Louisa Jane Di Felice. 2019. Complexity, Uncertainty and Ambi- guity: Implications for European Union Energy Governance. *Energy Research & Social Science* 53:159–169.

Kulovesi, Kati, and Sebastian Oberthür. 2020. Assessing the EU's 2030 Climate and Energy Policy Framework: Incremental Change toward Radical Transfor- mation? *Review of European, Comparative & International Environmental Law* 29(2):151–166.

Maltby, Tomas. 2013. European Union Energy Policy Integration: A Case of Euro- pean Commission Policy Entrepreneurship and Increasing Supranationalism. *Energy Policy* 55:435–444.

Meritet, Sophie. 2007. French Perspectives in the Emerging European Union Energy Policy. *Energy Policy* 35(10):4767–4771.

Ministry of Treasury and Finance. 2019. *Avrupa Birliği İklim Politikaları*. Ankara.

Misik, Matus, and Veronika Oravcova. 2022. Ex Ante Governance in the European Union: Energy and Climate Policy as a "Test Run" for the Post-Pandemic Recovery. *Energy Policy* 167(C):1–14.

Nature's Generator. 2023. *The Difference Between Nonrenewable and Renewable Energy*. Accessed July 27, 2023. https://naturesgenerator.com/blogs/news/the-difference-between-nonrenewable-and-renewable-energy#:~:text=Nonrenewable%20energy%20includes%20fossil%20fuels,will%20deplete%20and%20run%20out

Pacesila, Mihaela, Stefan Gabriel Burcea, and Sofia Elena Colesca. 2016. Analysis of Renewable Energies in European Union. *Renewable and Sustainable Energy Reviews* 56:156–170.

Petrović, Predrag, Sanja Filipović, and Mirjana Radovanović. 2018. Underlying Causal Factors of the European Union Energy Intensity: Econometric Evidence. *Renewable and Sustainable Energy Reviews* 89:216–227.

Ruble, Isabella. 2017. European Union Energy Supply Security: The Benefits of Natural Gas Imports from the Eastern Mediterranean. *Energy Policy* 105:341–353.

Sancar, M. Selçuk. 1992. *Avrupa Topluluğu'nda Enerji Arzı-Çevre Dengesinin Optimizasyonu ve Türkiye'deki Uygulanabilirliği*. Devlet Planlama Teşkilatı.

Sencar, Marko, Viljem Pozeb, and Tina Krope. 2014. Development of EU (European Union) Energy Market Agenda and Security of Supply. *Energy* 77(C):117–124.

Shao, Yu-Tong, and Kevin Sheng-Kai Ma. 2022. Renewable Energy Policies and the Design of Electricity Market for Energy Transition: Benefits, Challenges, and Strategies. *2022 International Conference on Green Energy, Computing and Sustainable Technology (GECOST)*, pp. 446–452.

Şimşek, Beste, İhsan Pençe, Azim Doğuş Tuncer, and Afşin Güngör. 2019. Avrupa Birliği Enerji Politikasında Yenilenebilir Enerji. In *Enerji, Çevre, İktisat Üzerine Güncel Araştırmalar*, edited by A. Güngör, C. Taşdoğan, Ş. Apaydın, M. Ş. Çeşmeli, A. D. Tuncer, İ. Başaran, . . . C. Karaman (pp. 25–33). Akademisyen Kitabevi.

Toke, David. 2011. Ecological Modernisation, Social Movements and Renewable Energy. *Environmental Politics* 20(1):60–77.

Türkeş, Murat, and Gönül Kılıç. 2004. Avrupa Birliği'nin İklim Değişikliği Politikaları ve Önlemleri. Çevre, Bilim ve Teknoloji, *Teknik Dergi* 2:35–52.

United Nations (UN). 2023. *Climate Action: What is Renewable Energy?* Accessed July 27, 2023. https://www.un.org/en/climatechange/what-is-renewable-energy?gclid=Cj0KCQjwiIOmBhDjARIsAP6YhSWnhjRLZ39geqycQRTezgJz6lqzKhsS2Rsbn8xciySdSsa_isG5di0aAkjREALw_wcB

Uslu, Kamil. 2004. Avrupa Birliği'nde Enerji ve Politikaları. *Marmara Üniversitesi İktisadi ve İdari Bilimler Dergisi* 19(1):155–172.

Vanham, Davy, Hrvoje Medarac, Joep F. Schyns, Rick J. Hogeboom, and Davide Magagna. 2019. The Consumptive Water Footprint of the European Union Energy Sector. *Environmental Research Letters* 14(10):104016.

Vavrek, Roman, and Jana Chovancová. 2020. Energy Performance of the European Union Countries in Terms of Reaching the European Energy Union Objectives. *Energies* 13(20):5317.

Vladimirov, Martin, and Bengisu Özenç. 2017. *Daha Güçlü AB-Türkiye Enerji Diyaloğuna Doğru Enerji Güvenliği Perspektifleri ve Riskleri Raporu.*

Yorkan, Arzu. 2009. Avrupa Birliği'nin Enerji Politikası ve Türkiye'ye Etkileri. *Bilge Strateji* 1(1):24–39.

Zajaczkowska, Magdalena. 2018. The Energy Union and European Union Energy Security. *Economics and Law* 17(3):319–328.

Green Transition in Europe

In the Context of Economy, Politics, and Energy Security

Çağatay Başarır and Altuğ Günar

INTRODUCTION

Europe has reached its present level of development by turning the difficulties it faced in the integration process into a success story. Europe was demolished after the Second World War and established peace on the continent by organising itself within the logic of economic integration. Today, the system known as the European Union (EU), which made European peace possible, is facing severe challenges. The war between Ukraine and Russia threatens European peace more than ever. In the last ten years, an anti-EU approach has been on the rise in the member states, seeking to disturb the peace and tranquillity built by its main motto, "In Varietate Concordia,"[1] by nurturing nationalism. The Euro debt crisis has severely damaged European prosperity, and EU competitiveness has suffered. As an alternative approach to counter the consequences of the current economic and political model, the green transition process, as an emerging approach in monetary policy and all other areas, envisages a radical transformation by being effective in all operations from the production model in the economy to policy-making in politics. The European Union began to turn towards increasing green awareness in the 2000s, but it was only with the "Green Deal" adopted by the European Commission in 2020 that it entered its central agenda.

The economic development/planning strategies have been criticised for their broad ten-year scope, and it has even been argued that these strategies cannot be effectively operated or implemented or that they are ineffective.[2] Launched in 2000, the "Lisbon Strategy" was created to make the European Union the most advanced knowledge-based, competitive, and innovation-rich economic block in the world, but due to the convergence and other policy instruments it put forward, the strategy could not go beyond being successful and could not transform the EU system nor prevent the Union from entering an economic and financial crisis in the face of the 2008 financial downfall of the USA.

A comparison between today and the 2000s shows that the international conjuncture was much more peaceful. The radically increased momentum of globalisation in the 2000s was dealt a significant blow by the 2008 crisis. The Lisbon Strategy was unsuccessful, and the European Union could not maintain its competitiveness against its competitors and could not realise its objectives. The EU 2020 strategy, which entered into force in 2010, aims to compensate for the effects and damages of the Euro debt crisis by adopting an economic development model based on innovation and digitalisation by acting with a more comprehensive and thematic structure and highly ambitious goals. Unlike the Lisbon Strategy, the EU 2020 strategy has achieved significant gains. Adopted in 2019, the Green Deal envisaged a radical transformation of the EU fight against climate change, combining a carbon-neutral policy with economic development. The development plan prepared quite comprehensively in the green transition process to be realised with the Green Deal faces difficulties in implementation due to the outbreak of war between Ukraine and Russia.

Today, EU members and European states face significant challenges due to the war between Russia and Ukraine. The COVID-19 pandemic in 2020, the Ukraine-Russia war in 2021, rising global inflation, and energy and food prices have brought the European Union to a turning point. On the other hand, the pressure of increasing innovations on development policy of the states in the world also forces political-economic change towards global structures, such as the European Union. The development of artificial intelligence puts it under pressure at many points, such as the rapid establishment of legal regulations in this field. It is obligatory to change structures, such as nation-states and the European Union, in the direction of evolving artificial intelligence and artificial intelligence-related technologies. In the process referred to as the green transition, it has emerged as a necessity. In addition to EU energy dependence on Russia, realising the activities determined for the Climate Goals is likely possible with an energy-free European Union. The energy shortage/crisis due to the war between Russia and Ukraine and the rapid emergence of a trend towards a return to fossil resources among EU members have concretely demonstrated how fragile the Union is regarding energy. Therefore, the study focuses on EU activities in the so-called green transition. It aims to analyse EU green transition effort/activities first in the economic and political and then in the context of energy, centring on the "Green Deal" adopted by the European Union.

GREEN TRANSITION IN THE WORLD AND
EUROPEAN UNION

The global reaction to climate events was formalised in the 1970s. The climate conference the United Nations (UN) organised was the first international event to preserve the world's natural bio-system. After the UN Conference, although issues such as climate change, sustainability, environmental protection, and effective and efficient use of energy resources have become the priority agendas of states, the failure to establish a global coercive system in this period has resulted in the issue being ignored by states. The increase in climatic events and the placement of environmental awareness on the worldwide agenda was realised with a striking report prepared by a group of scientists and researchers. The *Limits to Growth* report prepared by the Club of Rome revealed that the planet's resources are limited and that growth has limits. With the modelling made by the report, according to the data of 1972, it was concluded that the rapid continuation of industrialisation, resource consumption, pollution, and population growth rate in the world would result in the depletion of the world's resources within 100 years. The report has initiated a global "apocalypse" debate and rapidly began discussions on the environment, sustainable development, resource consumption, population control, and the search for alternative resources. By 2100, the world will lose its current resource capacity and ability to absorb pollution, and severe climate events and environmental destruction will begin globally (Newell, 2019, 79; Meadows et al., 1972, 23; Paterson, 2005, 239).

The striking results of the report put forward by the Club of Rome have begun to influence the planet's resources and economic development strategies globally. At the same time, after the report, studies such as *Blueprint for Survival*, a magazine of British origin, and Schumacher's *Small is Beautiful* initiated global discussions on green, planet, and nature-friendly measures and created a severe awareness that can be called a return to green (Spretnak and Capra, 1985, 163). As the global understanding of the planet's resources, nature, and pollution increased, green alternative movements centred on protecting nature and the environment replaced the accepted development paradigms. First, green theory started to develop, then it permeated economics, politics, and other fields. *The Ecologist* magazine has explained the need for action on the damage to nature globally; that the world needs radical reforms of protecting nature, resource use, and economic development; and that radical measures need to be implemented quickly. Related developments led to the emergence of green movements in Europe in particular, and a world was drawn towards the construction of a new society. Green movements, which penetrate the economy and politics, are based on a philosophical mindset in which self-sufficiency, appropriate technology, decentralisation, and population control are desired to be made effective (Günar, 2021, 244).

Green parties, which have been rising in Europe since the 1970s, are essential in politicising the issue. This rise has strengthened considerably by enabling green parties to become ruling partners all over Europe. However, the difference between the 1970s and today's understanding of politics and development has created the necessity for green parties to determine a political position. Although the number of green parties has increased and they have gained strength, they have to act together to change policies within the coalitions and parties that define themselves as right and left in the current politics (Besley and Persson, 2023, 1902).

When the green transition is defined in the context of the European Union, the concept encompasses a wide range of actions, from combatting climate change to reducing emission rates. The "Green Deal" programme prepared by the European Commission is at the centre of the process. The Green Deal text was accepted as a programme for the transition of the European welfare model to a competitive growth strategy with efficient use of energy resources by preventing climate change and environmental destruction. It was determined as the development strategy of the European Union. The programme, which is quite ambitious in terms of its targets, aims to make Europe climate-neutral by 2050 and includes many initiatives, such as preventing fossil energy pollution by using green technologies and establishing sustainable industries. The green transition, therefore, describes and covers all green transformation processes, including combatting climate change and sustainable development in the EU context (European Commission, 2023).

Economy

The economic disparities between the regions of the EU members could present a severe problem in the realisation of an economic green transformation. In particular, the target of reducing the greenhouse gas emission rate by 55 percent in 2030 compared to 1990 and becoming climate neutral in 2050,[3] which the European Commission adopted in the context of climate action, looks ambitious once the current situation is considered. Once EU members are taken into account on a regional basis, it can be seen that there are profound differences. For this reason, the European Commission has established essential support programmes and green financial instruments for the member states to achieve convergence to the targets set in the "Green Deal." In this context, the NextGenerationEU plan has allocated a budget of 600 billion Euros to achieve the "Green Deal" targets. It is expected that changes will occur in all areas with the decrease in dependence on fossil fuels and the changes in the scope of the green transition process that will appear in the member states. According to the European Commission, energy industries account for the majority of greenhouse gas emissions in the European Union (Maucorps et al., 2023). According to 2020 figures, four EU sectors account for 89.5 percent of total gas emissions in the European Union, with public electricity and other energy industries accounting for 31.4 percent of total emissions, transport for 29 percent, manufacturing and building/construction for 16.3 percent, and households for 12.8 percent (European Commission, 2022, 165).

The European Union sees the green transition process as a new industrial revolution. Technological innovations and new ways of doing business that will emerge in the context of its climate-neutral and carbon-pricing mechanism will broadly impact the economy, from investment to employment, from increased competitiveness to stability. Although studies show that having a climate-neutral economic structure has limited effects on gross domestic product, indirectly, policies to combat climate change are estimated to impact the economy positively, from investment to consumption. It is also emphasised that the green transition may cause adverse effects on the economy in the short term because it will cause a decrease in production and consumption. Some studies on reducing carbon ratios and the transition of production processes to low-carbon style reveal that shocks may occur in the direction of supply and demand (European Parliament, 2022, 1–2).

Studies on climate change and its economic effects emphasise welfare loss more than macroeconomic effects. The consequences of the changes that occur due to climate change and the increase in the world's temperature are considered to be much more severe than other economic consequences. As a result of not experiencing a green transformation globally, in other words, as a result of the failure of countries to harmonise their economic structures with climate change and green transformation processes, it is estimated that the current economy may experience an annual loss of 175 billion Euros as the global temperature level rises above 3 percent. According to the modelling made for the worldwide temperature level, if the temperature reaches 2 percent, the annual economic loss of welfare will be 83 billion Euros, and if the temperature level is limited and kept at 1.5 percent, a yearly loss of 42 billion Euros will be in question. In addition to the economic consequences, mortality rates are globally expected to increase due to the temperature rise (European Commission, 2020).

The economic consequences of climate change are predicted to be short-, medium-, and long-term. The financial results of weather and climate events that can be considered disasters can be sudden and severe. Although there is a risk that the situations arising from the rise in global temperature will be more permanent, it is estimated that the economic impact will occur in the medium term. In cases where measures for climate change or the green transition process are not implemented, or the transition process is prolonged, it is likely there will be a severe slowdown in the economy, low energy supply as a result of the low-carbon economy, and sudden and severe shocks for prices (Batten, 2018, 7).

The green transition process is being carried out in the European Union in the context of various support and regulation programmes. After becoming a partner of the Paris Climate Agreement, it has taken serious responsibility for combatting climate change and for an environmentally friendly economic development model. At the centre of the transition process is the "Green Deal." At the same time, the "European Climate Law" adopted in 2020, the "Climate Target Plan," and the "Fit for 55 Adaptation" package constitute the political pillar of the green transition process. At the centre of the economic pillar of the strategy is the EU emissions trading system, the obligation-sharing system/regulation between states, and the land and forestry regulation instruments. Energy security emerges as an imperative for the European Union to end its dependence on foreign and fossil resources within the low carbon-based economy model framework. Using fossil fuels in production causes high greenhouse gas emission rates and accelerates natural destruction due to global warming and climate change (European Parliament, 2020, 2).

It can be seen that the concrete steps taken towards the green transition in the European Union are the "Green Deal" prepared by the EU Commission and in force. In this context, the European Investment Bank (EIB) was put at the centre for the realisation of green transition investments and the provision of the necessary financing for the European Union, and it was planned to transform the bank into the "Climate Bank" quickly. With this decision taken in 2019, the necessary transformation tools have started to be created. EIB is the first organisation to issue "green bonds" financial instruments globally or as an international investment institution. Green bonds were published first in 2007 as "Climate Awareness Bonds." Once analysed from this point of view, EIB's investment of approximately EUR 6 million in 2007 in the field of climate change has shown a radical upward trend by 2020, reaching EUR 30.8 billion in "green bonds" (Ebeling, 2022, 1–2).

Furthermore, in its simplest form, the EU Emissions Trading System (ETS) had been adopted. ETS can be defined as a mechanism where the polluter pays and forces the relevant parties to reduce emissions and generates financial income for the EU green transition. Iceland, Liechtenstein, and Norway are included in the system, which covers 40 percent of the total calculated emissions in the European Union. Arrangements are being made to cover maritime transport emissions by 2024 within the system. The ETS has achieved a reduction of approximately 37 percent in the Union since 2005, while it operates fully market logic. Firms or companies must receive emission allowances from the upper limits every year. This emission allowance gives the relevant company the right to emit emissions.[4] Institutions or companies must receive allowances for as many emissions as possible yearly. Companies can exchange or sell the emission allowances they have received with each other. The system is operated in this way in an attempt to encourage the reduction of emission rates in the European Union. At the same time, the ETS has generated revenues of €152 billion since 2013, which are used for national green energy and transition projects of EU members or to modernise their infrastructure (European Commission, 2023a).

Moreover, another instrument of the green transition process is the EU obligation-sharing mechanism. The sharing mechanism envisages the reduction of emission rates in line with the targets set for EU members until 2030. In the areas of households, agricultural activities, small industries, and waste, member states, except for the aviation sector, act in line with their targets and within the framework of the obligation-sharing regulation. The regulation adopted in 2018 was later amended in 2023, and the member states' targets were updated. Thus, compared to 1990, member states have agreed to reduce their total emission rates by 55 percent (European Commission, 2023b).

In addition to the obligation-sharing mechanism, another economically important instrument in the green transition process is the EU regulation on "land use and forestry." The EU regulation includes basic land management rules such as agricultural land use, afforestation, and combatting deforestation. When the territories of the EU member states are considered, more than three-quarters of the lands within the EU borders are recognised as agricultural and forest lands. The protection of forests is vital in the fight against climate change. Since the removal of carbon dioxide from the air is inversely proportional to the size of forested areas, increasing forested areas directly reduces carbon dioxide emissions. At the same time, how land is used can be an essential tool in carbon reduction. Increasing the amount of grazing land and creating forests by planting trees are two of the best ways to remove carbon emissions from the atmosphere. In 2023, the EU land use and forestry law "Regulation on land, land use change and forestry" was reregulated and aimed to remove 310 million tonnes of CO_2 gas from the atmosphere by 2030. To achieve the stated targets, "LIFE," "Horizon Europe," "Soil Misson," and "EU Cohesion Fund" have been opened and encouraged by the European Union to be used in projects in carbon agriculture; additionally, it has introduced carbon sequestration certification to classify and measure carbon sequestration activities accurately (European Commission, 2023c).

Politics

The emission market arrangements established by the Green Deal plan have been criticised in many respects. The document was prepared by Frans

Tindemans during his term as Commissioner in 2019 and was supported by the two major political groups of the European Parliament—the European People's Party (EPP) and the Social Democrats and the Greens—while the left groups in the Parliament did not support it. The main reason for the lack of support for the Green Deal was because of the system that the document created for the green transition process in the context of the market mechanism. On the other hand, it has been argued that the Green Deal is a strategy to establish dominance over other countries with unequal power relations in the new period, as it was in the imperial period in Europe. The green transition or transformation process, which inherited the welfare understanding based on the colonisation of the resources and lands of other countries in the imperial period, aims to make Europe a global leader in the new process (Vela-Almeida et al., 2023, 2–3).

Although the Green Deal has been criticised in many respects, it is considered the most comprehensive transformation plan prepared by the European Union. In addition to the economic instruments created to make the green transition process possible, there is a need for political structuring in the field of implementation.

The European Union has focused primarily on basic regulations to promote the green transition process in the political field. In this context, the "European Climate Act" constitutes an essential framework for the green transition process and forms the political basis to achieve the 2030 and 2050 targets. It also provides for using a greenhouse gas emission budget to set the 2040 targets and establishes a scientific committee to work on climate change in Europe. The text approved by the EU Parliament entered into force in July 2021 (European Parliament, 2021).

Another instrument adopted to promote the green transition process from a political point of view is the "Fit for 55" package. As has already been emphasised, this package means the European Union will reduce its greenhouse gas emission rates by 55 percent by 2030. At the same time, the targets set with the "Fit for 55" package are planned to be transformed into climate laws and become legally binding. Compliance with 55 percent, a recommendation package, is vital for Europe to strengthen the European Union's determining role in global climate issues, to maintain EU competitiveness, to provide economic support to other countries, and to ensure a fair and social green transition process. As a matter of fact, within the scope of the targets set by the package, a "carbon limit adjustment mechanism" has been established, and a budget of 65 billion Euros has been allocated to the "Social Climate Fund" for households, relatively small businesses, and transport users (European Council, 2023, April 26). It is estimated that approximately 34 million people in the European Union are insufficient in terms of energy needs. Within the scope of the fund created with the package, it is planned to include new sectors in the emission trading system and transfer the funds to EU citizens or people who do not have energy sufficiency (European Council, 2023, July 25).

Energy

Energy security is one of the most critical issues that has occupied the EU agenda for a long time. For nearly twenty years, the European Union has endeavoured to reduce its dependence on foreign energy sources. However, the successive crises that it has faced have delayed the necessary transformation and the reliance on foreign energy has continued. The apparent increase in the need for energy in times of crisis reveals EU weakness in this area. Especially after the outbreak of war between Ukraine and Russia, the high dependence of EU member states on Russian gas has resulted in a severe threat to the European Union and Europe.

The importance of the green transition process in the context of EU energy security was clearly expressed by the President of the European Commission, Von der Leyen, in her "State of the Union" speech:

> We have not forgotten Putin's deliberate use of gas as a weapon and how it triggered fears of blackout and an energy crisis like in the 70s. Many thought we would not have enough energy to get through the winter. But we made it. Because we stayed united—pooling our demand and buying energy together. At the same time, unlike in the 70s, we used the crisis to invest in renewables and fast-track the clean transition massively. We used Europe's critical mass to decrease prices and secure our supply. The price for gas in Europe was over 300 euros per MWh one year ago. It is now around 35. (Leyen, 2023)

Leyen directly states that a rapid energy transition in the European Union and Europe must be achieved and that the key to this transition is the Green Deal.

The EU green transition process is designed as a long-term plan. As a matter of fact, there are many problems with linking economic growth and the green transition process by putting climate change, environment, and sustainability issues at the centre of the economy and moving to a climate-neutral economic production and consumption model. The point of energy and energy security also gains importance in this context.

The European Union's energy dependence on Russia and the current energy outlook clearly reveal the situation. After Russia invaded Ukraine in February 2022, the second question that came to the minds of EU decision-makers and the whole world was the Union's energy dependence on Russia and the future of economic sanctions. Russia's natural gas was undoubtedly predicted to be used as blackmail, which mobilised Europe quickly. After Russia played the energy card in the face of increasing EU economic sanctions levied against it due to the war, the European Union started to procure alternative energy sources. However, in 2020, it imported 57.5 percent of its fossil and solid fuel supplies, and the share of Russian energy in this ratio was 42.6 percent. As a natural consequence of this situation, Europe faced an energy crisis in which energy prices soared rapidly and shortages emerged (Eurostat, 2022).

Following Russia's interruption of energy deliveries via Nord Stream 1, Europe, which took action not as a union but in the context of its member states, quickly implemented national austerity measures. The countries with the highest natural gas consumption in the European Union are the Netherlands, Hungary, Italy, Belgium, and Germany (Netherlands' natural gas consumption is 38%, Hungary's 32.3%, Italy's 30.9%, Belgium's 29.3%, and Germany's 26.8%). The Nordic countries and the EU members in the north of Europe are fine regarding natural gas dependence. According to energy dependency statistics, the EU share of renewable energy sources remained at 22.1 percent in 2020. The resource-rich country in Europe regarding renewable energy is Iceland (which withdrew from candidate status in 2015) with 83.7 percent, while Malta is the EU member state with the lowest renewable energy ratio. Iceland is followed by Norway, Sweden, Albania, and Finland. For the European Union, heating is the main consumption area where energy is utilised. Renewable energy sources account for 23 percent of the energy used for heating. The share of natural gas in electricity generation is around 20 percent (Euronews, 2022).

As can be seen, the European Union continues to be dependent on foreign energy sources. For this reason, it is vital for it to end its energy dependence or reduce its reliance on foreign energy, which will be realised through the green transition. The European Union is at a very early stage for the outcome of the green transition process on energy and energy security. For this reason, it should be recognised that the main components of energy in the Union and in Europe are still nuclear form, natural gas, and coal—thus making decisions for a rapid green transition will create a direct challenge to EU energy sectors. As a matter of fact, when EU dependence on Russia is considered in the energy context, it does not seem possible to end reliance shortly; in other words, it will not be easy in the short-term to transform the EU energy structure. With the energy crisis, it is reasonable for EU member states to bring the use of nuclear energy and coal production back to the agenda, given the urgency of the current situation. Although the financial support programmes established by the European Union in the green transition process offer various opportunities for a fairer transition, nuclear energy and fossil resources should continue to be used for an easy energy transition (Joiţa et al., 2023).

According to 2021 figures, the European Union's dependence on Russia has declined over the last ten years. Russia is its fifth-largest trading partner in exports and the third-largest partner in imports. With the COVID-19 pandemic, the trade volume between the parties decreased. However, the product imported by the European Union from Russia was energy at a significant level. While energy accounted for 62 percent of EU imports in 2021, EU dependence on Russian energy decreased significantly between 2011 and 2021. There is a decline of approximately 14 percent over ten years (Eurostat, 2022). However, it is a challenge for the European Union to find alternative energy sources or to review the continuation of nuclear and coal power generation to achieve the energy transition required in the green transition process.

CONCLUSION

The Green Deal is a concrete transformation document for the European Union in the economic, political, and energy context. Although it is not possible to realise the targets within the scope of the Green Deal, which is at the centre of the process, in the short- and medium-term, the Union has begun a transformation in every field, especially in the economic area, with comprehensive regulations envisaged. The European Union, which has made good progress in combatting climate change and becoming a climate-neutral economy, has moved away from most of the targets set in the Green Deal due to the continuing war between Russia and Ukraine. With the outbreak of the war, the debate on EU energy dependence on Russia and the future of this dependence caused panic when Russia cut off its energy deliveries from Nord Stream 1; EU members quickly started to search for energy-saving measures and alternative energy sources, once they faced an energy crisis that affected most EU members from production to heating. Undoubtedly, the mechanisms designed by the European Union in the green transition process create numerous societal opportunities and set an example of pioneering initiatives globally; however, its previous claim of being a global leader and rule-maker in the fight against climate change and environmental issues has been shelved for a time due to the war between Russia and Ukraine. Considering current EU energy dependence, it is not easy to achieve the carbon emission and other targets set in the context of the European Green Deal, but the use of fossil resources, nuclear energy, and natural gas seems to be a necessity for a while longer to realise the economic, political, and energy targets, and dimensions in the green transition.

NOTES

1. The term refers to the EU motto which means "United in Diversity," first used in the 2000s. The term explains how Europeans come together in a single framework

called the European Union. For more information and the selection story of the
EU motto, please see https://european-union.europa.eu/principles-countries-history/
symbols/eu-motto_en; Fornäs, J. (2012). Motto. In *Signifying Europe* (pp. 103–114).
Intellect. https://doi.org/10.2307/j.ctv9hj915.9

2. For more information and resources on subject and critics: Günar, A. (2017).
Past Failure, New Future: An Analysis of the European Union Development Strate-
gies—From Lisbon to Europe 2020. In M. Khosrow-Pour, D.B.A. (Ed.), *Handbook
of Research on Global Enterprise Operations and Opportunities* (pp. 244–264). IGI
Global. https://doi.org/10.4018/978-1-5225-2245-4.ch015; Kok, W. (2004). *Facing the
Challenge: The Lisbon Strategy for Growth and Employment*. Report from the High
Level Group. Belgium: Office for Official Publications of the European Communities;
Pisani-Ferry, J., and Sapir, A. (2006, March 1). *The Last Exit to Lisbon*. Policy Brief.
Bruegel Policy Contribution, 1–22; Temin, P. (2002). The Golden Age of European
Growth Reconsidered. *European Review of Economic History* 6(1):3–22. https://www
.jstor.org/stable/41377908; Archibugi, D., and Coco, A. (2005). Is Europe Becoming
the Most Dynamic Knowledge Economy in the World? *Journal of Common Market
Studies* 43(3):433–459. https://ideas.repec.org/a/bla/jcmkts/v43y2005i3p433-459.html

3. To achieve the target adopted by the European Union, reducing greenhouse gas
emissions by 55 percent within the framework of the 2030 Climate Plan is expected
to help achieve the climate neutrality target in 2050. For more information, see https://
knowledge4policy.ec.europa.eu/publication/communication-com2020562-stepping
-europe%E2%80%99s-2030-climate-ambition-investing-climate_en

4. One allowance equals approximately one tonne of CO_2eq. For more information, see https://climate.ec.europa.eu/eu-action/eu-emissions-trading-system-eu-ets/
what-eu-ets_en

REFERENCES

Antoine, E. (2022). *European Investment Bank Loan Appraisal, the EU Climate
Bank?* Working Papers of BETA 2022-10. Bureau d'Economie Théorique et
Appliquée, UDS, Strasbourg.

Batten, S. (2018, January 12). Climate Change and the Macro-Economy: A Critical
Review. Bank of England Working Paper No. 706.

Besley, T., and Persson, T. (2023). The Political Economics of Green Transitions.
Quarterly Journal of Economics 138(3):1863–1906.

European Commission. (2020). *Supporting Policy with Scientific Evidence*. European
Commission. Retrieved from https://knowledge4policy.ec.europa.eu/publication/
communication-com2020562-stepping-europe%E2%80%99s-2030-climate-ambi-
tion-investing-climate_en

European Commission. (2022). *EU Energy in figures Statistical Pocketbook*. European Union. Luxembourg.

European Commission. (2023a). *What is the EU ETS?* European Commission.
Retrieved from https://climate.ec.europa.eu/eu-action/eu-emissions-trading-system
-eu-ets/what-eu-ets_en

European Commission. (2023b). *Effort-Sharing 2021–2030: Targets and Flexibilities*. European Commission. Retrieved from https://climate.ec.europa.eu/eu-action/effort-sharing-member-states-emission-targets/effort-sharing-2021-2030-targets-and-flexibilities_en

European Commission. (2023c). *Land Use Sector*. European Commission. Retrieved from https://climate.ec.europa.eu/eu-action/land-use-sector_en

European Council. (2023, April 26). *Infographic—Fit for 55: A Fund to Support the Most Affected Citizens and Businesses*. European Council: Council of the European Union. Retrieved September 29, 2023, from https://www.consilium.europa.eu/en/infographics/fit-for-55-social-climate-fund/

European Council. (2023, July 25). *Fit for 55*. European Council: Council of the European Union. Retrieved September 29, 2023, from https://www.consilium.europa.eu/en/policies/green-deal/fit-for-55-the-eu-plan-for-a-green-transition/

European Parliament. (2020, December 8). *EU Climate Target Plan: Raising the Level of Ambition for 2030*. Think Tank. European Parliament. Retrieved from https://www.europarl.europa.eu/thinktank/en/document/EPRS_BRI(2020)659370

European Parliament. (2021, August 31). *European Climate Law*. Think Tank. European Parliament. Retrieved from https://www.europarl.europa.eu/thinktank/en/document/EPRS_BRI(2020)649385

European Parliament. (2022). *Economic impacts of the green transition*. Retrieved from https://www.europarl.europa.eu/RegData/etudes/BRIE/2022/733623/EPRS_BRI(2022)733623_EN.pdf

Eurostat. (2022, March 7). *Energy Represented 62% of EU Imports from Russia*. Eurostat. European Union. Retrieved September 29, 2023, from https://ec.europa.eu/eurostat/web/products-eurostat-news/-/ddn-20220307-1

Euronews. (2022, October 3). *Avrupa'da elektrik krizi: Doğal gaz krizinden en az etkilenecek ülkeler hangisi?* Euronews. European Union. Retrieved September 29, 2023, from https://tr.euronews.com/2022/10/03/avrupada-elektrik-krizi-dogal-gaz-krizinden-en-az-etkilenecek-ulkeler-hangisi#:~:text=Malta%202020'de%20elektrik%20ihtiyacının,yüzde%2067'sini%20nükleerden%20karşılıyor

European Union. (n.d.). *Reform Support*. European Commission. https://reform-support.ec.europa.eu/what-we-do/green-transition_en

European Union. (n.d.). *Welfare Loss from Climate Change Impacts*. European Commission. https://joint-research-centre.ec.europa.eu/system/files/2020-09/14_pesetaiv_economic_impacts_sc_august2020_en.pdf

Fornäs, J. (2012). Motto. In *Signifying Europe* (pp. 103–114). Intellect. https://doi.org/10.2307/j.ctv9hj915.9

Günar, A. (2021). Green Theory in IR: A Theory for a Green World. In *Critical Approaches to International Relations* (pp. 240–265). Brill.

Joița, D., Panait, M., Dobrotă, C. E., Diniță, A., Neacșa, A., and Naghi, L. E. (2023). The European Dilemma—Energy Security or Green Transition. *Energies* 16(9):3849.

Leyen, V. D. (2023, September 13). *2023 State of the Union Address by President von der Leyen*. European Commission. Retrieved September 29, 2023, from https://ec.europa.eu/commission/presscorner/detail/ov/speech_23_4426

Maucorps, A., Römisch, R., Schwab, T., and Vujanović, N. (2023). The Impact of the Green and Digital Transition on Regional Cohesion in Europe. *Intereconomics* 58(2):102–110.

Meadows, D. H., Meadows, D. L., Rangers, J., and Behren, W. W. (1972). *The Limits to Growth: A Report for the Club of Rome's Projects on the Predicament of Mankind.* New York: Universe Books.

Newell, P. (2019). What is Green Politics? In *Global Green Politics* (pp. 21–48). Cambridge: Cambridge University Press.

Paterson, M. (2005). Green Politics. In S. Burchill et al., *Theories of International Relations.* Palgrave Macmillan.

Spretnak, C., and Capra, F. (1985). *Green Politics: The Global Promise.* London: Paladin, University Press.

Vela-Almeida, D. V., Kolinjivadi, V., Ferrando, T., Roy, B., Herrera, H., Gonçalves, M. V., and Van Hecken, G. (2023). The "Greening" of Empire: The European Green Deal as the EU First Agenda. *Political Geography* 105:102925.

4

European Energy Index Volatilities and Prices Forecasting in the Shadow of the Russia-Ukraine War

İhsan Erdem Kayral and Baki Rıza Balcı

INTRODUCTION

It is now accepted that the increased concentration of greenhouse gas emissions is caused by human activities. Greenhouse gas emissions are adversely affecting the environment, the economies of countries, and especially human health, leading to global warming and, more importantly, climate change.

The Kyoto Protocol was introduced by the United Nations in 1992 as a response to the risks posed by climate change and to establish an emissions trading system aimed at reducing greenhouse gases. The Kyoto Protocol was signed by more than 170 countries. Financial instruments are traded in various national and regional emission markets established within the framework of the Kyoto Protocol. The European Union (EU) has implemented a pan-European emissions trading scheme (EU ETS) aimed at mitigating carbon dioxide emissions from industries with high carbon intensity. The trade emission allowance system for reducing the environmental burden is one of the most important breakthroughs achieved across the European Union. CO_2 emission certificates have been traded as a new financial asset since 2005. Despite extensive research on many financial assets, there is still much to be explored in the carbon market (Byun and Cho, 2013).

Within the CO_2 trading framework, manufacturers have the opportunity to acquire emission allowances. These allowances assist them in minimising expenses linked to adapting production levels over time or avoiding depletion of their inventory. The sellers are required to limit their emissions below the level permitted, consequently, they have the option to sell any unused allowances to entities surpassing their allocated emission limits. The value of emission allowances is established by the equilibrium between the

43

availability and demand for them. The annual amount of emission allowances allocated is limited and is set by the EU Directive. EU ETS allows for the trading of spot, futures, and options on EU Allowances (EUA) and Certified Emission Reductions (CER), with EUA having a larger trading volume than CER. EUA is the legal aspect of the trading, while CER is voluntary (Byun and Cho, 2013).

As with any other asset market, traders face risks, and derivative instruments have been developed to overcome them. Because markets are volatile, it is necessary to hedge the risk. Derivative instruments like futures and forward contracts, options, swaps, and other derivatives are traded for this purpose. Futures contracts provide valuable information about these markets. Futures and options are traded on exchanges. Price risk affects futures prices. Nevertheless, within the context of managing energy-related risks, futures contracts are employed to provide protection against fluctuations in spot prices that transpire during delivery periods. Their purpose is to stabilise energy prices. Proficiency in the price dynamics of CO_2 emission certificates is essential for effective implementation of risk management strategies. Having a sound model for spot prices is essential for accurately valuing derivative instruments, which are the main instruments of European Union Allowances, and improving production costs, which include CO_2 costs, or supporting investment decisions for emissions.

Our research is limited to the European Energy Exchange (EEX). Established in 2002, the European Energy Exchange (EEX) operates in Germany and offers trading in energy contracts as well as European Union Allowances (EUA). It is widely regarded as one of the largest power markets in Europe. It operates spot and derivatives markets for power, natural gas, and emission allowances, as well as freight and agricultural products (Alt and Wende, 2020). In spot markets, trading occurs for near-term products set for delivery within periods spanning from 1 hour to 24 hours into the following day. Conversely, derivatives markets facilitate the trading of extended-term products, varying in maturity up to six years, contingent on the specific energy commodity involved (Kalantzis and Milonas, 2013). The derivatives market at EEX was launched in 2001, with futures contracts based on electricity indices. Options on these futures began trading three years later, and in 2005, futures on physical electricity and European Carbon Futures (ECFs) were introduced. EEX facilitates the trading of Phelix futures, Power futures, and Phelix options, which are futures contracts with cash or physical settlement and options contracts on financial futures in which Phelix means "Physical Electricity Index." Phelix futures are based on either the Phelix Base or Phelix Peak indices (Bauwens et al., 2011). In the derivatives market, various types of financial instruments are offered, such as futures contracts with physical delivery, financial futures, and options, which are priced through auctions or current price-setting mechanisms. Among them, electricity futures contracts come in two main types: futures with physical delivery and financial futures (Nedev, 2015). The price of a futures contract is specified in EUR per EUA (Pinho and Madaleno, 2014). The carbon market is becoming more mature. Because EUA futures have a high trading volume, studying the carbon market is valuable (Byun and Cho, 2013).

Since the beginning of the Russian-Ukrainian war, the prices of the energy market have been quite volatile, and the expansion of the derivatives trade in the energy market has continued. Conversely, pricing the derivatives of the energy market is quite challenging because it is characterised by high levels of volatility. The prices and inventories in these markets experience significant fluctuations on a weekly basis, partially in a predictable manner and partially in an unpredictable manner. Additionally, levels of volatility themselves vary over time. Price volatility fuels the demand for derivative instruments. The value of energy-based financial instruments, such as futures contracts, can be significantly influenced by the level of volatility. There is a lack of existing analytical approaches or complex methods to compute futures and volatility curves based on a general price model for the purpose of risk management (Vazquez et al., 2006).

Two main questions will be answered: i) what will be the volatility of the European Energy Index; and ii) how much will the prices of the index be soon in the scope of the Russia-Ukraine war?

Researchers commonly use univariate and multivariate generalised autoregressive conditional heteroskedasticity (GARCH), regime switching (RS), and stochastic volatility (SV) models as econometric methodologies to analyse the interrelations between time series. The univariate and multivariate GARCH models are the most often utilised of these models (Jonsson et al., 2017). If the volatility of the prices varies over time, it means that they exhibit the behaviour of returning to their mean. GARCH processes can be used to model this type of behaviour (Vazquez et al., 2006). GARCH-based models have gained widespread use in estimating the volatility of financial asset returns and are known for their strong performance (Byun and Cho, 2013). They are describing the volatility dynamics of commodities. Different types of GARCH models are utilised in GARCH-type models. ARCH and GARCH are models that account for heteroskedasticity, meaning they assume a stochastic process with conditional variance. Specifically, the GARCH model is used to model the conditional volatility of a time series. The model improves the hedging effectiveness. GARCH models provide an alternative approach to modelling the heteroskedasticity commonly observed in time series. The models used to estimate volatility should be flexible and capable of accurately representing the dynamics of variances and covariances. The literature on the GARCH model for analysing financial time series is extensive (Benz and

Trück, 2009). ARIMA (autoregressive integrated moving average) models are applied for price forecasting with a smaller number of observations and data up to one year (Jakasa et al., 2011). ARIMA models use lagged values of a variable to predict its present value and also use past errors to predict future errors. While ARIMA is commonly used for price forecasting, it may not be able to capture all the relevant characteristics of the electricity market. Seasonality and price spikes are two significant challenges in price forecasting. A precise forecast of a time series can be obtained by selecting an appropriate ARIMA model that can accurately capture the behaviour of the series under study (Kapoor, 2013). To capture the complexities of the electricity market, more advanced methods can be used, such as the GARCH model. This model is capable of forecasting changes in the variance of the error term by estimating it with an ARIMA process. As a result, two models are required, one for forecasting the original time series and the other for predicting the error term. This allows for the combination of ARIMA and GARCH models into a hybrid forecasting approach. So, combined ARIMA-GARCH models are utilised to capture the movement of prices over time (Diallo et al., 2018). Especially, due to the intricate nature of carbon markets and the distinct behaviour of EUA, it is recommended to employ a GARCH-type structure for predictive purposes (Paolella and Taschini, 2008).

The subsequent sections of the paper are structured as follows: Section two reviews the literature. In section three, the data and their stylised statistical characteristics are presented. Section four outlines the models designated for the empirical examination of spot and futures prices within the European Energy Exchange (EEX). This section presents and investigates the empirical findings. Finally, section five concludes.

LITERATURE REVIEW

Pindyck (2001) studied the futures market for energy items, finding evidence of high volatility. In the electricity futures market, Botterud, Bhattacharyya, and Ilic (2002) discovered a risk premium that is inverse in nature. Longstaff and Wang (2004) conducted an experiment to find out the relation between risk premia in electricity forward prices and the volatility of unexpected changes in demand, spot prices, and total revenue. Yield and risk relations were searched by Wei and Zhu (2006) in the US natural gas market. Price data obtained from the Nord Pool exchange market in Norway, the European Energy Exchange (EEX) in Germany, Powernext in France, and the Amsterdam Power Exchange (APX) in the Netherlands was analysed by Koopman, Ooms, and Carnero (2007). The prices that ensue are denoted as spot prices. The pricing of electricity futures at the European Energy Exchange (EEX) from 2002 to 2004 was examined by Wilkens and Wimschulte (2007). To evaluate the suitability of different one-factor and two-factor models for electricity spot prices, Bierbrauer et al. (2007) employed spot and futures price data from the German EEX power market. Paolella and Taschini (2008) investigated the forecastability of emission allowance prices for CO_2 in Europe and SO_2 in the United States. Their research focused on analysing returns in the emission allowance spot market, and they determined that the Pareto distribution is a suitable representation for the unconditional tails, while a GARCH-type structure can be used to estimate the conditional dynamics (Daskalakis et al., 2009). Seifert et al. (2008) found that CO_2 prices do not trace seasonal patterns and apply a stochastic equilibrium model. Daskalakis and Markellos (2009) conducted an empirical investigation into the trading of spot and derivative instruments in three prominent electricity and emission markets, namely the EEX, Nord Pool (NP), and Powernext (PWN), which operate under the EU ETS. The paper explored whether the introduction of the EU ETS has had an impact on the pricing of electricity forwards and futures.

Benz and Trück (2009) recommend the utilisation of Markov switching and AR-GARCH models for stochastic modelling, due to the distinct phases of price and volatility behaviour observed in the returns. Solibakke (2009) utilised Markov Chain Monte Carlo (MCMC) simulation methods to construct an all-encompassing stochastic volatility (SV) model in the context of the base and peak load EEX one-year forward electric power contracts. This was achieved through the application of a Bayesian estimator to capture both the mean and hidden volatility aspects. Tan et al. (2010) investigated a price forecasting approach that combines wavelet transforms with ARIMA and GARCH models. On the other hand, Zanotti, Gabbi, and Geranio (2010) conducted an examination of whether GARCH models result in a greater reduction in variance in a high time-varying volatility context within electricity markets. Ibikunle and Gregoriou (2011) investigated the liquidity effects following the initiation of trading in phase II of the EU-ETS for futures contracts of the European Union Allowances (EUA). Meanwhile, Bauwens, Hafner, and Pierret (2011) constructed a model for the dynamic volatility and correlation structure of electricity futures series in the European Energy Exchange index, utilising an asymmetric GARCH model to estimate volatilities and augmented dynamic conditional correlation (DCC) models for correlations. Chesney and Taschini (2012) developed an endogenous model that describes the dynamics of emission allowance spot prices and incorporates the possibility of asymmetric information in the market. Veka et al. (2012) conducted a study to determine the degree of correlation between Nordic electricity derivatives and European Energy Exchange (EEX) and Intercontinental Exchange (ICE) electricity contracts, as well as their price correlation with ICE gas,

Brent crude oil, coal, and carbon emission contracts, utilising a multivariate generalised autoregressive conditional heteroskedasticity (MGARCH) model. They employed this approach to analyse the volatility and conditional correlation between energy futures markets. Byun and Cho (2013) examine three approaches that possess volatility forecasting ability. The models being referred to are GARCH-type models that incorporate carbon futures prices, implied volatility from carbon options prices, and the k-nearest neighbour method. Additionally, they investigate whether the volatilities of energy markets can be forecasted based on the following day's carbon futures volatility. He et al. (2013) introduced a new analytical model to capture the presence of negative prices in the European Energy Exchange power markets by considering the structural changes that occur in these markets. Kalantzis and Milonas (2013) analysed the effect of the introduction of electricity futures on the volatility of spot prices in the French (Powernext) and German (EEX) electricity markets. They used a bivariate vector error correction model (VECM) and a GARCH model for their tests. Kapoor (2013) investigated the time-varying volatility of daily Certified Emission Reduction (CER) prices traded in the European Energy Exchange and proposed a forecasting method using Markov switching autoregressive integrated moving average (MSARIMA) and exponential generalised autoregressive conditional heteroskedasticity (EGARCH) models. Pinho and Madaleno (2014), investigated CO_2 emission allowances traded on EEX in terms of the compliance yield of spot and future contract returns and risk premiums. Paraschiv, Erni, and Pietsch (2014) investigated the influence of renewable energy sources on the day-ahead electricity prices in the European Energy Exchange (EEX). Their discovery revealed that the underlying factors influencing prices vary across hours characterised by distinct load profiles. Fanelli et al. (2016) searched for seasonality in the volatility of the futures traded in EEX and continue to investigate the same topic with options in their paper, which was announced in 2019 (Fanelli and Schmeck, 2019). Fanelli et al. (2016) provide a futures price model that allows looking into stochastic price volatility, and periodic behaviour in the power market. In 2016, Auer conducted a study on the volatility of the electricity market in Germany, focusing on the impact of the country's green energy policy. The study used data from the European Energy Exchange covering the period between 2000 and 2015. Latas and Jeremić (2017) investigated the use of scientifically validated methods to evaluate the effectiveness of options in liquid energy markets. Diallo, Kacsor, and Vancsa (2018) developed combined ARIMA-GARCH models to forecast the spread between Hungarian (HUPX) and German (EEX) day-ahead power prices. Chang et al. (2018) investigated the price predictability of tradable emission allowances. Leczycka (2020), in her doctoral thesis, tried to model the term structure of either prices or volatility in the electricity market. Casula and Masala (2021) examined empirical data from IDEX, the energy derivatives part of the Italian derivatives market IDEM. They conducted an investigation into potential correlations between futures and spot prices, leading to insights about significant indicators including the ex-post risk premium and the net convenience yield.

DATA

The European Energy Exchange, which is listed on the DAX index of Germany, the largest economy in the European Union, has expanded in a way that includes other major EU economies, and has started to be recognised as one of the important indicators of energy, especially clean energy, in the European Union. Therefore, the price and return series of the European Energy Exchange index between January 1, 2015, and November, 30, 2022, have been used in the study. The analysis period also has a separate importance due to including the war process between Russia and Ukraine. The return series are provided by using the equation $r_t = \log\left(\dfrac{P_t}{P_{t-1}}\right)$, where P_t represents the closing price of the index on day t.

This study, which utilises price and return series, has two main objectives:

i) to compare symmetric and asymmetric models in order to determine the best model for estimating the volatilities of the European Energy Exchange index, and

ii) to forecast the prices of the index.

During the analysis period, the price and return series of the index are shown in figure 4.1.

When examining the price series related to the index in figure 4.1, it can be observed that prices showed an upward trend one year after the pandemic

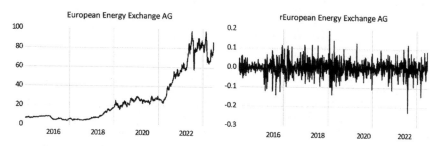

Figure 4.1 European Energy Exchange Index Prices and Return Series. *Source*: Thomson Reuters and authors' calculations.

began. Nonetheless, there was a decline and fluctuations due to the war that started between Russia and Ukraine. It can also be seen that prices have maintained a high level similar to the prewar period. In the return series examined within the scope of figure 4.1, although there were periodic fluctuations, the largest negative fluctuation was identified during the war period in 2022.

METHODOLOGY

In this study, evaluations were carried out using a two-stage analysis method. In the first stage, the volatilities of the return series were modelled, and in the second stage, analyses were applied to obtain predictions related to prices.

Accordingly, GARCH-type models were used to model the volatilities of the return series. To be able to use these models, the return series needed to meet the stationarity condition, not have autocorrelation issues, and exhibit heteroskedasticity. ADF (Dickey and Fuller, 1981) and PP (Phillips and Perron, 1988) unit root tests were used to test the stationarity condition, the Q-test statistic was used to examine the presence of autocorrelation issues, and the ARCH-LM test was used to investigate the presence of heteroskedasticity.

The ADF and PP unit root tests are used to evaluate whether the index returns contain a unit root or not, and if the null hypothesis is rejected, it can be said that the index does not contain a unit root and thus satisfies the stationarity condition.

If the probability value for the Q-test statistic is greater than the values of 1%, 5%, and 10%, there is no autocorrelation problem. However, if the hypothesis that the residuals from the simple regression model for the return series have constant variance (homoskedasticity) is rejected at similar probability values, it can be concluded that there is a problem of heteroskedasticity and the ARCH effect.

According to the assumptions being satisfied, GARCH-type volatility modelling can be performed. After evaluating the relevant assumptions, comparisons were made using GARCH (1,1) (Bollerslev, 1986) as a symmetric model and EGARCH (1,1) (Nelson, 1991); TARCH (1,1) (Zakoian, 1994); APARCH (1,1) (Ding et al., 1993); CGARCH (1,1) (Engle and Lee, 1993); and ACGARCH (1,1) (Engle and Lee, 1993) models as asymmetric models to estimate the index's volatilities. In determining the most appropriate model to calculate volatilities of the index, as a first objective of the study, among these models, in addition to the significance of the coefficients specific to the model, Akaike information criterion (AIC), Schwarz information criterion (SIC), and Hannan-Quinn information criterion (HQC) values will be examined, and the model with the smallest value will be presented as the best model.

In this context, the main difference between asymmetric models and the symmetric GARCH (1,1) model is that it allows for the examination of whether the effects of positive and negative shocks on the relevant index are different or not. In addition to this, it is also possible to examine the short-term (transitory effects) and relatively longer-term (persistent effects) movements of volatilities in the CGARCH and ACGARCH models.

In accordance with the second objective determined within the scope of the study, a hybrid and two-stage model was used, which combines the traditional ARIMA model with the multilayer perception (MLP) model, a nonlinear artificial neural network method, for the purpose of not only determining the most successful model in predicting volatilities, but also predicting index prices. Using this model, price predictions for the index were for a three-month period. While the ARIMA (Box and Jenkins, 1976) model generally makes predictions based on past price movements, MLP (Liébana-Cabanillas et al., 2017) is a nonlinear artificial neural network method with limited statistical assumptions. In the study, a prediction method was used that combines these two models and includes external variables.

As detected in the price and return series, although the pandemic has largely lost its impact on a global scale, it has been assessed that the ongoing Russia-Ukraine conflict at the EU border still has the potential to affect energy prices. Therefore, in price predictions, dummy variables were used to estimate the effects of the conflict for two different scenarios, one where war effects will continue and another where they will decrease. The hybrid model also implemented a ten-fold cross-validation technique to avoid overfitting neural network models (Liébana-Cabanillas et al., 2017). Cross-validation was used in training and testing data in the 70–30 percent ratio.

RESULTS

According to the Jarque-Bera test statistic (431.96), a normal distribution was not observed in the return series. However, the skewness value was close to 0 (-0.1911) and the kurtosis value was found to be 6.1039, indicating strong evidence that the return series of the index may exhibit a varying variance structure commonly encountered in financial time series.

The stationarity of the return series was examined using ADF and PP tests with the test statistics for stationary with trend (-32.1673 and -32.1718, respectively), and it was found that the return series were stationary at the 1% significance level.

After evaluating the preliminary data, different models were tested for the return series based on the significance of the coefficients, and it was decided to use a model with only a constant. The results of the ARCH-LM test and Q test were then examined using the simple regression model obtained. According to the ARCH (2) results (16.6543), there is an ARCH effect (a heteroskedasticity problem) at the 1% significance level, while the Q (2) test results (0.8317) indicate that there is no autocorrelation problem.

The results for volatility models for index returns are presented in table 4.1. The table also includes test results for the presence of heteroskedasticity (ARCH-LM test) and autocorrelation (Q-test statistic) in the fluctuations.

According to the results shown in table 4.1, among the examined models for estimating the volatility of the European Energy Exchange index return series, the CGARCH (1,1) model was identified as the model with the smallest Akaike, Schwarz, and Hannan-Quinn Information Criteria. Accordingly, the CGARCH (1,1) model was determined to be the best model for predicting the volatilities of the European Energy Exchange index during the analysis period. All coefficients in this model were found to be significant at the 1% level. In other models that include asymmetric effects, all coefficients except those evaluating the leverage effect were found to be statistically significant. According to these findings, there is no leverage effect in the index, and the impact of positive and negative shocks on volatilities does not differ. Additionally, it was observed that the heteroskedasticity problem was eliminated in the obtained volatilities according to the ARCH-LM test results, and there was no autocorrelation problem. The volatilities obtained from the best model identified after evaluations of conditional variance models are shown in figure 4.2.

According to figure 4.2, it can be seen that the volatility of the index varies over time, and the highest fluctuation was observed at the beginning of 2022, when the war between Russia and Ukraine started. In this regard, it is believed that the potential risks that may arise in terms of energy supply and the creation of alternative sources in the European Union, given the significant energy dependence on Russia, play a role. In the CGARCH model, the components of volatility are classified as short-term (transitory) and relatively longer-term (persistent). According to this, it can be seen from figure 4.2 that the temporary effects have a limited impact on the total volatility, and the total volatilities and permanent effects (relatively longer-term effects) move almost together in a single graph due to this reason. The fact that volatilities reached their highest levels during the Russia-Ukraine war period has increased the importance of price movement predictions based on scenarios of the war continuing or ending in the price forecasts of the index. In the second part of the empirical study, the time series obtained for price forecasts using only the traditional ARIMA model and the hybrid model (ARIMA and the MLP model, a nonlinear ANN method applied together) are shown in figure 4.3.

Table 4.1 Test Results for Volatility Models for Index Returns

Parameters	GARCH (1,1)	EGARCH (1,1)	TARCH (1,1)	APARCH (1,1)	CGARCH (1,1)	ACGARCH (1,1)
c	0.0027**	0.0027***	0.0028***	0.0028***	0.0028***	0.0028***
ω	0.0001***	-0.5307***	0.0001***	0.0001	0.0017***	0.0017***
α	0.0832***	0.2043***	0.0907***	0.0863***	0.0540***	0.0359***
β	0.8966***	0.9422***	0.8986***	0.8978***	0.3731***	0.4572***
EGARCH (δ)	–	-0.0026	–	–	–	–
TARCH (γ)	–	–	-0.0154	–	–	–
APARCH (δ)	–	–	–	1.8558***	–	–
APARCH (γ)	–	–	–	-0.0447	–	–
CGARCH (ρ)	–	–	–	–	0.9690***	–
CGARCH (θ)	–	–	–	–	0.0990***	–
ACGARCH (ρ)	–	–	–	–	–	0.9665***
ACGARCH (θ)	–	–	–	–	–	0.0987***
ACGARCH (γ)	–	–	–	–	–	-0.0235
Akaike	-3.7911	-3.7885	-3.7897	-3.7879	**-3.7909**	-3.7893
Schwarz	-3.7724	-3.7651	-3.7663	-3.7599	**-3.7729**	-3.7664
Hannan-Quinn	-3.7840	-3.7796	-3.7808	-3.7773	**-3.7803**	-3.7798
ARCH (2) (F)	1.7819	1.5906	1.7303	1.8656	0.4582	0.4248
Q (2)	2.2759	2.0355	2.4478	2.4023	2.4254	2.3291

Note: *, **, *** significance at 10%, 5%, and 1%, respectively.
Source: Authors' calculations

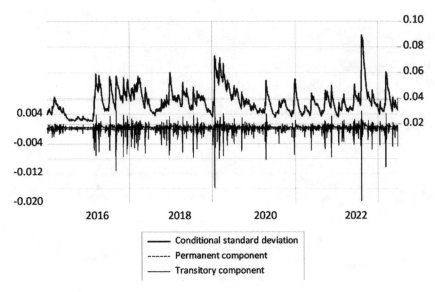

Figure 4.2   European Energy Exchange Index Volatility Series. *Source:* Authors' calculations

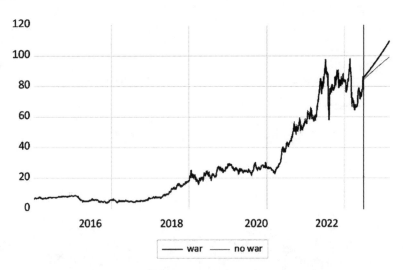

Figure 4.3   European Energy Exchange Index Price Forecastings. *Source:* Authors' calculations

According to the price movements observed at the beginning of the war in February 2022, similar to many parameters in financial markets, the index prices showed a declining tendency but later recovered and saw price increases. According to the price forecasts shown in figure 4.3, it is predicted that the index prices will continue to increase in both scenarios (continuation or cessation of war conditions). Therefore, the potential for inflationary pressures to persist in many member countries, including Germany, the largest economy in the European Union, is considered one of the factors.

According to the results obtained from figure 4.3, another conclusion is that in the scenario where the effects of the war continue, price increases are expected to be higher. One potential reason for this is the possibility that in the scenario where the war conditions continue, possible problems in energy supply due to the prolongation of the process could create upward pressure on energy contracts and increase index prices even more.

CONCLUSIONS

The environment is being negatively impacted by greenhouse gas emissions, which in turn have detrimental effects on the economies of nations and pose significant risks to human health. These emissions contribute to global warming and, more significantly, drive climate change. So, green energy, also known as renewable energy, plays a pivotal role in addressing the pressing challenges of climate change and sustainable development. Its importance lies in its ability to provide clean, reliable, and abundant power while significantly reducing greenhouse gas emissions and minimising environmental impact.

In short, our empirical analysis relies on examining the volatility of the European Energy Index and forecasting the potential price movements of the index in the near future, specifically in the context of the Russia-Ukraine war. This analysis takes into account the significance of green energy and its implications for the energy sector amidst geopolitical tensions.

The European Energy Exchange has started to be recognised as an important indicator for energy-related issues in the European Union. Therefore, in this study, the price and return series of the European Energy Exchange index between January 1, 2015, and November, 30, 2022, were used. The analysis period is also of particular importance due to the inclusion of the war period between Russia and Ukraine.

When examining the price series, it can be observed that approximately one year after the start of the pandemic, prices entered an upward trend, but a decline and fluctuation occurred with the outbreak of the war between Russia and Ukraine. However, it can be seen that prices have maintained a high level similar to the prewar period. According to the return series, although there were periodic fluctuations, the biggest negative fluctuation was observed during the war period in 2022.

The potential for the Russia-Ukraine war on the EU border to affect energy prices is still considered significant.

The best model for predicting the volatility of the European Energy Exchange index during the analysis period was determined to be the CGARCH (1,1) model.

There is no leverage effect in the index, and there is no significant coefficient; the impact of positive and negative shocks on volatilities does not differ. In addition, according to the results of the ARCH-LM test on the obtained volatilities, the heteroskedasticity problem has been eliminated, and there is no autocorrelation problem.

The analysis reveals that the highest volatility in index fluctuations was observed at the beginning of 2022, when the war between Russia and Ukraine broke out. In this case, potential risks are seen in terms of energy supply and the creation of alternative sources in the context of the European Union.

The fact that the volatilities reached their highest levels during the period of the Russia-Ukraine war has increased the importance of price forecasts based on scenarios of the continuation or end of the war in terms of predicting price movements in the index.

According to price forecasts, it is predicted that the index prices will continue to increase in both scenarios (continuation or cessation of war conditions). In this case, the potential for inflationary pressures to persist in EU countries has been evaluated as one of the factors. An increase in prices is observed to be greater in the scenario where the effects of the war conditions continue.

In future studies, the importance of research on energy prices and the volatility and price forecasting of related indices will be maintained. The relationships between these indices and other markets can be investigated as well.

REFERENCES

Alt, Rainer, and Erik Wende. (2020). Blockchain Technology in Energy Markets—An Interview with the European Energy Exchange. *Electronic Markets* 30(2):325–30. https://doi.org/10.1007/s12525-020-00423-6

Auer, Benjamin R. (2016). How Does Germany's Green Energy Policy Affect Electricity Market Volatility? An Application of Conditional Autoregressive Range Models. *Energy Policy* 98(C):621–28.

Bauwens, Luc, Christian M. Hafner, and Diane Pierret. (2011). Multivariate Volatility Modeling of Electricity Futures. *Journal of Applied Econometrics* 28(5):743–761. https://doi.org/10.1002/jae.2280

Benz, Eva, and Stefan Trück. (2009). Modeling the Price Dynamics of CO_2 Emission Allowances. *Energy Economics* 31:4–15.

Bierbrauer, Michael, Christian Menn, Svetlozar Rachev, and Stefan Trück. (2007). Spot and Derivative Pricing in the EEX Power Market. *Journal of Banking & Finance* 31(11):3462–3485.

Bollerslev, Tim. (1986). Generalized Autoregressive Conditional Heteroskedasticity. *Journal of Econometrics* 31(3):307–327.

Botterud, Audun, Arnob K. Bhattacharyya, and Marija Ilic. (2002). Futures and Spot Prices—An Analysis of the Scandinavian Electricity Market. In *Proceedings of the North American Power Symposium 2002*, 1–8. Tempe, Arizona.

Box, George E. P., and Gwilym M. Jenkins. (1976). *Time Series Analysis: Forecasting and Control*. Revised edition. San Francisco: Holden-Day.

Byun, Suk Joon, and Hangjun Cho. (2013). Forecasting Carbon Futures Volatility Using GARCH Models with Energy Volatilities. *Energy Economics* 40(C):207–221.

Casula, Laura, and Giovanni Masala. (2021). Electricity Derivatives: An Application to the Futures Italian Market. *Empirical Economics* 61(2):637–666. https://doi.org /10.1007/s00181-020-01915-2

Chang, Chia-Lin, Jukka Homaki, Hannu Laurila, and Michael McAleer. (2018). Moving Average Market Timing in European Energy Markets: Production Versus Emissions. *Energies* 11(12):1–24.

Chesney, Marc, and Luca Taschini. (2012). The Endogenous Price Dynamics of Emission Allowances and an Application to CO_2 Option Pricing. *Applied Mathematical Finance* 19(5):447–475.

Daskalakis, George, and Raphael N. Markellos. (2009). Are Electricity Risk Premia Affected by Emission Allowance Prices? Evidence from the EEX, Nord Pool and Powernext. *Energy Policy* 37(7):2594–2604.

Daskalakis, George, Dimitris Psychoyios, and Raphael N. Markellos. (2009). Modeling CO_2 Emisson Allowance Prices and Derivatives: Evidence from the European Trading Scheme. *Journal of Banking & Finance* 33(7):1230–1241.

Diallo, Alfa, Enikö Kacsor, and Milan Vancsa. (2018). Forecasting the Spread between HUPX and EEX DAM Prices: The Case of Hungarian and German Wholesale Electricity Prices. In *15th International Conference on the European Energy Market (EEM)*, 1–5. Lodz-Poland.

Dickey, David A., and Wayne A. Fuller. (1981). Likelihood Ratio Statistics for Autoregressive Time Series with a Unit Root. *Econometrica* 49(4):1057–1072.

Ding, Zhuanxin, Clive W. J. Granger, and Robert F. Engle. (1993). A Long Memory Property of Stock Market Returns and a New Model. *Journal of Empirical Finance* 1(1):83–106.

Engle, Robert F., and Gary G. J. Lee. (1993). A Permanent and Transitory Component Model of Stock Return Volatility. Discussion Paper 92-44R. San Diego: University of California.

Fanelli, Viviana, and Maren Diane Schmeck. (2019). On the Seasonality in the Implied Volatility of Electricity Options. *Quantitative Finance* 19(8):1321–1337.

Fanelli, Viviana, Lucia Maddalena, and Silvana Musti. (2016). Modelling Electricity Futures Prices Using Seasonal Path-Dependent Volatility. *Applied Energy* 173(C):92–102.

He, Yang, Marcus Hidmann, Florian Herzog, and Göran Andersson. (2013). Modeling the Merit Order Curve of the European Energy Exchange Power Market in Germany. *IEEE Transactions on Power Systems* 28(3):3155–3164.

Ibikunle, Gbenga, and Andros Gregoriou. (2011). European Union Emissions Trading Scheme (EU-ETS) Futures Liquidity Effects: Evidence from the European Energy Exchange (EEX). In *8th International Conference on Advances in Applied Financial Economics*, 1–9. https://www.researchgate.net/publication/278009609 _European_Union_Emissions_Trading_Scheme_EU-ETS_Futures_Liquidity _Effects_Evidence_from_the_European_Energy_Exchange_EEX

Jakasa, Tina, Ivan Androcec, and Petar Sprčić. (2011). Electricity Price Forecasting—ARIMA Model Approach. In *8th International Conference on the European Energy Market (EEM)*, 222–225. Zagreb-Croatia.

Jonsson, Erlendur, Sindre Lorentzen, and Roy Endre Dahl. (2017). Volatility Spillovers in EU Electricity Markets. In *15th IAEE European Conference*, 1–17.

Kalantzis, Fotis G., and Nikolaos T. Milonas. (2013). Analyzing the Impact of Futures Trading on Spot Price Volatility: Evidence from the Spot Electricity Market in France and Germany. *Energy Economics* 36(C):454–463.

Kapoor, Nimisha. (2013). Modelling Daily CER Price Volatility in European Energy Exchange: Evidence from MSARIMA-EGARCH Model. *Vision* 17(4):279–284.

Koopman, Siem Jan, Marius Ooms, and M. Angeles Carnero. (2007). Periodic Seasonal Reg-ARFIMA–GARCH Models for Daily Electricity Spot Prices. *Journal of the American Statistical Association* 102(477):16–27.

Latas, Tatjana, and Zoran Jeremić. (2017). The Option on Electric Energy for the Decrease of Risk on the Example of EEX (European Energy Exchange). *European Journal of Applied Economics* 14(2):43–57. https://doi.org/10.5937/ejae14-14849

Leczycka, Katarzyna. (2020). Modelling Term Structure of Prices and Volatility on Electricity Market. Wroclaw University of Economics and Business.

Liébana-Cabanillas, Francisco, Veljko Marinković, and Zoran Kalinić. (2017). A SEM-Neural Network Approach for Predicting Antecedents of m-Commerce Acceptance. *International Journal of Information Management* 37(2):14–24. https://www.sciencedirect.com/science/article/abs/pii/S0268401216303103

Longstaff, Francis A., and Ashley W. Wang. (2004). Electricity Forward Prices: A High-Frequency Empirical Analysis. *Journal of Finance* 59(4):1877–1900.

Nedev, Todor S. (2015). Issues of the Bulgarian Electricity Market and Possibilities of Risk Management by Financial Futures at the European Energy Exchange-EEX. *Economics and Finance*, 6–10.

Nelson, Daniel B. (1991). Conditional Heteroskedasticity in Asset Returns: A New Approach. *Econometrica* 59(2):347–370.

Paolella, Marc S., and Luca Taschini. (2008). An Econometric Analysis of Emission Allowance Prices. *Journal of Banking & Finance* 32(10):2022–2032.

Paraschiv, Florentina, David Erni, and Ralf Pietsch. (2014). The Impact of Renewable Energies on EEX Day-Ahead Electricity Prices. *Energy Policy* 73:196–210.

Phillips, Peter C., and Pierre Perron. (1988). Testing for a Unit Root in Time Series Regressiontle. *Biometrika* 75(2):335–346.

Pindyck, Robert S. (2001). The Dynamics of Commodity Spot and Futures Markets: A Primer. *Energy Journal* 22(3):1–29.

Pinho, Carlos, and Mara Madaleno. (2014). CO_2 Risk Premium and Convenience Yield Determination: Considering Spot Volatility in the EEX Market.

Seifert, Jan, Marliese Uhrig-Homburg, and Michael Wagner. (2008). Dynamic Behavior of CO_2 Spot Prices. *Journal of Environmental Economics and Management* 56:180–194.

Solibakke, Per Bjarte. (2009). EEX Base and Peak Load One-Year Forward Contracts: Stochastic Volatility. In *6th International Conference on the European Energy Market*, 1–17. Leuven-Belgium.

Tan, Zhongfu, Jinliang Zhang, Jianhui Wang, and Jun Xu. (2010). Day-Ahead Electricity Price Forecasting Using Wavelet Transform Combined with ARIMA and GARCH Models. *Applied Energy* 87(11): 3606–3610.

Vazquez, Miguel, Julian Barquín, and Carlos Batlle. (2006). Electricity Forward and Volatility Curves Computation Based on Monte Carlo Simulation. In *9th International Conference on Probabilistic Methods Applied to Power Systems KTH*, 1–5. Stockholm-Sweden.

Veka, Steinar, Gudbrand Lien, Sjur Westgaard, and Helen Higgs. (2012). Time-Varying Dependency in European Energy Markets: An Analysis of Nord Pool, European Energy Exchange and Intercontinental Exchange Energy Commodities. *Journal of Energy Markets* 5(2):3–32.

Wei, Song Zan Chiou, and Zhen Zhu. (2006). Commodity Convenience Yield and Risk Premium Determination: The Case of the U.S. Natural Gas Market. *Energy Economics* 28:523–534.

Wilkens, Sascha, and Jens Wimschulte. (2007). The Pricing of Electricity Futures Evidence from the European Energy Exchange. *Journal of Futures Markets* 27(4):387–410.

Zakoian, Jean-Michel. (1994). Threshold Heteroskedasticity Models. *Journal of Economic Dynamics and Control* 18(5):931–955.

Zanotti, Giovanna, Giampaolo Gabbi, and Manuela Geranio. (2010). Hedging with Futures: Efficacy of GARCH Correlation Models to European Electricity Markets Giovanna. *Journal of International Financial Markets, Institutions and Money* 20(2):135–418.

The European Green Deal on the "Nature-Efficiency" Dichotomy

Samet Zenginoğlu and Ferhat Apaydın

INTRODUCTION

Throughout history, the human-nature relationship has been a field of "harmony" on the one hand and "competition" on the other. However, it has been observed that competition has become a more dominant factor since the periods when market conditions increased their effectiveness instead of natural conditions. Especially with the Industrial Revolution, it is possible to say that the human-nature relationship has evolved into a very different dimension. As a matter of fact, with a production and efficiency-oriented perspective, intensive energy consumption has led to the destruction of both underground and aboveground resources. Since the second half of the twentieth century, criticisms against this result have been on the rise. Since the 1970s, criticisms against the "development against all odds" approach, both in the development literature and in international circles, have been the main agenda of the global public opinion. In this context, criticisms focus on two points. The first dimension of the criticisms is related to the development of human capacity, such as meeting basic human needs in the face of increasing unemployment, poverty, and inequality. The second dimension has been related to the environmental sustainability aspect of development such as increasing population, depleting natural resources, and environmental destruction (Yüksel Acı, 2023, 1–4).

Although "human-environment-nature"-oriented awareness has been on the rise, the fact that a comprehensive, permanent, and effective solution mechanism has not been established until the twenty-first century represents another reality. Although international and regional organisations and states, especially the United Nations (UN), have taken steps under the headings of climate change and global warming, it does not seem possible to state that a stable result has been achieved yet. Existing data also confirm this view. For example, it is reported that the economic damage caused by climate-related disasters in 2017 was approximately 283 billion Euros. According to the IPCC report published in October 2018, the world is warming by approximately 0.2°C in each decade. Global temperatures, which have increased by more than 1°C since the Industrial Revolution, are projected to increase by at least 2°C by 2060 unless necessary measures are taken (Baydemir, 2021, 14).

It is known that the capitalist context has an undeniable impact on such an outcome. Indeed, from the perspective of sustainable environment and future generations, capitalism or its mutated form neoliberalism is a system that will lead to environmental disasters and thus traumatic consequences. Ataöv (2009) emphasises that the ecological science of capitalism and the neoliberal capitalist order are in conflict with each other, thus neoliberalism puts the human at the centre, not the environment. The emphasis on any means being permissible for the sake of profit is the basis of the capitalist system. Reparations made on the environment will further strengthen capitalism, thus serving the destruction of the environment. According to Foster and Magdoff (2014), since capitalism does not have a soul, it will never, ever be environmentalist. The sole purpose of capitalism is to ensure ever-increasing capital accumulation, to aim for a continuous profit maximisation and thus to transform everything in the world into a commodity with a price.

So, why is it, despite all these realities and solution-oriented initiatives, that a permanent and stable process and result cannot be mentioned? It is thought that the biggest factor that can be given as an answer to this question is the focus on "efficiency"—because it is known that, since the Industrial Revolution, global systematics have basically been built on efficiency. Therefore, the existence of a context that ignores efficiency in a completely environment-nature oriented approach cannot be accepted. This study aims to analyse the European Green Deal (EGD) in the nature-efficiency dilemma by focusing on this very conflict.

With the EGD announced by the President of the European Commission Ursula von der Leyen in December 2019, the European Union (EU) comes to the fore as an influential actor in terms of becoming climate neutral in 2050 (net-zero greenhouse gases, preservation of industrial employment and industrial production, and reduction of global greenhouse gases, etc.). However, the prominence of a climate-neutral target here allows us to infer that the main concern of the EGD is not ecological. In other words, it is known that the EGD includes issues such as economy, employment, health, food, and social justice along with ecology. In the declaration of December 11, 2019, it is understood that the EGD focuses on current questions on climate change and includes a new growth strategy to offer the European Union a fairer and more prosperous life. Moreover, it was stated that this growth would be a growth strategy that would revitalise a modern, resource-efficient, competitive economy (Aşıcı, 2022, 136).

The text of the EGD concerns EU members and other countries that have any relations with the European Union. In this context, the steps taken by countries that trade with the European Union, countries on the way to EU membership, and all countries that have social, political, and economic relations with it in terms of harmonisation with the EGD are important. Considering that the European Union has prepared this agreement not only on ecological values but also on various economic and political concerns, it would not be wrong to think that it expects to obtain various gains (tax, etc.) from other countries in this process, just like the negative expectations such as the danger of resource depletion and the tendency of future profit rates to decrease have included developed countries in the adventure of sustainable development. Within this general framework, the study consists of two main sections. The first part analyses the relationship between capitalism and ecology from a theoretical perspective. The second part draws attention to the clues in the EGD in relation to the main subject of the study.

CAPITALISM AND ECOLOGY: A THEORETICAL BACKGROUND

The process of economic development is closely related to the development of capitalism. In this process, production is indispensable for the survival of societies. At the point of ensuring and sustaining this production, the increasing need for energy, especially in the period after the Industrial Revolution, and the aim of establishing this need in a continuous and secure context have come to the fore. It is accepted that the most important process in the rise of capitalism is the Industrial Revolution. In this context, it is considered necessary to present a general perspective in terms of the basic functioning of capitalism and neoliberalism before the transformation of capitalism in the nature-environment focus.

Roy (2015, 31–42) summarised his neoliberal criticism of the Indian economy in his book *Capitalism: A Ghost Story* summarised his critique of neoliberalism on the Indian economy as follows. Under neoliberalism, massive slaughter of people and the environment for more profit has become commonplace. The so-called charitable foundations established by capitalist corporations have played a crucial role in the transformation of money into power. Foundations are tax-free organisations with enormous resources, unlimited powers, and complete lack of transparency. In fact, they are the instruments set up by usurers to rule the world. International organisations such as the World Bank (WB) and the International Monetary Fund (IMF) are the guardians of capitalism in the world. From their very inception, they have ensured the strengthening of global capital and the spread of a free market, with the dollar as the sole reserve currency. To this end, they have spent huge sums of money to promote good governance (provided they have the reins in their own hands), the establishment of the rule of law (provided they have a say in the law), and many anti-corruption programmes (to keep their own programmes flowing). They demand transparency and accountability from poor countries, but they themselves remain the most closed organisation in the world. They exert overt and covert pressure on poor countries to open their economies to global finance. It is therefore not for nothing that the world admires corporate and foundation philanthropy.

The core of the capitalist system is surplus value and the basis of injustice in this context is capitalist exploitation. In ideal capitalism, value is created solely and exclusively by the labour factor. Natural resources create the basis for wealth. However, under extractive capitalism, not only labourers but also resources are exploited. Thus, nature is exploited and destroyed as an input for resource production. After all, given that resources are scarce and the world population is increasing, such exploitation means the impoverishment of future generations (Skirberkk, 2000, 53). Unfortunately, exploitation in the capitalist system is not only for the present but also for future generations. An oil exploration company, a gold or other mineral exploration company, or a hydroelectric power plant (HEPP) to be built on a river are the best examples of this.

One of the important strengths of capitalism or neoliberalism is that it presents itself as a kind of great chain of being. Bourdieu (2021) drew attention to this issue with a theological metaphor. At the top is God, and it is a process of passing through a series of links to the most ordinary realities. At the top of the neoliberal cloud (in God's place) is a mathematician, and below is an ideologue. In other words, this is someone who does not know much about economics but creates the perception that he knows something, thanks to the prominence of his technical vocabulary. This chain has a strong authority. This chain expresses an authority extending from mathematician to banker, from banker to philosopher, from essayist to journalist. This situation emerges with people who provide ideological services in exchange for a position of power. The fact that the secret relations between some foundations, organisations, and journals, even those who work in their own columns, come to light from time to time adds a different dimension to the process. On the other hand, the fatalistic speech given by these people collectively in an atmosphere of consensus consists of transforming economic orientations into fate. However, it is known that social and economic laws are realised only if they are allowed to have an effect. The reason why conservatives in particular are in favour of the slogan "let them do" is that they need this slogan in order to preserve such laws.

There is also the unshakable reality of how money influences electoral politics regarding the inequality of capitalism. As is well known, political campaigns involve a considerable expenditure of money. The financing of these political campaigns, that is, those who donate to the parties, is of course realised thanks to rich minorities. The fact that the rich also spend this money to buy power or for other interests creates a kind of feedback effect. This positive feedback loop leads to the realisation of policies in favour of the rich and thus to a power policy or even a state policy that makes the rich even richer. In other words, the rich are the largest group whose voices are listened to by politicians (Milanovic, 2018, 204). This situation leads to inequality problems that are even more difficult to solve. To put it bluntly, a system has been created in which not everyone has one vote; it is a system in which those who have money actually turn it into votes. Although this new capitalism theoretically allows everyone to cast one vote in a democratic way, after the election, it actually realises the practice that only the rich vote. This gives rise to the concept of plutocracy[1] where elected public officials listen to the voice of the rich. In a nutshell, rather than following a vicious circle between environmental problems and productivity, capitalism continues to implement policies that increase inequality with its pro-productivity policies.

With the rise of capitalism, environmental problems and concerns have also started to increase. Looking at the history of environmental problems, it was initially thought that these problems were specific to advanced industrial countries due to factors such as inhumane urbanisation, increasing pollution caused by automobile emissions, pollution caused by industry and similar organisations. However, it was later realised that the roots of environmental problems stem from the production styles of countries, in other words, from the capitalist economic and social order (Amin, 2018). In this context, the Industrial Revolution created a very important momentum during the rise of capitalism. In this period, a series of technical innovations, which added mechanical power (water and steam power) to production, moved the production process from the home or workshop to the factory and transformed it into mass production and completely changed the production process. Of course, this important change is not so simple and monotonous that it can be explained by technical innovations alone. Because in this process, in addition to technical innovations, the existence of capital owners who are ready to apply these innovations for production and market purposes is important (Dobb, 1973, 21). In fact, what is meant here is that the Industrial Revolution is a product of maturation rather than a sudden transformation. In other words, even within the fabric of feudal society, significant changes had already begun to emerge in the forces of production, trade, and thus in the merchant mentality. In other words, compared to the previous two centuries, this process accelerated greatly with the widespread technical developments of the Industrial Revolution and moved to a tremendously advanced stage.

On the other hand, capitalism is a system based on inequality. Moreover, this inequality has increased even more after the Industrial Revolution. In all modern capitalist societies, capital is largely concentrated in the hands of very few individuals. Especially in the recent period, the increase in the share of capital in national income and the concentration of this capital among very few individuals exacerbate income inequality. In today's capitalism, the inequality gap between families has widened and the problem has become chronic. If we take into account that rich families attach great importance to education, provide their children with the best education, so that their children will be employed in high-paying jobs in the future, and that these children inherit a large amount of capital from their families, this inequality resembles meritocracy. Therefore, it will not be possible to break this inequality. In this new capitalism, rich capitalists will actually appear as rich workers. Therefore, the acceptability of this meritocratic order has spread over a wide area, because rich people are also working people. In fact, it is seen as a system in which well-educated people work in jobs suitable for their education and receive the wages they deserve (Milanovic, 2018). As can be understood, inequality in the old capitalism has changed in the new capitalism. While it was easy to criticise the inequality between rentiers, who earned income without working, and the poor in the old capitalism, it has become difficult to criticise a certain percentage of the richest in the new capitalism. In this context, it has also become politically and ideologically difficult to reduce this inequality disguised as meritocracy. Since this rich minority is educated and conscious, all negative environmental problems will fall on poor people. Even if the rich pollute the environment, they will be comfortable within the framework of the "polluter pays" principle. They will already have the opportunity to use all environmentally friendly products without even needing to do so.

The tension between nature and economic value goes back long before the capitalist system of production. However, the capitalist system has reproduced environmental and other problems that existed before it in its own way of functioning, and has also reconstructed their content and dimension. Capitalism has become more efficient over time through technical change. In fact, capitalism proceeds from the fact that greater utilisation of modern technical progress and higher productivity is an urgent necessity. This can be expressed in relation to the process of economic growth. Daly (1974) attributes this state of the world to "growthmania." At this point, the preference for the technosphere over the ecosphere leads the world into an unpredictable growth process. According to Burkett (2011), the market mechanism, whose production is motivated by profit, has to rely on growth. In simple terms, making money is only possible if the money obtained at the end of the process is greater than the initial money, which implies growth. However, it should be noted that something that is rational in the ecological system becomes irrational for the market mechanism. Because while an ecological system adopts a profitless economy, this is contrary to the logic of the market.

Capitalism's ability to survive despite the destruction of the environment and even to prosper through new and more moneymaking methods implies a kind of environmental crisis. This environmental crisis is a crisis in the quality of natural wealth as a condition for human development. The production of goods and services designed to manage and cope with the destruction of the environment is itself a profitable field for capital investment. In this context, the rapid development of the waste management and environmental pollution control industry and the huge profits generated for the treatment of diseases such as asthma triggered by the polluted air of the cities serve as examples. In addition, the contribution of global warming and cooling to air conditioning production should not be overlooked, because all of these are the result of activities created by human beings. Ultimately, this environmental crisis, unlike scarcities in the supply of goods, is permanent and intensifying. Unless there is an intervention against private profit and competition in favour of human social needs as the main priority behind the organisation of production, it is not possible to solve or even temporarily soften this crisis (Burkett, 2011, 190).

O'Connor (2000) explains that sustainable capitalism is not possible. According to him, capitalism is self-destructive and in times of crisis more hungry, poor, and miserable people appear in the world economy. It is not possible for peasants and especially labourers to endure the crisis for a long time. In this context, nature is under attack everywhere and ecological sustainability begins to disappear. It is well known that many environmental movements are seeking to harmonise the economic activities of conglomerates with the sustainability of forest areas rich in biodiversity, water quality, wildlife, atmospheric conditions, and so on. However, it is seen that the main emphasis of most of these movements is on issues such as production process, technology, recycling, reuse, profitability, and efficiency. It is clear that all environmentalist practices are actually based on economic motives. The rhetoric and practices of recycling facilitate the reuse of the obsolete with the image of being environmentally friendly, thus legitimising consumption fetishism and serving the continuation of profitability and efficiency. In short, even many green movements are thought to restructure nature by making it more usable. In fact, by turning nature into a commodity, it is an undeniable fact that the green movement forces capital to move from the exploitation of nature to a "capitalistised" environment/nature that it restructures in line with its own interests.

In the context of efficiency, it is thought that elements such as energy efficiency and recycling, which seem very sweet and environmentalist to us, actually serve profitability, not the environment. As O'Connor mentioned above, the main purpose of especially environmentally friendly products is nothing more than inventing a capitalistised environment rather than thinking about the environment. In O'Connor's (2000) words, by restructuring nature in the form of "sinks" and "taps"[2] and making them more easily usable, sustainable profit and the continuation of capitalist accumulation are ensured, not sustainable environment. This approach has political, ideological, economic, and ecological repercussions. Some examples of these repercussions are afforestation equivalent to the skyscrapers erected in cities, changing genetics to increase soil crops, polluter pays, environmentally friendly fuel technology, health-friendly paint chemistry, and many other so-called green movements. Therefore, it does not seem possible in the capitalist system that there will not be a losing side in the dilemma of "efficiency" and "nature." Although supranational institutions (such as the EU) are involved in some green movements, it is thought that they actually serve an expanding capitalism. In the capitalist system, it is known that the most ideal solution for capital accumulation is to structure production conditions in a way to increase "efficiency." The logic of capital, which is always focussed on growth, is admittedly not environmental, urban, and social.

EUROPEAN GREEN DEAL

It is possible to see the beginning of the European Union's institutional moves in the field of "environment" since the 1970s. In this sense, the "United Nations Environment Programme" (UNEP) was adopted as a result of the Conference held in Stockholm in 1972. The European Union also put forward the necessity of determining an environmental policy at the Paris Summit held on October 19–20, 1972. The legalisation of the institutional moves was realised in 1987 with the Single European Act. In the following process, the field of environmental policy was expanded with the Maastricht Treaty, which entered into force in 1993. Following the Maastricht Treaty, the Amsterdam Treaty, which entered into force on May 1, 1999, took the issue one step further by making sustainable development one of the objectives of the European Community (see Mutlu and Zenginoğlu, 2019). However, since the 2000s, issues related to environment, climate, and energy have increased their influence in the field of EU policies. At this point, the influence of green politics, which has been on the rise in European politics, should not be ignored, because green parties have shown a remarkable increase both in the parliaments of member states and in the European Parliament. Therefore, green policies and green economy have taken their place among the important agenda items of the European Union (Kakışım, 2022, 7).

Since 2010, the European Union has started to adopt the green economy model in the field of environment and energy in a significant way. With the adoption of the Paris Climate Agreement in 2015, it has focussed on two objectives: (a) keeping the global temperature increase below 1.5°C and (b) adapting to the impacts of climate change (Küçük and Yüce Dural, 2022, 139). In addition to the institutional and legal developments in this context, the European Union has taken one of the most recent and most comprehensive steps in the "nature-environment" focus with the EGD. Declared on December 11, 2019, the EGD put forward a comprehensive and effective "road map" on the "nature-environment" axis (https://www.eur-lex.europa .eu, 2019). At the outset, it should be noted that the EGD has two main objectives, short-term and long-term. Firstly, the short-term goal is to reduce greenhouse gas reductions by 55 percent by 2030 compared to 1990. Here again, zero-pollution targets can be added as an important detail among the 2030 targets (Nurgün, 2023, 158). Secondly, the long-term goal is to reduce net greenhouse gas emissions to zero (climate neutral) by 2050 (Ersoy Mirici and Berberoğlu, 2022, 157).

It is also possible to evaluate the EGD as a vision document. It sets out the basic parameters for transforming the EU economy for a sustainable future. However, it is important to note that the EGD is not a law but rather an empowered political movement and, most importantly, Europe's largest decarbonisation commitment to date (Ecer et al., 2021, 128). In this sense, it should be emphasised that the European Union, together with the EGD, intensively draws attention to the following objectives (see https://www.eeas .europa.eu/_en, 2023): (a) Working with nature to protect our planet, (b) Using clean energy systems, (c) Leading the third industrial revolution, (d) Making transport sustainable for all, (e) Renovating buildings for greener lifestyles, (f) Strengthening global climate action, (g) Transforming the economy and society. Again, within the scope of the relevant text, the following headings should be mentioned as forward-looking action areas: climate law, biodiversity, sustainable agriculture, clean energy, sustainable industry, reducing pollution, protecting nature, financing green projects, transforming buildings into energy efficient, ensuring fair transition for all, leading the green change globally (role model) (Küçük and Yüce Dural, 2022, 143). In this sense, the focus on "EU leading the way" is important because with this plan, the European Union will reduce carbon emissions by switching to a new order called the green order and turn this transformation into a business and growth opportunity at the same time. In this way, the European Union aims to become a "world leader" in the field of circular economy, clean technologies, and decarbonised energy-intensive sectors (Türkoğlu Üstün, 2021, 333).

One of the main parameters of the EGD is the "circular economy." The circular economy replacing the linear economy based on fossil fuels represents the economic aspect of the consensus. This aspect is a guide for both EU countries and other countries that have economic-trade relations with them (Ecer et al., 2021, 131–132). In a close relationship with the circular economy, the green economy focus here is also the means of transition to a low-carbon economy and ensuring environmental sustainability (Küçük and Yüce Dural, 2022, 140). In addition to the circular economy, another prominent parameter is the Carbon Border Adjustment (CBA). The Carbon Border Adjustment was published by the European Commission on July 14, 2021, in order to reduce carbon leakage. As per its decision taken on March 10, 2021, the European Parliament announced that the CBA will be compatible with the WTO (World Trade Organization) and will be implemented in 2023 at the latest. In this context, the obligations to be imposed for selected sectors will be determined by taking into account the carbon content of the goods and it will be established to tax the products to be exported to Europe at rates to be determined (Arısoy, 2021, 7). Therefore, carbon tax constitutes an important position in the transition to a zero-carbon economy within the scope of the EGD. Here, a content that will be valid for both EU members and countries that have trade relations with the European Union is mentioned. According to the EGD, countries that have trade relations with EU countries will have to transition to a low-carbon economy in order to continue their trade with the European Union, even if they do not aim for zero emissions. However, in this context, it should be criticised that green taxes, including the carbon tax, do not have a widespread use at this stage. As to the reasons for this situation, the following points are generally shared: (a) Public scepticism and prejudices about the purpose of taxes and the use of revenues, (b) Asymmetric information between policy-makers and society about environmental problems and alternative environmental policies, (c) The negative impact of carbon tax on carbon-intensive sectors and the concern that this may reflect on competition, (d) The regressive nature of the carbon tax, that is, the structure of the carbon tax that affects low-income groups more negatively (Uyduranoğlu, 2023, 353–361).

It is evident that the EGD is not only a roadmap that the European Union is trying to implement within its own context. At the same time, this process has a scope of international cooperation on the basis of which other actors are or should be involved (Çayırağası and Sakıcı, 2021, 1923). It is possible to evaluate examples such as "working with international partners to improve global environmental standards," which is one of the main objectives of the EU climate neutrality target by 2050, and the mobilisation of all sectors in the EU economy (Ecer et al., 2021, 129). As a matter of fact, the fact that the European Union has declared itself to be a "role model" at this point is considered important in terms of the course of relations with the EGD.

Two questions can be raised here in particular. Firstly, is it possible to find a solution to the global environmental problem only with the plans and practices of the European Union? Secondly, does the European Green Deal envisage a "fully protectionist" or "integrated with nature" structure towards nature/environment? The following answer can be given to the first question: Experiences since the twentieth century have shown that national legal regulations are not sufficient in establishing legal policies towards nature/environment (Türkoğlu Üstün, 2021, 332), because the solutions to a global problem are also expected to be on a global axis. Of course, unlike national law, the possibility and situation for the European Union, which has a supranational structure, to take more effective steps at this point is much higher. However, it does not seem realistic to talk about a global solution only with the reflections of the European Union and its economic, commercial, and legal relations in this direction. Secondly, as the primary problematic of the study, the main emphasis is on nature or efficiency. It should be noted that the EGD does not envisage a completely and directly green economy-policy area, and that there are a number of stages here. This is because the EGD has an impact on many areas, from industry to agriculture and from foreign trade to transport. In order to achieve the climate target in such a wide area, low-cost carbon reduction activities alone will not be sufficient; investments in new decarbonisation technologies will also be required (Türkoğlu Üstün, 2021, 342). Such an approach will bring the topics of investment and sustainable efficiency back to the agenda and the main discussion area may become a cycle.

CONCLUSION

One of the most striking features of the European Union in the international arena is its capacity to update itself in the face of crises on economic, political, sociocultural, or legal grounds. It is possible to encounter many examples in this direction throughout the EU history. As a matter of fact, in this study, it is considered that the EGD has a similar character in the face of the nature-environment orientated global crisis. First of all, it should be underlined that such a move is an important initiative in terms of its reflections on a global scale. Although the question of how successful solution initiatives with a focus on nature-environment can be if they are not on a global axis comes to the fore, the goals of the European Union and its steps towards these goals should not be ignored. Despite this positive picture, in the context of this study, the EGD's "nature-efficiency" dichotomy is analysed within a theoretical background and a critical perspective is presented. In fact, when the text of the EGD is analysed in the light of keywords, it is seen that the words "environment" and "climate" are used intensively, while the similarly intensive use of words such as "sustainability" and "investment" can be read as another issue that confirms the dilemma.

Apart from this theoretical and legal basis, the following points should be shared in order to build a "future" oriented context: Thinking about what will happen thousands of years from now is the best legacy to be left to the world. While leaving this legacy, concrete steps should be taken as much as possible on what should be done. It would be a more concrete step to stand against the ideology of growth than to act against profit-driven companies and the system. In other words, people must first create their own self-discipline by limiting the growth of their desires; what underlies this unlimited desire for economic growth is in fact people's own ambitions that lie in their nature. In this context, instead of producing policies with a single dogma for a sustainable future, it is necessary to create various institutional prescriptions needed to make room for different ecological values and to use the pluralism of different disciplinary perspectives.

The uncontrolled capital accumulation process of the capitalist system lies at the root of environmental destruction in the global context. This is because capitalism focuses on investing in areas where short-term profits are high rather than long-term. However, an economic policy that is in harmony with the environment, not at war with it, requires long-term planning. In fact, in the very long term, it is an economic policy in which future generations will receive their rights at least as much as current generations. In addition, in capitalism, some measures are taken after problems arise. However, long-term planning is possible through preventive policies (Demirer et al., 2000). No result can be achieved by imposing ecological values from the top on abstract models of the capitalist system. What needs to be done is to support the struggle of workers and other communities to improve their material-social conditions and human development. The necessary socioeconomic institutions and ecological values are to put an end to the alienation in the conditions of human production, to initiate a process by which everyone participates in collective-democratic struggles, moving from exploitative conditions of moneymaking to sustainable human development (Burkett, 2011). With the concepts of economy and ecology coming from the same root (*oikos*), it is necessary to somehow focus on the concept of "world ecology"[3] rather than green movements made by a group or institution or even an international organisation. Because, economically, the future guarantee of almost all living things depends on nature.

NOTES

1. For more detailed information on this issue, see Apaydın and Zenginoğlu, "Hiç Kimse Eşit Değildir," 283–307.
2. The term "sink" here means waste disposal and "tap" means raw material utilisation.
3. For detailed explanations on this subject, see Deleage and Hemery, "From Ecological History," 21–36.

REFERENCES

Amin, Samir. (2018). *Emperyalizm ve Eşitsiz Gelişme*. Translated by Semih Lim. İstanbul: Yordam Kitap.

Apaydın, Ferhat, and Zenginoğlu, Samet. (2022). "Hiç Kimse Eşit Değildir Ancak Bazıları Daha Eşit Değildir": Byung-Chul Han ve Neoliberalizmin Geleceğini Yeniden Düşünmek. *Akademik Hassasiyetler* 9(20):283–307.

Arısoy, Hasan. (2021). Avrupa Yeşil Mutabakatı. *ATED*: 6–12.

Aşıcı, Ahmet Atıl. (2022). Çare Türkiye Yeşil Mutabakatı mı? In *Ekoloji: Bir Arada Yaşamanın Geleceği*, edited by Didem Bayındır ve Mine Yıldırım (pp. 127–145). İstanbul: Tellekt.

Ataöv, Türkkaya. (2009). *Kapitalizm ve Çevre: Kapitalist Emperyalizmin Çevre Soygunu*. İstanbul: İleri Yayınları.

"Avrupa Yeşil Mutabakatı." (n.d.). Accessed May 2, 2023. https://www.eeas.europa .eu/delegations/t%C3%BCrkiye/avrupa-ye%C5%9Fil-mutabakat%C4%B1_tr

Baydemir, Tuncay. (2021). Avrupa Yeşil Mutabakatı: Temiz Dünya Vizyonu ile Büyüme Stratejisi. *Bilim ve Teknik* 644:12–29.

Bourdieu, Pierre. (2021). *Karşı Ateşler-Neoliberal İstilaya Karşı Direnişe Hizmet Edecek Sözler*. Translated by Sertaç Canbolat. İstanbul: Sel Yayıncılık.

Burkett, Paul. (2011). *Marksizm ve Ekolojik İktisat: Kızıl ve Yeşil Bir Ekonomi Politiğe Doğru*. Translated by Ertan Günçiner. İstanbul: Yordam Kitap.

Çayırağası, Filiz, and Sakıcı, Şehnaz. (2021). Avrupa Yeşil Mutabakatı (Green Deal) ve Birleşmiş Milletler Sürdürülebilir Kalkınma Hedefleri Perspektifinde Sürdürülebilir Dijital Pazarlama Stratejileri. *Gaziantep University Journal of Social Sciences* 20(4):1916–1937.

Daly, Herman E. (1974). The Economics of the Steady State. *American Economic Review* 64(2):15–21.

Deleage, Jean-Paul, and Hemery, Daniel. (1990). From Ecological History to World Ecology. In *The Silent Countdown*, edited by Peter Brimblecombe and Christian Pfister (pp. 21–36). Berlin: Springer.

Demirer, Göksel N., Duran, Metin, and Torunoğlu, Ethem. (2000). Marksist Ekoloji Anlayışı Üzerine. In *Marksizm ve Ekoloji*, edited by Göksel N. Demirer, Metin Duran, ve Gökçer Özgür (pp. 166–193). Ankara: Öteki Yayınevi.

Dobb, Maurice. (1973). *Kapitalizm Sosyalizm Az Gelişmiş Ülkeler ve İktisadi Kalkınma*. Translated by Mehmet Selik. Ankara: Doğan Yayınevi.

Ecer, Kübra, Güner, Oğuz, and Çetin, Murat. (2021). Avrupa Yeşil Mutabakatı ve Türkiye Ekonomisinin Uyum Politikaları. *İşletme ve İktisat Çalışmaları Dergisi* 9(2):125–144.

Ersoy Mirici, Merve, and Berberoğlu, Süha. (2022). Türkiye Perspektifinde Yeşil Mutabakat ve Karbon Ayak İzi: Tehdit mi? Fırsat mı? *Artvin Çoruh Üniversitesi Doğal Afetler Uygulama ve Araştırma Merkezi Doğal Afetler ve Çevre Dergisi* 8(1):156–164.

European Commission. (2019). *The European Green Deal*. European Commission. Brussels, 11.12.2019: COM(2019) 640 final. Accessed April 11, 2023. https://eur -lex.europa.eu/resource.html?uri=cellar:b828d165-1c22-11ea-8c1f-01aa75ed71a1 .0002.02/DOC_1&format=PDF

Foster, John Bellamy, and Magdoff, Fred. (2014). *Her Çevrecinin Kapitalizm Hakkında Bilmesi Gerekenler: Kapitalizm ve Çevre Üzerine Bir Rehber*. Translated by Özgün Aksakal. İstanbul: Patika Kitap.

Kakışım, Cemal. (2022). Avrupa Yeşil Mutabakatı: Yeşil Teori Perspektifinden Bir Analiz. *Stratejik ve Sosyal Araştırmalar Dergisi* 6(1):1–16.

Küçük, Gülay, and Yüce Dural, Betül. (2022). Avrupa Yeşil Mutabakatı ve Yeşil Ekonomiye Geçiş: Enerji Senaryoları Üzerinden Bir Değerlendirme. *Anadolu Üniversitesi Sosyal Bilimler Dergisi* 22(1):137–156.

Milanovic, Branko. (2018). *Küresel Eşitsizlik: Küreselleşme Çağı İçin Yeni Bir Yaklaşım*. Translated by Meneviş Uzbay and Mustafa Pirili. Ankara: Efil Yayınevi.

Mutlu, Mustafa, and Zenginoğlu, Samet. (2019). Yeşil Teori Perspektifinden Avrupa Birliği Çevre Politikası. *Asos Journal* 7(88):459–469.

Nurgün, Müge. (2023). Toksik İçermeyen Bir Çevre İçin Sıfır Kirlilik Hedefi. In *Avrupa Yeşil Mutabakatı Kapsamında Yeşil Ekonomi,* edited by Funda H. Sezgin, Esra Yüksel Acı, Rana Atabay Kuşçu (pp. 151–169). Ankara: Nobel Yayınları.

O'Connor, James. (2000). Sürdürülebilir Kapitalizm Mümkün mü? In *Marksizm ve Ekoloji,* edited by Göksel N. Demirer, Metin Duran, ve Gökçer Özgür (pp. 15–48). Ankara: Öteki Yayınevi.

Roy, Arundhati. (2015). *Kapitalizm: Bir Hayalet Hikayesi*. Translated by Çiçek Öztek. İstanbul: Sel Yayıncılık.

Skirberkk, Gunnar. (2000). Marksizm ve Ekoloji. In *Marksizm ve Ekoloji,* edited by Göksel N. Demirer, Metin Duran, ve Gökçer Özgür (pp. 49–60). Ankara: Öteki Yayınevi.

Türkoğlu Üstün, Kamile. (2021). Yeni Bir Dönemin Başlangıcı: Avrupa Yeşil Mutabakatı ve Türk Çevre Hukuku ve Politikalarına Etkileri. *Memleket Siyaset Yönetim* 16(36):329–366.

Uyduranoğlu, Ayşe. (2023). Avrupa Yeşil Muatabakatı'nda Uygulanması Gereken Karbon Vergisinin Önündeki Engeller: Asimetrik Bilgi ve Ön Yargı. In *Avrupa Yeşil Mutabakatı Kapsamında Yeşil Ekonomi,* edited by Funda H. Sezgin, Esra Yüksel Acı, Rana Atabay Kuşçu (pp. 351–374). Ankara: Nobel Yayınları.

Yüksel Acı, Esra. (2023). Sürdürülebilir İnsani Kalkınma Perspektifinden Yeşil Ekonomi ve Avrupa Yeşil Mutabakatı. In *Avrupa Yeşil Mutabakatı Kapsamında Yeşil Ekonomi*, edited by Funda H. Sezgin, Esra Yüksel Acı, Rana Atabay Kuşçu (pp. 1–17). Ankara: Nobel Yayınları.

6

The Role of Green Bonds in Driving the Sustainable Financial Transformation of the European Union's Economy

Kaan Çelikok and Gülden Poyraz

INTRODUCTION

Significant transformations in economic and social systems are imperative to achieve the challenging goal of restricting the increase in global temperature to 1.5°C. The integration of environmental considerations into financial decision-making is anticipated to be a vital mechanism in facilitating the transformation to a low-carbon economy, and financial markets are anticipated to have a significant influence in this regard. The issuance of green bonds is acknowledged as an essential tool for mobilising financial resources toward achieving the goals of the Paris Agreement because they have the dual benefits of offering financial returns to investors while also encouraging a consistent demand in financial markets. There have been several green bond issuances since the European Investment Bank issued its first one in 2007 (Gianfrate and Peri, 2019, 2–3; Turguttopbaş, 2020, 275).

The study aims to investigate and assess how green bonds fit into Europe's sustainable economy's financial transformation. It is concentrated on examining how green bonds may assist in developing and implementing the European Green Deal and their potential to contribute a sustainable economic transformation in this environment.

The study begins by establishing a firm conceptual foundation for green bonds through an extensive review of pertinent literature. It then delves into green bonds' origins, evolution, practical applications, advantages, and potential drawbacks. Furthermore, it is aimed to provide insights into how the use of green bonds can support the European Union's broader sustainability objectives. The study also identifies the challenges and opportunities associated with the use of green bonds in the context of the European Green Deal, including regulatory and market-related issues. Specifically, the study provides a comprehensive understanding of EU policies, regulations, and initiatives related to green bonds, including the Green Bond Standard and the EU Taxonomy. An extra focus is placed on EU initiatives to promote the issuing of green bonds by member states, supranational organisations, and businesses in order to support ecologically sound initiatives and the shift to a low-carbon economy.

A COMPREHENSIVE OVERVIEW OF GREEN BONDS: DEFINITION AND CLASSIFICATION

A unique class of fixed-income financial instruments known as green bonds is created to fund or refinance projects, possessions, or commercial endeavours that have a positive environmental impact (Hyun et al., 2019, 129). They are a subset of climate bonds that can be issued by governments, multinational banks, or corporations just like regular bonds—that's why green bonds are similar to other types of bonds in that they are a form of debt financing. That means that they are similar to traditional bonds but the proceeds are used exclusively for projects that promote sustainability and address environmental challenges, making them more attractive to environmentally conscious investors. They also provide companies and governments with a source of capital to finance green projects that may not be profitable on their own. In contrast, other types of bonds are not necessarily used for green projects and may not have a direct environmental benefit, making them less attractive to environmentally conscious investors (Ehlers and Packer, 2017, 89).

The two most popular guidelines for green bonds are the Green Bond Principles (GBP) and the Climate Bonds Standard. Green bonds are any bonds that will only be used to finance or refinance new or existing qualifying green projects, according to the GBP (OECD, 2017, 23). An investor-focused, nonprofit group called the Climate Bonds Initiative is aiming to organise the global bond market in order to spur and expand climate funding. A green bond, according to the Initiative, is used to finance initiatives that help the environment, such as pollution reduction, renewable energy, or energy efficiency (Climate Bonds Initiative, 2018).

Due to unfamiliarity, several nations have major challenges while implementing global green bond criteria. Furthermore, it's possible that regulators, potential issuers, and investors do not completely understand the advantages of the green bond market. Even seasoned financial experts might not be familiar with green bonds. Multilateral Development Banks (MDBs) and supranational organisations may assist in informing diverse stakeholders, including institutional investors, commercial banks, municipalities, and some of the biggest enterprises in the world, about the benefits of green bonds (Banga, 2019, 19).

Green bonds are issued in accordance with the Paris Agreement framework, which was ratified in 2015 with the purpose of constraining the detrimental impacts of climate change and global warming. This is accomplished by mitigating the quantity of greenhouse gas emissions discharged into the atmosphere. The financial resources generated from the distribution of green bonds are allocated towards financing environmental projects, such as renewable energy, energy efficiency, sustainable transportation, waste management, and other ventures that advance climate and environmental protection. Green bonds may be used by both companies and governments to finance green infrastructure initiatives and help make their operations more environmentally friendly (United Nations, 2015).

Rizzello (2022, 29) classified green bonds into three groups: The first of these, the Climate Bonds Initiative, has distinguished itself among green bonds, with a special emphasis on financing projects aimed at addressing climate change mitigation and adaptation. Green Income Bonds represent a specific category of debt instruments, where the credit risk linked with the bond is contingent upon the cash flows generated by a specific project or income stream, such as fees or taxes, rather than being borne by the issuer. This implies that the responsibility of repaying the bond lies with the cash flows generated by the green project funded by the bond, rather than the issuer. As a result, investors solely rely on the cash flows generated by the green project to receive repayment for the bond. The third group, Green Securitised Bonds, are created using the conventional securitisation structure, where a vehicle that holds the bond purchases debt portfolios that are secured by renewable energy projects from banks. The securitised bonds are considered "green" if they meet the requirements for labelling a green bond at the time of issuance. This means that the proceeds from the issuance of green securitised bonds must be used for environmentally sustainable projects and meet the disclosure requirements for green bonds.

An examination of green financial instruments was carried out by Frydrych (2021, 245–251), who categorised them based on the type of coupon they offer. It was observed that fixed coupons were the most prevalent type of coupon in the study, and they held the top position in the ranking. Subsequently, the other types of coupons, such as discount or zero-coupon instruments and floating coupon instruments, followed behind fixed coupons in the ranking.

AN EXPLORATION OF THE HISTORICAL BACKGROUND AND DEVELOPMENTAL TRAJECTORY OF GREEN BONDS

Following the release of a study by the Intergovernmental Panel on Climate Change (IPCC), green bonds first appeared in 2007. The study revealed a link between human activity and climate change. A number of Swedish pension funds indicated interest in funding initiatives that help to mitigate climate change in the wake of this research. In November 2008, the World Bank issued the first green bond, aiming to raise money from fixed-income investors to support qualified climate-focused initiatives. In response to investors' increasing interest in fixed-income investments connected to the environment, the International Finance Corporation (IFC) issued its first green bonds in 2010. In 2013, the IFC released two $1 billion-sized green bonds, which were the first of their kind in the market. These green bonds, which were the biggest of their kind when they were issued, greatly contributed to setting a standard and bolstering the green bond market (World Bank, 2021).

The GBP, which were established in 2014 by a number of international organisations with the intention of encouraging the development of green bond markets globally, provide issuers with a comprehensive set of best practices for the issuance of green bonds and are designed to promote integrity and transparency in the market (World Bank, 2019).

THE BENEFITS OF GREEN BONDS IN SUPPORTING ENVIRONMENTAL SUSTAINABILITY AND ECONOMIC GROWTH

The ability of green bonds to allow investors to support environmentally beneficial activities while simultaneously providing them with a financial return on their investment is its major advantage. They also let businesses and organisations finance green projects and show stakeholders their dedication to sustainability. Issuing green bonds can be particularly beneficial for companies that are not purely focused on sustainability, as it can help integrate sustainability into the overall operations of the organisation by linking sustainability and financial management functions (Maltais and Nykvist, 2020, 11).

Schmittmann and Chua (2021, 17–20) found that companies issuing green bonds generally have lower CO_2 emissions in relation to their revenue and assets compared to those who do not issue green bonds. Companies or entities that issue green bonds are also more likely to disclose their carbon emissions to investors and the public, as part of their commitment to transparency and accountability in the context of sustainable finance. The positive effect of green bonds is consistent across various industries. Additionally, environmental rating rankings are often higher for green bond issuers than for non-issuers. Companies that seek external reviews for their green bond issuances tend to have lower CO_2 emissions than those that do not.

In the wake of the Paris Climate Agreement, green bonds may be a powerful tool for businesses to communicate their sustainability strategy and enhance their brand. Companies may show their dedication to sustainability and transparency by issuing green bonds, and they can also get access to a rising market of investors that give environmental, social, and governance (ESG) concerns a high priority when choosing which investments to make (Shishlov et al., 2016, 9–10).

Green bonds provide investors with increased transparency regarding the impact of their funds and the utilisation of proceeds. This enables investors to develop better-informed investment strategies and risk assessments. This helps investors to better understand issuers' environments and strategies, leading to enhanced communication between issuers and lenders. Green bonds also help institutional investors with long-term outlooks to diversify their investment portfolios by providing the essential data on the effects of investment items on the environment. Green bonds can serve as a means for socially responsible investors to broaden their investment portfolio by investing in companies that may not meet their usual screening criteria, as long as the proceeds from the bond issuance are utilised to finance a project that aligns with their screening criteria (Shishlov et al., 2016, 9–10).

The systemic benefits of green bonds include bridging knowledge gaps on ESG issues, improving capital allocation, and better linking securities with tangible investments. However, green bonds alone cannot stimulate the low-carbon transition without other policies that incentivise the creation of green project initiatives. To make the green bond market meaningful, it needs to be sufficiently large and supported by both public and private stakeholders. Governments and regulatory bodies have the potential to act as key actors in promoting and ensuring the longevity and sustainability of the green bond market (Shishlov et al., 2016, 9–10).

Green bonds have played a significant role in the development of the green finance sector since their introduction in 2007. These innovative green bonds have sparked the creation of a wide range of other sustainable financial products and services. Many different entities, including international financial institutions, large corporations, banks, national governments, and municipalities, are now issuing green bonds. The issuing of new green bonds increased in popularity, reaching USD 155.5 billion in 2017. Green bonds are used to finance projects that have a positive impact on the environment, such as those that use renewable energy, sustainably manage natural resources, are energy efficient (including building renovations), and prevent and control pollution. Green bond purchasers have the certainty that the proceeds of the issue will be utilised for the intended purpose, and the largest buyers of green bonds are institutions. Green bonds have played an important role in mobilising private funding for green initiatives and in achieving sustainable development objectives (Berrou et al., 2019, 15–16).

EXAMINING THE RISKS AND CHALLENGES OF GREEN BONDS IN SUPPORTING SUSTAINABLE FINANCE: IMPLICATIONS FOR INVESTORS AND ISSUERS

As a financial tool to promote sustainable financing and develop ecologically sustainable activities, green bonds have grown in popularity in recent years. However, green bonds do come with risks and difficulties for both investors and issuers, just like any other financial product.

The green bond market faces several risks, including lack of awareness among potential issuers and investors, small market size and low liquidity, absence of absolute standards and limited legal regulations, additional costs associated with green bond labelling and reporting, and doubts about the green qualities of bonds issued. These challenges can lead to increased costs of funds, reputation damage for issuers, and investor demand for penalties if green principles are not upheld (Kandır and Yakar, 2017, 163–164).

While green bonds are an increasingly popular tool for financing environmentally friendly projects and initiatives, there are still some uncertainties and potential downsides to consider. One potential challenge is the issue of pricing and return uncertainties, as the market for green bonds is still relatively new and may not yet be fully developed or understood by all investors. This could lead to greater volatility or uncertainty in pricing and returns (Coskun and Unalmis, 2022, 74).

There is a risk of "greenwashing" where issuers may claim that their bonds are green or sustainable without providing adequate evidence to support these claims. Investors need to carefully assess the green credentials of the issuer and the project being financed by the bond. If the issuers exaggerate the environmental benefits of the projects being funded by these bonds, this can mislead investors and undermine the credibility of the green bond market (Banga, 2019, 27).

THE EUROPEAN UNION'S APPROACH TO GREEN BONDS

Historical Perspectives, Policy Priorities, and Strategic Goals

The regulations adopted in accordance with Article 322 of the Treaty on the Functioning of the European Union set down the requirements for Member States' control and auditing, as well as the specific guidelines for each institution's duties with regard to carrying out its own expenditures. The Commission is in charge of carrying out the budget within the allocated funds and in accordance with good financial management practices, working together with the Member States. The Commission may, within the budget and within the limits and circumstances stated, shift appropriations from one chapter or subdivision to another. To make sure that the funds are spent in conformity with the principles of good financial management, the Member States must work with the Commission (Official Journal of the European Union, 2016, C 202/186).

In Europe, green bonds have grown in importance as a mechanism for funding ecologically friendly initiatives including renewable energy, sustainable transportation, and green structures. Green bond issuance is encouraged and their environmental credentials are verified by the EU Green Bond Standard and other programs. The development of the green bond market in Europe has been accelerated by the European Green Deal. This market is aimed at funding projects that are crucial in attaining climate neutrality by the year 2050. The emergence of verifiers and assurance providers has examined the process and environmental integrity, and standardisation efforts have borne fruit through self-regulatory initiatives like the Green Bond Principles and Climate Bond Standards, recognised and backed by public financial institutions and development banks (OECD, 2017).

The GBP provide a framework for issuers of green bonds to disclose information about the environmental criteria used to select the projects, the management of the proceeds raised, and the ongoing reporting and monitoring of the environmental impacts of the funded projects (ICMA, 2021).

The European Commission plans to raise up to €250 billion via green bonds, which represents 30 percent of the NextGenerationEU funds. This move is expected to bring several benefits, such as the introduction of a highly rated and liquid green asset to the market, as well as expanding the range of investors who can access green investments. Additionally, this will allow investors to diversify their portfolio of green investments with a highly rated and liquid asset, which may accelerate sustainable investments. Furthermore, this move confirms the European Commission's commitment to sustainable finance, boosts the green bond market, and sets an example

for other issuers to follow. Lastly, it is expected to enhance the position of
the European Union and the euro currency in the sustainable finance markets
(European Commission, 2021b).

Investors are given extra reassurance by external reviews that the issuer's
Green Bond Framework is reliable and compliant with GBP. The Green Bond
Principles (GBP) 2021 edition advises issuers to enlist the help of an outside
reviewer to carry out an unbiased analysis of the Green Bond Framework
and determine the issuer's compliance with the GBP. To guarantee that the
funds are used as intended, accreditation by third-party organisations is also
a regular practice in the green bond market. These agencies confirm that the
green bond–funded projects adhere to strict environmental standards, such
as lowering greenhouse gas emissions, protecting natural resources, or supporting sustainable land use. The Climate Bonds Initiative, the International
Capital Market Association, and the Sustainability Bond Guidelines are some
instances of third parties that certify green bonds (ICMA, 2021).

In June 2021, the GBP was updated to provide more guidance on the use
of proceeds, reporting, and transparency, and to include new sustainability-
linked bond principles. The key updates to the GBP 2021 include:

When issuing green bonds, issuers should take into consideration all four
of the following basic components that are included in the 2021 version of the
Green Bond Principles: the use of proceeds, the process for project appraisal
and selection, management of proceeds, and reporting and assurance.

In addition to these fundamental elements, the edition of 2021 specifies
crucial suggestions with respect to Green Bond Frameworks and External
Reviews (ICMA, 2021):

Use of proceeds: GBP 2021 gives greater clarification on the criteria that
should be met by qualified green projects and contains additional guidelines
on the application of revenues to social initiatives. It is required that the revenues from the sale of the bonds be used only for the purpose of financing
existing or new initiatives that promote climate change adaptation, mitigation, or both. Projects related to renewable energy, energy efficiency, sustainable agriculture, forestry, water management, and low-carbon transportation
may be considered eligible for funding. Disclosure of how profits from green
bonds are used is done both to prevent "greenwashing," which is making misleading or inflated assertions regarding a product or service's environmental
advantages in order to establish credibility in the market for green bonds
(Nemes et al., 2022, 10).

Project evaluation and selection: The projects to be financed must undergo
a rigorous evaluation process that considers their environmental impact, technical feasibility, and financial sustainability. The projects must also comply
with applicable environmental and social standards and regulations.

Management of proceeds: The proceeds from the bond issuance must be managed separately from the issuer's other funds, and the use of the funds must be tracked and reported on a regular basis.

Reporting and transparency: The revised criteria demand more thorough and consistent reporting on how supported projects affect the environment, including the use of third-party verifiers. According to the principles of green bonds, it is the issuer's responsibility to provide regular disclosures on the use of funds and the environmental effects of the projects that have been funded. Additionally, the issuer should also furnish any other pertinent information that would assist investors in evaluating the environmental soundness of the bond.

Sustainability-Linked Bond Principles (SLBPs): This is a new set of principles that expand the GBP to include bonds where the proceeds are not earmarked for specific green projects, but are instead tied to the issuer's sustainability performance.

The purpose of establishing such criteria is to instil in investors a heightened level of assurance that their investment in green bonds will result in tangible environmental advantages and facilitate the shift towards a low-carbon economy.

It is abundantly obvious that the urgent need to address climate change and other environmental challenges is intimately linked to the development of the green bond market as well as its further expansion. Investors are given the chance to support environmental efforts while still experiencing economic advantages via the purchase of "green bonds," which provide organisations with a method for raising funds that may be utilised for projects with the goal of lowering carbon emissions and other effects on the environment. Additionally, green bonds give businesses a way to raise funds for these kinds of initiatives. In 2007, the European Investment Bank (EIB) was responsible for the issuance of the world's first green bond. Since then, the cumulative issuance of green, social, and sustainability (GSS) bonds has been close to €2.2 trillion, which is a number that emphasises the pertinence of the EIB's fifteen-year-old effort (European Investment Bank, 2022). Additionally, the market has been opened up to private enterprises, with Environmental Defense Fund (EDF) issuing the very first corporate green bond in the year 2013. The market expansion can be attributed, in part, to the acknowledgment of the significance of capital markets in promoting sustainable economic growth, as well as the necessity for novel funding mechanisms to confront exigent environmental predicaments (Broadstock et al., 2021, 120–121).

In addition, the European Union is thinking about using monetary policy to make money available for green investment possibilities. The European Central Bank (ECB) has given its approval to use its large asset purchase scheme to pursue green objectives, and it is currently investigating various potential ways to do so. These potential ways include concentrating on green bond purchases, applying less stringent risk-mitigation measures to green assets used as collateral, and imposing lower capital charges on green assets held by banks. Isabel Schnabel, a member of the board of directors of the ECB, has outlined three primary routes via which the ECB might assist in the fight against climate change. These avenues include considering climate factors when formulating and conducting monetary policy operations. However, there is a discussion going on in the realm of monetary policy over whether or not market neutrality should be prioritised above taking into consideration the threats that climate change brings to the stability of prices (Tagliapietra and Veugelers, 2020, 72–74).

EU Regulatory Framework for Green Bonds

The European Green Consensus (2019) recommends that the European Union should develop a green bond standard to make sustainable investment easier and more convenient. The market for green bonds is growing rapidly as investors become more interested in sustainable investing. In light of the need for substantial backing from both public and private entities, the European Green Deal Investment Plan (EGDIP) has been put forward by the Commission as a sustainable European Investment Plan, which aims at a fair and green transition. The EGDIP will assist in the development of a European Green Bond Standard, which will outline the requirements for green bond issuance and the benchmarks for investor trust. The transition to a low-carbon and climate-resilient economy will be financed by a €500 billion investment plan and a combination of public and private funding will be used to pay. The EIB will make the government investment. This will offer a uniform framework for the issuing of green bonds throughout the European Union (European Parliament, 2020, 5). The European Green Bond Standard will cover the following areas (Norton Rose Fulbright, 2023):

• Clear definitions of eligible green investments and sustainable projects
• Transparency and disclosure requirements
• Assessment and reporting mechanisms
• Governance structures
• Alignment with the European Union's Paris Agreement commitments
• Oversight and enforcement mechanisms

The European Green Bond Standard has been formulated with the objective of furnishing issuers and investors with a framework to follow, and is anticipated to serve as a benchmark for the establishment of additional green bond standards at the national and regional levels. Furthermore, it is expected to serve as a touchstone for the creation of green bond products and markets. The Standard is designed to be flexible enough to accommodate the needs of a wide range of issuers, investors, and markets. The Standard offers a structure for the creation, administration, and reporting of green bonds. It outlines the standards for a green bond to be considered a European Green Bond as well as the issuer reporting obligations. The Standard also outlines the process for determining whether a bond qualifies for the "green bond" designation. It is designed to be a voluntary, market-driven effort, and its adoption is not meant to result in any new governmental obligations. It is anticipated to offer issuers and investors a blueprint to adhere to, and is designed to function as a point of reference for the evolution of supplementary national and regional green bond standards (KPMG, n.d.).

The EU Taxonomy Regulation was fully implemented on July 12, 2020, after being officially published in the Official Gazette on June 22, 2020. The EU Taxonomy's main goal is to support sustainable finance policies by providing a collection of performance criteria that includes these distinct goals: pollution prevention and control, biodiversity conservation, adaptation to climate change, wise use and protection of water and marine resources, and transition to a circular economy. The objective is to educate businesses and investors on sustainable capital management practices (Official Journal of the European Union, 2020).

The EU Taxonomy is a reliable tool that creates a common language around green activities and translates climate and environmental objectives into clear criteria. It will support companies in planning and financing their transition towards sustainability, while mitigating market fragmentation, protecting against greenwashing, and accelerating financing for sustainable and transitional projects. It is an essential element of a broader sustainable finance framework that provides a complete toolkit for financing the transition. Its value is predicated on the ability to increase investment in green projects that are deemed essential for the successful execution of the European Green Deal (European Commission, 2021a, 2).

On July 6, 2021, the Commission put forward a proposition for a regulatory framework aimed at instituting European green bonds. The "European Green Bond" or EuGB application area for bonds that promote ecologically friendly goals is to be regulated under the EuGB proposal. It aims to establish a system for the registration and auditing of entities acting as external auditors for the EuGB and to frame the EuGB issue audits (Council of the EU, 2023).

On April 8, 2022, the Council endorsed its stance on the proposal, indicating its willingness to engage in talks with the European Parliament to achieve consensus on the definitive draft of the regulation (Council of the European Union, 2022).

Green Bond Regulations in EU Member States

As of 2022, most EU member states have established regulations or guidelines for issuing green bonds. However, the specific regulations and guidelines vary by country.

France's Green OATs (Obligations Assimilables du Trésor) are a type of sovereign bond that is specifically issued to raise funds to finance green investments and projects that are geared towards addressing environmental concerns and climate change. The first Green OAT was launched in 2017 and was followed by a second Green OAT in 2021. The funds raised from these bonds are used to finance central government budget expenditure and expenditure under the "Invest for the Future" programme to fight climate change, protect biodiversity, adapt to climate change, and fight pollution. The Green OATs of France are administered in accordance with the general budget guideline and treated like monies from a traditional OAT. The maximum amount of Green OATs that may be issued in a given year is determined by the sum of the Green Eligible Expenditures in that year and the monies earned through Green OATs. This implies that the money earned through Green OATs is devoted solely to green endeavours, helping to guarantee that they are advancing the objectives of the Paris Climate Agreement (Agence France Trésor, 2023).

Germany has also established guidelines for green bond issuances, which include requirements for the use of proceeds, reporting and verification, and external reviews. Other EU member states, like Sweden, have created optional standards for green bond issuances that offer guidance on how to utilise the revenues and how to report on the environmental effect. In general, more regulation and uniformity in green bond issuances are being sought by EU member states.

CONCLUSION

Green bonds are a financial tool used to fund environmentally sustainable projects, providing an opportunity for investors to support sustainable initiatives while earning a return on their investment and for issuers to demonstrate their commitment to sustainability.

The preferential treatment of green bonds, such as acceptance as part of central bank reserves or as highly liquid capital components by prudential authorities, may have both positive and negative impacts on the stability of the financial sector. On the positive side, the promotion of green finance through the preferential treatment of green bonds can lead to a more sustainable and environmentally friendly economy, which is increasingly prioritised by governments and societies around the world. This can help to reduce the risks associated with climate change, such as the physical risks from natural disasters, and the transition risks associated with the shift towards a low-carbon economy. Furthermore, green bonds can help to diversify the portfolios of financial institutions, reducing their exposure to traditional high-carbon assets that may become stranded as a result of changing regulations and consumer preferences. On the negative side, there is a risk that the preferential treatment of green bonds may create a bubble in the market, leading to overvaluation and misallocation of resources. This may result in a sudden collapse of the market, with potential implications for financial stability. Furthermore, there is a risk that the preferential treatment of green bonds may crowd out other types of investments that are also important for sustainable development, such as social infrastructure or education. This could potentially lead to a suboptimal allocation of resources, which could have negative implications for economic growth and welfare. Overall, it is important to carefully consider the potential benefits and risks of preferential treatment of green bonds for financial stability and to develop appropriate policies and regulations to ensure a balanced and sustainable development of the market.

The development of the green bond market is a critical step towards achieving the ambitious goals of the European Green Deal and transitioning to a more sustainable economy. By providing dedicated financing for environmentally friendly projects, green bonds can help to accelerate the transition to a low-carbon future and support the broader goals of sustainable development.

The process of allocating the required financial resources for green initiatives involves the European Union, which is an important player. By virtue of its monetary policy, regulatory framework, and measures relevant to the formation of standards, the European Union has the capacity to nurture an environment that is favourable for the growth of the green bond market and the green finance industry as a whole.

REFERENCES

Agence France Trésor. (2023). Green OATs. Accessed March 22, 2023. https://www.aft.gouv.fr/en/green-oat

Banga, J. (2019). The Green Bond Market: A Potential Source of Climate Finance for Developing Countries. *Journal of Sustainable Finance & Investment* 9(1):17–32.

Berrou, R., Dessertine, P., and Migliorelli, M. (2019). An Overview of Green Finance. In *The Rise of Green Finance in Europe: Opportunities and Challenges for Issuers, Investors and Marketplaces* (pp. 3–29). Palgrave MacMillan.

Broadstock, D. C., Cheng, L. T., and Wang, T. (2021). Understanding Green Bond Challenges: A Stakeholder's Perspective. In *Green Finance, Sustainable Development, and the Belt and Road Initiative* (pp. 119–155). Routledge.

Climate Bonds Initiative. (2018). Green Bonds: The State of the Market. https://www .climatebonds.net/files/reports/cbi_gbm_final_032019_web.pdf

Coskun, Y., and Unalmis, I. (2022). Role of Governments in Enhancing Green Digital Finance for Meeting the SDGs. In *Green Digital Finance and Sustainable Development Goals* (pp. 69–88). Singapore: Springer Nature.

Council of the European Union. (2022). Regulation of the European Parliament and the Council on European Green Bonds: Mandate for Negotiations with the European Parliament. Brussels: Interinstitutional File 2021/0191 (COD).

Council of the European Union. (2023). European Green Bonds: Council adopts new regulation to promote sustainable finance. Press release. October 24, 2023. https:// www.consilium.europa.eu/en/press/press-releases/2023/10/24/european-green-bonds-council-adopts-new-regulation-to-promote-sustainable-finance/

Ehlers, T., and Packer, F. (2017). Green Bond Finance and Certification. *BIS Quarterly Review* September.

European Commission. (2021a). FAQ: What Is the EU Taxonomy and How Will It Work in Practice? Accessed April 16, 2023. https://finance.ec.europa.eu/system/ files/2021-04/sustainable-finance-taxonomy-faq_en.pdf

European Commission. (2021b). Questions and Answers: NextGenerationEU Green Bond Framework and Funding Plan Update. Accessed April 3, 2023. https://ec .europa.eu/commission/presscorner/detail/hu/QANDA_21_4567

European Investment Bank. (2022). 15 Years of EIB Green Bonds: Leading Sustainable Investment from Niche to Mainstream. Accessed April 3, 2023. https://www .eib.org/en/press/all/2022-308-15-years-of-eib-green-bonds-leading-sustainable -investment-from-niche-to-mainstream

European Parliament. (2020). European Green Deal Investment Plan: Main Elements and Possible Impact of the Coronavirus Pandemic. Briefing by Alessandro D'Alfonso, Members' Research Service, PE 649.371, April 2020. https://www .europarl.europa.eu/RegData/etudes/BRIE/2020/649371/EPRS_BRI(2020)649371 _EN.pdf

Frydrych, S. (2021). Green Bonds as an Instrument for Financing in Europe. *Ekonomia i Prawo. Economics and Law* 20(2):239–255.

Gianfrate, G., and Peri, M. (2019). The Green Advantage: Exploring the Convenience of Issuing Green Bonds. *Journal of Cleaner Production* 219:127–135.

Hyun, S., Park, D., and Tian, S. (2019). Differences Between Green Bonds Versus Conventional Bonds: An Empirical Exploration. In *Handbook of Green Finance: Energy Security and Sustainable Development* (pp. 127–154). Singapore: Springer.

International Capital Market Association (ICMA). (2021). Green Bond Principles (GBP): Voluntary Process Guidelines for Issuing Green Bonds. Paris: ICMA.

Kandır, S. Y., and Yakar, S. (2017). Yeşil Tahvil Piyasaları: Türkiye'de Yeşil Tahvil Piyasasının Geliştirilebilmesi İçin Öneriler. *Çukurova Üniversitesi Sosyal Bilimler Enstitüsü Dergisi* 26(2):159–175.

KPMG. (n.d.). EU Sustainable Finance Explained—Green Bonds. Accessed April 15, 2023. https://kpmg.com/fi/fi/home/Pinnalla/2019/11/eu-sustainable-finance -explained-green-bonds.html

Maltais, A., and Nykvist, B. (2020). Understanding the Role of Green Bonds in Advancing Sustainability. *Journal of Sustainable Finance & Investment*: 1–20.

Nemes, N., Scanlon, S. J., Smith, P., Smith, T., Aronczyk, M., Hill, S., . . . Stabinsky, D. (2022). An Integrated Framework to Assess Greenwashing. *Sustainability* 14(8):4431.

Norton Rose Fulbright. (2023). Update: Provisional Agreement Reached on the European Green Bond Standard. Accessed April 15, 2023. https://www.nortonrose-fulbright.com/en/knowledge/publications/3a31a991/update-provisional-agreement -reached-on-the-european-green-bond-standard

OECD. (2017). *Green Finance and Investment: Mobilising Bond Markets for a Low-Carbon Transition*. OECD Publishing, Paris. http://dx.doi.org/10.1787 /9789264272323-en

Official Journal of the European Union. (2016). Consolidated Versions of the Treaty on European Union and the Treaty on the Functioning of the European Union (2016/C 202/01).

Official Journal of the European Union. (2020). Regulation (EU) 2020/852 of the European Parliament and of the Council of 18 June 2020 on the establishment of a framework to facilitate sustainable investment, and amending Regulation (EU) 2019/2088.

Rizzello, A. (2022). *Green Investing: Changing Paradigms and Future Directions*. Springer Nature.

Schmittmann, J., and Chua, H. T. (2021). *How Green are Green Debt Issuers?* International Monetary Fund. IMF Working Paper No. 2021/194.

Shishlov, I., Morel, R., and Cochran, I. (2016). *Beyond Transparency: Unlocking the Full Potential of Green Bonds* (pp. 1–28). Institute for Climate Economics.

Tagliapietra, S., and Veugelers, R. (2020). *A Green Industrial Policy for Europe*. Bruegel.

Turguttopbaş, N. (2020). Sürdürülebilirlik, Yeşil Finans ve İlk Türk Yeşil Tahvil İhracı. *Finansal Araştırmalar ve Çalışmalar Dergisi* 12(22):267–283.

United Nations. (2015). Paris Agreement. Accessed March 10, 2023. https://unfccc .int/sites/default/files/english_paris_agreement.pdf

World Bank. (2019). 10 Years of Green Bonds: Creating the Blueprint for Sustainability Across Capital Markets. https://www.worldbank.org/en/news/immersive -story/2019/03/18/10-years-of-green-bonds-creating-the-blueprint-for-sustainabil-ity-across-capital-markets.

World Bank. (2021). What You Need to Know About IFC's Green Bonds. Climate Explainer Series. Accessed April 15, 2023. https://www.worldbank.org/en/news/ feature/2021/12/08/what-you-need-to-know-about-ifc-s-green-bonds

Digital Green Economy and Green Finance Under the Scope of Sustainability

Arzu Alvan

INTRODUCTION

There are many areas of study that can be used to study the sustainability movement, such as economics, finance, production, consumption, social life, trade, etc. Green economy and green finance, two topics that have gained popularity recently, fall under the main umbrella of sustainability and the Green New Deal. At first, the green deal does not appear to be a priority that governments are eager to accept. Therefore, the general perception is that investors are not confident about green investments. The government priorities environmental goals before considering future unemployment and crises before considering environmental goals. Additionally, governments have never had as much public money to invest in their economies as they do now. It is for economic recovery, repair, and rebuilding that governments have money for Green New Deal investments. Greener and more digital economies are clearly the goals of this money (Loiseau et al., 2016). This money is intended to be used to invest in renewable energy sources, energy efficiency, green infrastructure, research and development of new technologies, and public transportation. It is also intended to create jobs in the green sector, help to retrain workers, and shift towards a more sustainable economy. This money will be spent in accordance with the Green New Deal and digitalisation goals, which can explain how it will be spent. As of yet, no action has been taken. Governments must accept this.

We are in the midst of a global economic crisis, which is forcing industries to make great efforts to survive. As a result, some of them can no longer withstand the resistance and are compelled to cease operations. The economy has not yet recovered. Despite this, a mass collapse was averted. As of now, it is unclear whether the Green New Deal will be a success or a risk. For this study, future predictions will be scripted in a sense, examining ways in which the Green New Deal could have a significant impact on the economy in the short-term and long-term. In the short-term, it could lead to increased economic growth, job creation, and a reduction in emissions. In the long-term, it could lead to greater economic resilience, lower energy costs, and a reduced reliance on fossil fuels. Ultimately, the success of the Green New Deal will depend on how well it is implemented and how it is embraced by the public (Slatin, 2019).

As part of the Green New Deal, governments are required to invest in assets that contribute to a clean future and zero emissions by 2050. This is exactly what the Green New Deal aims to accomplish. It appears, however, that governments are not yet very eager to comply. Meanwhile, they are satisfied with high-level statements about the Green New Deal and the importance of climate change mitigation. Initially, governments hesitated because they were interested in the details. Future generations will actually repay investments made with the Green New Deal. Governments are taking a step back at this point. They are well aware of the fact that the success of the agreement will be judged by future generations. Therefore, they are taking a cautious approach and are reluctant to make any commitments before carefully considering the potential consequences of their decisions. This is because the investments to be made are expected to have long-term impacts and the governments want to make sure that they are making the right decisions so that future generations do not have to pay for them. They also want to ensure that the agreement is successful, and that it will bring long-term benefits in the form of reduced emissions and increased sustainability. It is expected that governments will spend more than 30 percent of their budgets on climate measures. The principle of doing no harm, which prevents harmful investments such as in fossil fuels, should be clear in the incentives for investments. As a result, bailout-supported companies must commit to implementing net-zero transition plans. By doing so, taxpayer money will be utilised responsibly and invested in companies and projects that are committed to achieving zero emissions. This helps to reduce the global carbon footprint and encourages companies to shift away from fossil fuels and towards cleaner and greener energy sources. By investing in these technologies, companies are able to reduce their emissions and become more sustainable (Miller, 2020; Pettifor, 2020).

A sustainable future involves moving away from outdated structures, creating new roads, and using technology to its full potential. Economies and finance can be greened under the broader context of digitalisation that has recently taken hold around the world. Digitalisation has reached a point where the latest technological developments are necessary to ensure the most effective use of resources to shape the future of financial and economic life

(Barefoot et al., 2018). As part of green financing decisions, ESG (environmental, social, and governance) factors have been taken into account. Leasing plays an important role in mobilising investments in environmentally friendly projects in this context. With this financing method, companies are now able to shape their future with green practices. As part of the Green New Deal, the USA has already spent more than 10 trillion dollars on projects with sustainability goals. Business evaluates new business opportunities on the path to digitisation as a natural way to achieve sustainable development goals (Weybrecht, 2010).

In the European Union, a budget of 560 billion Euros was proposed two years ago. There should be a resilience and remediation facility with a proposed budget, climatic conditions are optional, and climate neutrality should be a mandatory principle in flexible remediation plans. These plans should include ambitious objectives and measures to reduce emissions, promote energy efficiency and renewable energy, and invest in nature-based solutions and other technological solutions. Furthermore, these plans should be accompanied by a well-defined timeline for implementation.

The green new agreement's improvement package proposal should not scale back climate conditionality. Furthermore, all fossil fuel investments, even the new generation, should be excluded from all government financing. As one of the potential risks of the Green New Deal, ignoring these principles will leave future generations with unbearable debt levels and an unrecoverable climate emergency. Conversely, if these principles are followed, the economy, jobs, and the environment will be more secure in the future.

The focus of the study is to explore how digitalisation of the economy and finance can contribute to the sustainability goals set out by the green new agreement and how it can be handled in a way that has minimal environmental impact.

GREEN NEW DEAL

The Green New Deal is not an offer that appeared out of nowhere. It is a proposal that can be further developed. It is also part of the framework for foreign policy. Considering the Green New Deal starts with understanding its basic provisions. A summary of these provisions can be divided into two main categories. The first is to decarbonise the economies, and the second is to make an economic plan to deal with some of the fallout that will result. First, in order to decarbonise economies, the agreement calls for large-scale investments in renewable energy sources and energy efficiency. Moreover, existing power plants and other industrial processes are also called upon to comply with stricter emissions regulations. In addition, stronger enforcement of current emissions standards is necessary to ensure compliance. A combination of green infrastructure investments, training and education, and social safety nets is proposed to address economic fallout. In addition, we need clean, renewable, and emission-free energy. Finally, we must repair and upgrade the electricity grid, the buildings, and the infrastructure. This will allow for the transition to cleaner energy sources and reduce emissions, while also providing jobs and economic stability. The investments in green infrastructure and technology will also create a more resilient, energy-efficient, and sustainable society. Additionally, zero-emission vehicle infrastructure and overhauls of public transportation and high-speed rail systems are priorities. Green energy would create tens of thousands of jobs and reduce carbon emissions that harm the environment. It would also help to create a more efficient transportation system, which would reduce our dependence on fossil fuels. Finally, investing in infrastructure would benefit communities across the country, as it would create more safe and reliable systems for people to use. Last but not least, clean production and the elimination of greenhouse gas emissions from production and agriculture are essential. Additionally, fossil fuel withdrawal must be accompanied by an economic program. This includes investments in renewable energy, energy efficiency and storage, and research and development of new technologies. Governments should also provide incentives to businesses to transition to clean energy sources. Finally, regulations should be put in place to ensure compliance with clean energy standards (Pettifor, 2020; Zycher, 2011).

What governments are doing in terms of resource management seems unsustainable and dangerous. With solar panels, you're not just generating energy, you're also balancing the power grid. Fossil fuels and the power and money they represent are the biggest obstacles.

Carbon neutrality is unequivocally committed to by the Council of Europe in these policy frameworks. There are many binding regulations mandating a reduction of greenhouse gas emissions by at least 40 percent by 2030. The legislation also requires the development of an ambitious long-term strategy to achieve carbon neutrality by 2050. The Green New Deal also requires the continued promotion of renewable energy sources and energy efficiency measures. Additionally, it also calls for the implementation of policies that reduce energy poverty. This is part of the European Green Deal which aims to make Europe the world's first climate-neutral continent by 2050. It seeks to tackle climate change and improve the quality of life of citizens by investing in green infrastructure, innovation, and research as well as creating jobs in the green economy. The goal is to ensure that Europe is able to reach its climate targets while also achieving social and economic objectives. A number of tools are used by the European Green Deal to achieve this goal, including the European Investment Plan, the European Green Bond Standard, and the Just

Transition Mechanism. The Green New Deal aims to reduce carbon emissions by half by 2050 (E. B. Barbier, 2010; Luke, 2009).

As a result of the Green New Deal, governments are expected to increase the reduction of carbon emissions to 50 or 55 percent. It is expected that they will prepare a logistics plan for this purpose. It is another matter of debate, however, as to how far this climate law can be extended. The Green New Deal is an ambitious plan and requires global cooperation and understanding from all stakeholders involved. It must also include incentives to promote sustainable development and an equitable approach to reducing emissions. Developing a comprehensive strategy is essential because it helps to ensure that all stakeholders have a shared understanding of the goals, know what needs to be done, and are held accountable for their actions. Additionally, incentives can help to ensure that everyone is motivated to reach the goals and that sustainable development is supported. Finally, monitoring and enforcement of the policies is necessary to ensure that the goals are met in a timely manner (E. Barbier, 2010; Mazzucato, 2022).

Governments are expected to develop separate hydrogen, energy system integration, and renewal wave strategies under the Green New Deal. Despite the fact that governments have produced energy and climate plans so far, little progress has been made in implementing them. They will be criticised in this regard by the Commission. Governments must now take the necessary steps to put their plans into action. They must also work together to ensure that the goals of the green new agreement are met. It is up to them to ensure that the world moves towards a more sustainable future. To this end, governments must ensure that they have both the capacity and the will to execute their plans in a timely manner, while also collaborating with one another to ensure that their efforts are not wasted. However, if we look at world trade covered by the Green New Deal, we can say that it is full of tensions. Despite claims by trade theorists, world trade has never been smooth. Tariffs and other protectionist measures are a major obstacle to global trade (Bloomfield and Steward, 2020; Zycher, 2011).

Sustainability under the Green New Deal

Implementation of a comprehensive package of legislation is the goal of the Green New Deal. As part of the plan, net-zero greenhouse gas emissions are to be achieved, millions of high-wage jobs will be created, infrastructure will be improved, and social justice will be promoted. As a result of the Green New Deal, communities of colour, low-income communities, and Indigenous populations will be helped (Bretschger, 2011; Levidow, 2022).

It also aims to create high-paying jobs in the renewable energy industry and investment in infrastructure that can withstand the effects of climate change.

Additionally, it calls for a shift away from fossil fuels to cleaner, renewable energy sources. A more sustainable world is the purpose of the Green New Deal. Creating a sustainable energy system is of paramount importance. Sustainable energy refers to the process of using renewable natural resources over time without depleting them. The energy from sunlight, rain, and wind can be converted into sustainable energy sources. As the use of renewable energy resources increases, the use of fossil fuels (natural gas, oil, coal) will decrease (Quaschning, 2016; Sorensen, 2004).

In the Green New Deal, there is a strong emphasis on sustainability as a key component, which seeks to reconcile environmental sustainability with a socially more equitable economic system. It proposes a number of measures to help promote sustainable development, including the investment in renewable energy, the improvement of energy efficiency, and the promotion of sustainable agriculture among its goals. Governments will be required to invest in energy-efficient buildings and transportation as part of the Green New Deal. To achieve this goal, public and private sectors must work together to invest in renewable energy sources and develop incentives to drive economic growth. Infrastructure, renewable energy sources, and energy-saving technologies will all be required to achieve this.

Further, renewable energy sources such as solar and wind energy will need to be increased. Solar energy is one of the most promising renewable energy sources, as it is abundant, reliable, and cost-effective. Solar energy can be used to generate electricity, to heat buildings, and to provide hot water for domestic and industrial uses. Furthermore, solar energy can be used to power transportation systems, such as electric cars and buses (Mastini et al., 2021).

In order to ensure sustainability, there is a clear goal above all others—we must achieve net zero, which doesn't solve biodiversity and other problems but actually stabilises the planet. It is essential that markets are organised in a certain way. What is the process by which a public institution establishes its jurisdiction? In reality, the deal partly involves redesigning the social contract, public-private relations, and allowing social movements more freedom to operate (Bretschger, 2011). In order to establish the jurisdiction of a public institution, it is necessary to decide who will be responsible for regulating the market and what levels of regulation should be put in place. This requires a careful consideration of the interests of all involved parties, including private companies, citizens, and public institutions, in order to ensure a fair and equitable system is established. To ensure all interests are balanced, a thorough and unbiased analysis of the possible outcomes should be conducted before any decision is made. There needs to be a clear understanding of what a Green New Deal means for government structures, private structures, their interrelationships, and the agreement at its core. This is because the Green New Deal seeks to reduce carbon emissions, create more renewable energy jobs, and invest in green infrastructure. To achieve these goals, there must be a shift from government-funded projects to private-sector investments, and a new understanding of the interrelationship between private and government entities.

A large amount of liquidity was introduced into the financial system in order to alleviate the crisis in 2008. In giving the system liquidity this time, the goal is to build better—where "better" comprises an enormous green and sustainable transition. In order to ensure that this injected money lands on the concrete structures, it has to be handled differently. In fact, receiving recovery funds is a step towards a sustainable transition. It is a design issue, and it can be solved. This means that the funds need to be distributed in ways that prioritise green and sustainable investments, such as renewable energy and green infrastructure. This can be done by providing incentives for companies to invest in green initiatives and by focusing on projects that will have a positive environmental impact (Norton, 2023).

DIGITALISATION AND INDUSTRY 4.0

Financialisation of the economy has accelerated since the 2008 financial crash. Currently, we are in the midst of a technological revolution that goes back much further than that date. Financialisation of the economy is also accelerated by technological changes. In the economy, we are now experiencing two major connections: digital and sustainable. It doesn't matter how we define them, they will lead to large shifts in value. What is most critical here is how the government will frame the issues and make the market work for broader values. In what proportion does the market get its share, and in what proportion does the state get its share? What are the components of the Green New Deal? What kind of incentives should be provided to encourage companies to switch to green technologies? How can we ensure a just transition and that those who are most affected by the changes are taken into consideration? Who should be held responsible for environmental damage? (Yuan et al., 2021).

Information is converted from analogue format to digital format via digitalisation. Digitalisation can help make data storage, sharing, and access much more efficient and secure. Digital technologies have been integrated into manufacturing processes in Industry 4.0, which is also known as the Fourth Industrial Revolution. By developing smart factories, we can create more efficient, flexible, and responsive factories for our customers. Through digitalisation, vast amounts of data can be collected, analysed, and shared. This data can be used to create predictive analytics that allow companies to anticipate customer needs and optimise production. Even further optimisation

is possible with these systems, resulting in cost reductions and higher efficiency. Industry 4.0 is enabled by digitalisation, as it provides the data needed
to optimise manufacturing processes and improve product quality. Through
digitalisation, vast amounts of data can be collected, analysed, and shared
(Afonasova et al., 2019). Companies can use this data to optimise production
and anticipate customer needs. Digitalisation enables innovation and collaboration while reducing greenhouse gas emissions and optimising resource use.
The Internet of Things (IoT) provides a unique opportunity for the solution
of long-term sustainability challenges. In order to combat climate change,
digital technology may be the most powerful, scalable tool available. A 15
percent reduction in global emissions in 2030 can be achieved using it as an
accelerator (Sharma et al., 2022).

Digital technologies used in Industry 4.0 include the IoT, artificial intelligence (AI), machine learning, and big data analytics. In order to improve
product quality and optimise manufacturing processes, these technologies are
used to collect and analyse data (Ghobakhloo, 2020). Additionally, Industry
4.0 technologies can be used to help achieve the goals of the Green New
Deal, by providing the data and insights needed to create a more sustainable
and environmentally conscious manufacturing process. Machine learning
and data analytics can be used by Industry 4.0 technologies to identify waste,
increase efficiency, and reduce energy consumption. Sensors can also be used
to monitor the environment and identify potential risks, enabling businesses
to reduce their environmental impacts. Circular economies involve reusing
and recycling materials, thereby moving away from an economy based on
environmental resource extraction (Castelo-Branco et al., 2019).

As part of the Green New Deal, environmental and climate goals will be
established, with the reduction of carbon emissions being the main target
for sustainability. For this purpose, economic growth based on non-resource
usage is sought, eliminating the concept of scarcity of resources based on
the law of diminishing returns in the classical system. This involves a shift
towards the circular economy, where materials are reused and recycled,
and away from an economy based on the extraction of finite resources from
the environment. This approach is expected to reduce emissions and create jobs in the green economy, while also providing economic growth that
does not depend on the use of resources. All of these initiatives will require
widespread use of digitalisation to achieve environmental and climate targets, improve energy efficiency and reduce energy consumption, develop
renewable energy sources, and improve the energy infrastructure to more
effectively use renewable energy sources (Aksin-Sivrikaya and Bhattacharya,
2017; Hegyes et al., 2017).

Economic and Financial Digitalisation under Green New Deal Scope

We have built up an unmanageable amount of credit assets in the financial and monetary system we are currently in and which is coming to an end. A link between credit creation and the price of a loan with an interest rate, as well as the relationship between it and the accumulation of debt and finance, will ultimately lead to emissions accumulation. There will be further greenhouse gas emissions if credit is used to consume, extract fossil fuels, or increase purchasing power. A new monetary and financial system is needed to combat climate degradation and biodiversity loss—two of the most pressing issues facing our planet today. Entrepreneurial capitalism exists to create new assets, but we need a new kind of monetary and financial system to effectively manage the risk associated with climate change and ensure that resources are allocated responsibly to guarantee that future generations can enjoy economic stability and prosperity (Lindenberg, 2014).

Through blockchain technology, decentralised finance (DE-FI) promises to provide more secure and traceable financial transactions. While digitalisation is accelerated by financial technologies, decentralisation is also brought to the fore. Innovations brought about by Industry 4.0 include decentralised and digitalised finance. A major goal of the Green New Deal is to make financial transactions environmentally friendly. A digitalised financial system is the foundation of the financial system of the future (Ozili, 2021). Switching to digital finance will therefore make it easier for companies targeted by the Green New Deal to access the funds they need. Digital finance offers the advantage of speed, cost-efficiency, and improved customer experience. It also has the potential to reduce environmental damage as it eliminates the need for physical documents, reduces paper consumption, and enables more efficient tracking of customer transactions.

E-commerce, e-marketplaces, online educational courses, streaming platforms, social media, video conferencing, work-from-home options, and e-health are all included in the digital economy. All of these technologies have allowed people to conduct business, learn, interact, and access health care from their own homes, without having to travel or be physically present. This has drastically changed the way people work and live, and has had a huge impact on the global economy. This shift has presented many opportunities for businesses, which have had to quickly adapt to the new environment, and has also opened up many new paths for individuals to pursue in order to succeed in the digital economy. As well as making the world more sustainable, the digital economy has also opened up new opportunities (Ciocoiu, 2011).

CONCLUSION

The biggest challenge of this century is how to deal with the effects of global warming. Governments began adapting our lives after signing the Green New Deal to preserve a sustainable planet. It is imperative that we reduce our carbon footprint, invest in renewable energy, and reduce waste production in order to ensure the success of this agreement. The aim of this study was to examine the points of economic and financial digitalisation in the context of a more sustainable and carbon-neutral society. Digital transformation strategies that are based on long-term thinking, sustainability, resilience, and a commitment to zero-carbon economies are essential. Sustainable economic and financial systems should be created by using digital technologies to support the Green New Deal. Our lives have been transformed by digitalisation in recent years, as technology has been integrated into our daily lives. Many different types of crises plaguing the world have been addressed via digitalisation. The Green New Deal is seeking to reduce global emissions and address climate change by utilising technology, such as artificial intelligence and machine learning. This area has been identified as one of the most problematic due to the alarming rate at which digital solutions are affecting human life. Because of this, sustainability and digitalisation are at odds with each other. For a more sustainable future, digital solutions must fill this gap. As a result, organisations are encouraged to prioritise the development of ethical and environmentally friendly digital solutions.

REFERENCES

Afonasova, M. A., Panfilova, E. E., Galichkina, M. A., and Ślusarczyk, B. (2019). Digitalization in Economy and Innovation: The Effect on Social and Economic Processes. *Polish Journal of Management Studies* 19(2):22–32.

Aksin-Sivrikaya, S., and Bhattacharya, C. (2017). Where Digitalization Meets Sustainability: Opportunities and Challenges. In *Sustainability in a Digital World: New Opportunities Through New Technologies*, edited by T. Osburg and C. Lohrmann (pp. 37–49). Springer International.

Barbier, E. (2010). How is the Global Green New Deal Going? *Nature* 464(7290):832–833.

Barbier, E. B. (2010). *A Global Green New Deal: Rethinking the Economic Recovery.* Cambridge University Press.

Barefoot, K., Curtis, D., Jolliff, W., Nicholson, J. R., and Omohundro, R. (2018). Defining and Measuring the Digital Economy. Working paper. US Department of Commerce Bureau of Economic Analysis, Washington, DC, 15.

Bloomfield, J., and Steward, F. (2020). The Politics of the Green New Deal. *Political Quarterly* 91(4):770–779.

Bretschger, L. (2011). Sustainability Economics, Resource Efficiency, and the Green New Deal. In *International Economics of Resource Efficiency: Eco-Innovation Policies for a Green Economy* (pp. 3–17). Springer Nature.

Castelo-Branco, I., Cruz-Jesus, F., and Oliveira, T. (2019). Assessing Industry 4.0 Readiness in Manufacturing: Evidence for the European Union. *Computers in Industry* 107:22–32.

Ciocoiu, C. N. (2011). Integrating Digital Economy and Green Economy: Opportunities for Sustainable Development. *Theoretical and Empirical Researches in Urban Management* 6(1):33–43.

Ghobakhloo, M. (2020). Industry 4.0, Digitization, and Opportunities for Sustainability. *Journal of Cleaner Production* 252:119869.

Hegyes, É. G., Csapó, I., & Farkas, M. F. (2017). Some Aspects of Digitalization and Sustainability in the European Union. *Journal of Management* 36(2):37–46.

Levidow, L. (2022). Green New Deals: What Shapes Green and Deal? *Capitalism Nature Socialism* 33(3):76–97. doi:10.1080/10455752.2022.2062675.

Lindenberg, N. (2014). Definition of Green Finance. Green Finance Network. Collaboration for Development. World Bank.

Loiseau, E., Saikku, L., Antikainen, R., Droste, N., Hansjürgens, B., Pitkänen, K., . . . Thomsen, M. (2016). Green Economy and Related Concepts: An Overview. *Journal of Cleaner Production* 139:361–371.

Luke, T. W. (2009). A Green New Deal: Why Green, How New, and What is the Deal? *Critical Policy Studies* 3(1):14–28.

Mastini, R., Kallis, G., and Hickel, J. (2021). A Green New Deal Without Growth? *Ecological Economics* 179:106832.

Mazzucato, M. (2022). Financing the Green New Deal. *Nature Sustainability* 5(2):93–94.

Miller, C. (2020). An Ideological Criticism of the Green New Deal and Media Responses. *UNLV Theses, Dissertations, Professional Papers, and Capstones.* 3929. University of Nevada, Las Vegas.

Norton, M. G. (2023). A Green New Deal. In *A Modern History of Materials: From Stability to Sustainability* (pp. 187–206): Springer.

Ozili, P. K. (2021). Digital Finance, Green Finance and Social Finance: Is There a Link? *Financial Internet Quarterly* 17(1):1–7.

Pettifor, A. (2020). *The Case for the Green New Deal.* Verso Books.

Quaschning, V. (2016). *Understanding Renewable Energy Systems.* Routledge.

Sharma, R., Lopes de Sousa Jabbour, A. B., Jain, V., and Shishodia, A. (2022). The Role of Digital Technologies to Unleash a Green Recovery: Pathways and Pitfalls to Achieve the European Green Deal. *Journal of Enterprise Information Management* 35(1):266–294.

Slatin, C. (2019). The Green New Deal—A Revolutionary Concept. *New Solutions: A Journal of Environmental and Occupational Health Policy* 29(2):133–137.

Sorensen, B. (2004). *Renewable Energy.* 3rd edition. Elsevier.

Weybrecht, G. (2010). *The Sustainable MBA: The Manager's Guide to Green Business.* John Wiley & Sons.

Yuan, S., Musibau, H. O., Genç, S. Y., Shaheen, R., Ameen, A., and Tan, Z. (2021). Digitalization of Economy is the Key Factor Behind Fourth Industrial Revolution: How G7 Countries are Overcoming with the Financing Issues? *Technological Forecasting and Social Change* 165:120533.

Zycher, B. (2011). *The Green New Deal: Economics and Policy Analytics.* AEI Press.

8

Environmental Pollution and Sustainable Development

An Assessment for G7 Countries

Seher Suluk and Serdar Öztürk[*]

INTRODUCTION

Humans have always tried to influence and benefit from nature by making fire, cultivating the land, developing hunting methods, and so on to survive. However, in the industrialisation process that started with the Industrial Revolution, people began to seriously exploit natural resources and energy in order to create more wealth and prosperity for themselves (Høher-Larsen, 2017). In today's world, the increase in the intensity of the disruption of the human-environment balance and the deepening of the environmental crisis have led to an increase in research on the human-nature relationship (Çelikkıran, 1995; Porsmose, 1992, 38).

Climate crisis, global warming, environmental pollution, decrease or loss of biodiversity, depletion of the ozone layer, depletion of natural resources, deforestation, and desertification are among the most important threats of our age. These environmental problems negatively affect both human health and all living things. Although the main cause is human activities, increasing destruction of nature and environmental problems have begun to be felt day by day due to rapid population growth, industrialisation, urbanisation, globalisation, technological developments, economic growth, and especially the desire to make a profit, which is at the core of the capitalism.

Putting the environment in the background for the sake of creating economic growth has brought about serious and various problems, and as a result of the understanding that the point reached is "unsustainable," it is understood that it is necessary and significant to move to a "sustainable" world

---

[*] This study is derived from the doctoral dissertation prepared by Seher Suluk under the advisory of Prof. Dr. Serdar Öztürk at Nevşehir Hacı Bektaş Veli University, Department of Economics. New variables have been added and the graphs and comments have been updated.

order (Yücel and Kurnaz, 2021, 20). Hereby, it can be said that the concept of sustainable development has emerged due to the damage to the ecosystem and the gradual degradation of the natural environment. These problems have reached such serious and important dimensions that they cannot be ignored. Sustainable development aims to ensure a balance between the economy, society, and the environment.

The current climate crisis and other ecological crises, which are mostly the result of human activities, threaten all living things (UNESCO, 2021, 6). However, living in a healthy and clean environment is a fundamental right of every human being. Therefore, in order to leave a liveable world to both current and future generations, it is of great importance to protect nature and to continue our existence in harmony with nature and the environment. The G7 countries (Canada, France, Germany, Italy, Japan, the United Kingdom, and the United States) are among the most developed economies in the world. These countries are also among those with the highest CO_2 emissions (Pata and Aydın, 2023, 15268). In this context, this study aims to assess the sustainable development status of G7 countries. For this reason, the conceptual and historical framework of sustainable development will be explained in the next section. Then, G7 countries will be evaluated within the framework of environmentally sustainable development with the help of graphs. Finally, the study will end with the conclusion section.

CONCEPTUAL AND HISTORICAL FRAMEWORK OF SUSTAINABLE DEVELOPMENT

Sustainability, which can be defined as the continuation and continuity of a situation or something, comes from the Latin word *sustinere*, which means "to maintain," "to continue," "to support" (Can, 2017, 138–139; Nystad et al., 2008). Although it is not known when the idea of sustainability, a widely used concept today, was contemplated for the first time, it was likely applied in the early 1700s in areas like forestry and then fishing, to prevent the destruction of forests and fish and to ensure continuity in meeting human needs. It has been understood that the destruction of forests and fish is unsustainable. Therefore, it can be said that sustainability aims to solve the resource problem and ensure the continuation of human welfare. Generally, the development of the concept of sustainability outside of forestry and fisheries has been limited. Sustainability, which emerged as a response to the environmental degradation concern, has been used in a wider area in the more recent periods (Tıraş, 2012, 59; Kılıç, 2006, 84; Can, 2017, 138; Kopnina and Shoreman-Ouimet, 2015).

In today's world, environmental problems are increasing gradually and continue to make their impacts felt intensely in all areas of our lives. The main reason for this is that human beings are in a dominant position in the human-environment relationship and pollute the environment without regard (Yaşaroğlu, 2020, 245). With the emergence of environmental concerns, the concept of sustainable development entered the world agenda in the twentieth century and has become a significant concept (Yeni, 2014, 183). Today, the point reached by the globalisation process and the activities of countries or companies are likely to affect each other. In other words, from an environmental point of view, the environmental destruction caused by the activities of industrialised countries or non-environmentally sensitive businesses and the wastes they create can spread in nature and have negative effects on both natural life and all humanity, regardless of country or nation. And this situation threatens future generations. For this reason, it is significant to support the sustainable development strategy with development policies compatible with the environment (Alagöz, 2007, 7–8). Within this scope, maintaining a balance between economic, social, and environmental dimensions is vital in the sustainable development process. Economic growth alone is not enough; it is necessary to distribute the wealth created fairly among the people who make up the society, and while doing this, to protect the environmental values (Kandemir, 2021, 614). Any action taken in this context is interconnected with its economic, social, and environmental aspects. Considering only one of these is likely to result in "unsustainable consequences." To give an example, disregarding social and environmental dimensions and focusing only on economic growth and profit margins will cause damage to the society and the environment that will be costly for the society in the long run (OECD, 2008, 2). From this point of view, if we briefly talk about the three dimensions of sustainable development, an economically sustainable system should be able to consistently deliver goods and services, to maintain manageable levels of government and external debt, and to prevent excessive sectoral imbalances (Rosiek, 2016, 554). Economic sustainability requires strong and robust economic growth, low and stable inflation, great investment and innovation capacity, and financial stability (Uysal, 2013, 115). The main goals of achieving sustainable economic development are to increase the standard of living and reduce poverty around the world by providing means of income; to reduce environmental degradation; and to prevent resource degradation, cultural degradation, and social instability (Yurtsal, 2019, 63–64). The social dimension of sustainable development is people-oriented and is significant in terms of ensuring the continuity of social and cultural systems. Significant requirements of the social dimension include ensuring human rights and intercommunal equality (reducing poverty) as well as protecting pluralism and cultural diversity, etc. (Gürlük, 2010, 87). A healthy environment is a significant key indicator of sustainable development (Ibimilua, 2011, 482). The environmental dimension of sustainability includes maintaining ecosystem integrity, carrying capacity, and biodiversity (Basiago, 1998, 150). Environmental sustainability is necessary for people's well-being and includes the protection and conscientious development of limited natural resources. Making both production and consumption sustainable is necessary to safeguard environmental sustainability (Atvur, 2009, 232).

A report titled *The Limits to Growth* was published by the Club of Rome in 1972. The report made a huge impact by emphasising the fact that the world's natural resources are limited and some of them are nonrenewable (Çankır et al., 2012, 375). In addition, issues related to population growth, agriculture, and the resources of the world, air and environmental pollution were discussed in detail and it was emphasised that humanity was in danger of extinction due to these problems (Cansever, 2021, 636). In the same year, the United Nations Conference on the Human Environment was held in Stockholm, Sweden. It is accepted that this conference was the first conference where environmental issues were discussed on a global scale (Ezer, 2022, 32). The main topics covered in this conference, which laid the foundations of the concept of sustainable development, can be listed as: environmental planning and environmental management in residential areas; environmentally oriented conservation perspective in the use of natural riches; detection and control of harmful substances released into the environment at the international level; education, information, and cultural policies in relation to environmental problems, development, and environment; and involvement of international organisations in environmental actions (Karacan, 2007; Çankır et al., 2014, 3). At the end of the conference, a Declaration of the United Nations Conference on the Human Environment was accepted. Additionally, as a result of this conference, which is the major conference to deal with the environment, it was decided to establish the United Nations Environment Programme (UNEP), to establish the Environment Fund, and to accept June 5 as World Environment Day (https://www.mfa.gov.tr; Alada et al., 1993, 93).

In 1979, the first World Climate Conference took place in Geneva, Switzerland, and the importance of the global warming problem was shared with all the countries in the world (Şanlı et al., 2017, 202). The concept of sustainable development was for the first time defined in 1987 as "development that meets current needs without compromising the ability of future generations to meet their needs" by the World Commission on Environment and Development in the Brundtland Report, also known as "Our Common Future" (https://bu.dk). The concept has begun to be widely accepted and used since then, promoting support of economic and social development without jeopardising the environment and the opportunities of future generations (Husted et al., 2020, 1). Sustainable development includes some basic objectives, which were determined within the framework of environmental and development policies. These goals can be listed as follows: reviving growth; changing the quality of growth; meeting essential needs for water, sanitation, food, energy, and jobs; providing a sustainable population level; maintaining and enhancing the resource base; reorienting technology and managing risk; and merging the environment and economics in decision-making (Yıldırım and Nuri, 2018, 3). In 1992, the United Nations Conference on Environment and Development was held in Rio de Janeiro, Brazil. Evaluating the developments in the twenty-year period and determining the policies for the future has been the main purpose of this conference (Çankır et al., 2012, 377). The World Summit for Social Development took place in Copenhagen, the capital of Denmark in 1995. At the mentioned summit, governments reached a new consensus on the need to put people at the centre of development. Topics and priority objectives addressed at the summit include conquest of poverty; ensuring full employment; and fostering stable, secure, and just societies (United Nations, 2023).

In 1997, the Kyoto Protocol, which aims to combat global warming and climate change, was signed in Kyoto, Japan (Cömert et al., 2015, 884). The Kyoto Protocol, which entered into force in 2005, is an international agreement aimed at reducing harmful greenhouse gas emissions (https://www .globalis.dk). The United Nations Millennium Summit was held in New York in 2000 and the Millennium Declaration, which consisted of several goals expected to be achieved by 2015, was signed (Çelik et al., 2016, 337). In 2012, the United Nations Conference on Sustainable Development took place in Rio de Janeiro, Brazil. At the end of the Rio+20 summit, a final document titled "The Future We Want," which was a roadmap for development, was accepted. In 2015, the United Nations Sustainable Development Summit was held in New York. At the summit, "Agenda 2030: UN Sustainable Development Goals" was adopted as 17 goals and 169 subgoals planned to be achieved by 2030 (https://www.mfa.gov.tr). These goals are the following: no poverty; zero hunger; good health and well-being; quality education; gender equality; clean water and sanitation; affordable and clean energy; decent work and economic growth; industry, innovation and infrastructure; reduced inequalities; sustainable cities and communities; responsible consumption and production; climate action; life below water; life on land; peace, justice, and strong institutions and partnerships for the goals (UNDP, 2023).

In 2015, the Paris Agreement was accepted. This agreement aims to combat climate change and was adopted at the 21st Conference of the Parties to the United Nations Framework Convention on Climate Change in Paris, the capital of France, and entered into force in 2016 (Avrupa Birliği Türkiye Delegasyonu, 2016; United Nations Climate Change, 2023). The main objective of the agreement is to limit the increase in global temperature to well below 2°C, and to 1.5°C or below as much as possible (Çetinkaya and Akar, 2022, 37).

Chapter 8

ASSESSMENT OF G7 COUNTRIES WITHIN THE FRAMEWORK OF SUSTAINABLE DEVELOPMENT

In this section of the study, G7 countries have been evaluated within the scope of environmentally sustainable development. G7 countries, which represent the most developed industrialised countries, constitute about 10 percent of the global population, account for more than 60 percent of the world's net wealth, and approximately 50 percent of the world's GDP (Li and Haneklaus, 2022; Voumik et al., 2023). Additionally, G7 countries consume nearly one-third of the world's energy each year and discharge about a quarter of the global greenhouse gas emissions generated from the use of these energy resources (Ahmed et al., 2022). The global recession caused CO_2 emissions to drop, realised as 31.56 billion metric tons in 2009. Again, due to various restrictions and measures like quarantine caused by the COVID-19 pandemic that occurred in 2019, transportation and industrial activities were reduced significantly, thus CO_2 emissions decreased in 2020. The global CO_2 emissions decreased to 35.26 billion metric tons in 2020. However, global CO_2 emissions from fossil fuels and industry have increased significantly since 1990, reaching 37.12 billion metric tons in 2021, which is a record level. Global CO_2 emissions have increased by more than 60 percent since 1990 (Statista, 2023).

In the graph in figure 8.1, the population growth rates of the G7 country group for the years of 2007–2021 is given. In 2007, the country with the highest population growth rate was Canada, while Germany had the lowest. While the country with the highest population growth rate in 2021 was

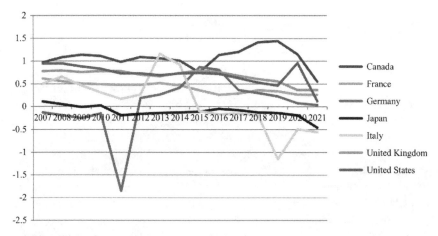

Figure 8.1   Population Growth Rates of the G7 Countries between 2007–2021. *Source:* World Bank: Population growth (annual %), https://data.worldbank.org (accessed March 28, 2023)

Canada again, the lowest population growth rate observed belongs to Italy. Over the years, it is observed that the population growth rate has decreased, albeit slightly, in all other countries except Germany, while it has fallen to negative in Japan and Italy.

The economic growth rates of G7 countries for the years 2007–2021 are given in the graph in figure 8.2. Accordingly, the economic growth rates of G7 countries fluctuate between −11% and 7.5% on average in the period in question. Germany had the highest growth rate of 2.98% in 2007, and Italy had the lowest growth rate of 1.49% in the same year among G7 countries. The economic growth rates of all countries slowed down in 2009 and dropped to negative values due to the impact of the global economic crisis. After 2009, there was an increase again and it followed a fluctuating course in general. In 2020, there were declines in economic growth rates; this can be attributed to the COVID-19 pandemic that occurred in 2019. It is observed that there is an improvement in the growth rates of all countries in 2021. The United Kingdom had the highest growth rate in 2021 with 7.52%, and Japan had the lowest growth rate in the same year.

The foreign direct investment inflows as a percentage of GDP of G7 countries between 2007 and 2021 is given in the graph in figure 8.3. It is observed that G7 countries' foreign direct investment inflows range between −1% and 12% on average in the period in question. Canada was the country that received the highest foreign direct investment inflow in 2007 with 8.20%. The global financial crisis has reduced foreign direct investment inflows of many G7 countries. Foreign direct investments, which in general follow a fluctuating course, decreased overall from 2007 to 2021. In 2021, the country

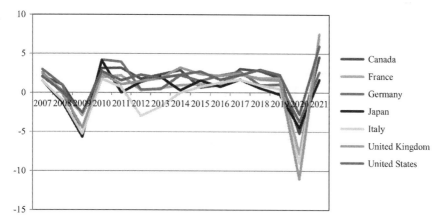

Figure 8.2   Economic Growth Rates of the G7 Countries between 2007–2021. *Source:* World Bank: GDP growth (annual %), https://data.worldbank.org (accessed March 20, 2023)

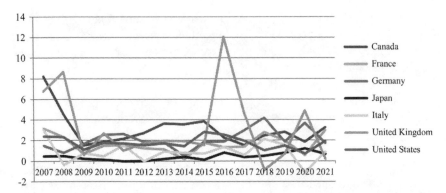

Figure 8.3   Foreign Direct Investment Inflows of the G7 Countries (% of GDP), 2007–2021. *Source:* World Bank: Foreign direct investment, net inflows (% of GDP), https://data.worldbank.org (accessed March 20, 2023)

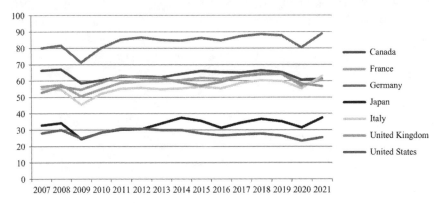

Figure 8.4   Trade of the G7 Countries (% of GDP), 2007–2021. *Source:* World Bank: Trade of the G7 Countries (% of GDP), https://data.worldbank.org (accessed March 28, 2023)

with the highest foreign direct investment was Canada again with 3.26%. In spite of that, with 0.19%, the United Kingdom had the least foreign direct investment.

The ratio of trade to GDP of G7 countries for the same period is given in the graph in figure 8.4. Accordingly, while Germany's ratio of trade to GDP is higher than other G7 countries, it is seen to be low in the United States. It is observed that the ratio of trade to GDP of all the countries generally follows a horizontal course in the period in question, but there is a decrease in 2009 and 2020.

Fossil fuel and excessive energy use are among the factors that increase CO_2 emissions and environmental problems. As a matter of fact, fossil fuel energy consumption increases greenhouse gas emissions, which brings about climate crisis and other environmental concerns as well as causing economic and social development problems. According to the World Bank data, while France consumed the least fossil fuel energy among G7 countries between 2007–2015, Japan's fossil fuel energy consumption increased, especially after 2010, and has followed a horizontal course since 2012. The United States follows Japan. In other words, the United States consumes the most fossil fuel energy after Japan in 2015 among G7 countries. Since fossil fuel–based energy consumption causes many environmental problems, it is important to abandon these and instead use environmentally friendly energy sources.

The G7 country group is among the most-polluting countries in the world. Indeed, they are responsible for almost a quarter of global CO_2 emissions (https://ocean-energyresources.com). CO_2 emissions cause critical environmental problems and comprise the largest share among the greenhouse gases. The graph in figure 8.5 shows CO_2 emission data of G7 countries for the period of 2007–2019. As shown in figure 8.5, all G7 countries except the United States follow a horizontal course in CO_2 emissions. Noticeably, CO_2 emissions in the United States are on a downward trend. But in spite of that, it is by far the country that emits the most CO_2 among G7 countries. The United States is followed by Japan, which consumes the most fossil fuel energy among G7 countries. It has been determined that the country among the G7 group with the lowest level of CO_2 emissions is France.

The ecological footprint is accepted as one of the main indicators of environmental sustainability and is widely used in measuring countries. In this context,

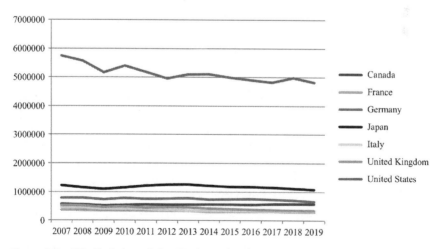

Figure 8.5 CO_2 Emission of the G7 Countries (kt), 2007–2019. *Source:* World Bank: CO_2 Emission of the G7 Countries (kt), 2007–2019, https://data.worldbank.org (accessed March 20, 2023)

according to the ecological footprint data, the United States has the highest ecological footprint among G7 countries. The United States, which does not rank well in the environmental performance index, is among the countries discharging the most CO_2, as well as consuming the most fossil fuel energy and the least renewable energy. The country with the least ecological footprint among G7 countries is Italy.

G7 countries are committed to attain 60 percent of electricity from renewable energy sources by 2030 to achieve their net-zero targets. But considering the current situation, it does not seem very encouraging. Because in 2020, only 20 percent of the total electricity outputs of these countries were provided by renewable energy (Ahmed et al., 2022). According to the World Bank data, the share of renewable energy consumption in the total final energy consumption has an increasing trend in G7 countries between 2007–2019. In this context, Canada is the country that consumes the most renewable energy among G7 countries. Those consuming the least renewable energy are Japan and the United States; these two countries also consume the most fossil fuel energy and have the highest levels of CO_2 emissions.

The 2022 environmental performance index, calculated for 180 countries, ranks countries on a scale of 0–100 from worst to best performance (Wolf et al., 2022). In 2022, among G7 countries, the United Kingdom showed the best performance with 77.70 score in the environmental performance index, ranking second after Denmark. However, Canada and the United States showed the worst performance among G7 countries (Environmental Performance Index, 2022).

CONCLUSION

In the human-nature relationship, the balance has greatly deteriorated. The negative impacts of this imbalance on nature and the environment have become more evident day by day, with the effects beginning to be felt more and more. It took a long time for humanity to recognise the damage it has caused to the environment. However, human beings have not been very willing to address and eliminate these problems. Considering the data obtained, the reports prepared, and the academic studies conducted, it is clear that there has not been a successful performance in addressing the environmental problems that have been identified and urgently expressed, especially since the second half of the twentieth century (Sağır, 2020, 74).

G7 countries are among the most economically developed countries in the world. But with strong economic growth, environmental conditions have also deteriorated in these countries (Olanrewaju et al., 2022, 1). Since the commitments adopted in 2015, G7 countries are not progressing at the speed they need to fulfil the United Nations 2030 Agenda. Although most have started to take measures to promote sustainability and fight against climate change, it is clear that these efforts are not enough (https://www.activesustainability .com). Despite promises of a commitment to green recovery, G7 countries have spent more on fossil fuels than on clean energy since the COVID-19 pandemic. In other words, G7 countries have set targets to reduce their CO_2 emissions (https://ocean-energyresources.com; Bhattacharya et al., 2021, 14). However, while CO_2 emissions of G7 countries have decreased in general as of the period under consideration, considering the fact that these countries are among the biggest CO_2 emitters, and that the first conference dealing with the environmental issue was held in Stockholm in 1972, it is clearly not enough to reach the desired targets. It can be said that these countries value growth-oriented development, and that they do not demonstrate the care required to reduce environmental pollution in this process.

In this context, the negative consequences of environmental pollution and other environmental problems threaten all living things. Therefore, the significance of being sensitive to the environment is understood in today's world when we feel the climate crisis and other environmental problems. It is a well-known fact that the increase in environmental pollution brings with it serious problems. Therefore, in order to protect the health of all living things and the environment, it is important and necessary to seriously develop and implement policies and strategies to prevent environmental pollution. For this reason, G7 countries should attach more importance to actualising and implementing environmentally friendly policies and practices.

REFERENCES

Ahmed, Z., Ahmad, M., Murshed, M., Shah, M. I., Mahmood, H., and Abbas, S. (2022). How Do Green Energy Technology Investments, Technological Innovation, and Trade Globalization Enhance Green Energy Supply and Stimulate Environmental Sustainability in the G7 Countries?, *Gondwana Research* 112:105–115.
Alada, A. B., Gürpınar, E. & Budak, S. (1993). Rio Konferansı Üzerine Düşünceler. *İstanbul Üniversitesi Siyasal Bilgiler Fakültesi Dergisi* 3-4-5:93–108.
Alagöz, M. (2007). Sürdürülebilir Kalkınmada Çevre Faktörü: Teorik Bir Bakış. *Akademik Bakış* 11:1–12.
Atvur, S. (2009). Yerel Gündem 21 ve Çevre: Antalya Kent Konseyi Örneği. *C. Ü. Sosyal Bilimler Dergisi* 35(2):231–241.
Avrupa Birliği Türkiye Delegasyonu. (2016). Geleceğe Dair: Paris İklim Anlaşması. Ankara.
Basiago, A. D. (1998). Economic, Social, and Environmental Sustainability in Development Theory and Urban Planning Practice. *Environmentalist* 19:145–161.
Bhattacharya, A., Ivanyna, M., Oman, W., and Stern, N. (2021). Climate Action to Unlock the Inclusive Growth Story of the 21st Century. IMF Working Paper 2021/147. International Monetary Fund.

Can, F. (2017). Sürdürülebilir Kalkınmanın Yeni Boyutları. *International Journal of Academic Value Studies* 3(10):138–146.

Çankır, B., Fındık, H., and Koçak, Ö. E. (2012). Sürdürülebilirlik ve Sürdürülebilir Organizasyon Yönetimi, 1st International Conference on Sustainable Business and Transitions for Sustainable Development, 11–13 October, Konya, Turkey, 375–385.

Çankır, B., Semiz, D., and Aktaş, A. (2014). Sürdürülebilir Yönetim Anlayışı Çerçevesinde Gönüllü Karbon Piyasalarında Kullanılan Standartlar ve Bu Standartların Karşılaştırmalı Analizi. *Journal of Economics, Finance and Accounting* 1(1):1–12.

Cansever, İ. H. (2021). Sürdürülebilir Kalkınma ve Sağlık: Türkiye'nin 2023 Hedefleri ile Karşılaştırmalı Bir Değerlendirme. *Hacettepe Sağlık İdaresi Dergisi* 24(3):633–650.

Çelik, H., Çelik, A. D., and Fisunoğlu, M. (2016). 1990–2015 Yılları Arasında Bin Yıl Kalkınma Hedefleri ve Yoksulluk: Türkiye Örneği, International Conference on Eurasian Economies, 336–341.

Çelikkıran, A. (1995). İnsan, Çevre, Eğitim. *Kuram ve Uygulamada Eğitim Yönetimi* 4(4):569–572.

Çetinkaya, G., and Akar, S. (2022). Türkiye'nin Küresel Karbon Bütçesindeki Payı: Öngörü Senaryoları ile Bir Değerlendirme. *Maliye Çalışmaları Dergisi* 68:33–50.

Cömert, R., Bilget, Ö., and Çabuk, A. (2015). Kyoto Protokolüne İmza Atan G20 Ülkelerinin Yıllara Göre Karbon Salınımlarının (1990–2012) Coğrafi Bilgi Sistemleri Yardımı ile Analizi. Anadolu Üniversitesi, Yer ve Uzay Bilimleri Enstitüsü, 883–891.

Environmental Performance Index. (2022). 2022 EPI Results. Accessed March 27, 2023. https://epi.yale.edu/epi-results/2022/component/epi

Ezer, A. I. (2022). Çevre Etiği Bağlamında Sürdürülebilir Kalkınma ve Yeşil Büyüme: Sermayenin Sürdürülebilirliği mi? Doğal Varlıkların mı?, TÜCAUM 2022 Uluslararası Coğrafya Sempozyumu, 12–14 Ekim 2022, Ankara, 30–46.

Global Footprint Network. (2023). Accessed March 28, 2023. https://www.footprint-network.org

Gürlük, S. (2010). Sürdürülebilir Kalkınma Gelişmekte Olan Ülkelerde Uygulanabilir Mi? *Eskişehir Osmangazi Üniversitesi İktisadi ve İdari Bilimler Dergisi* 5(2):85–100.

Høher-Larsen, M. (2017). Menneskets Forhold Til Naturen. Accessed March 28, 2023. https://faktalink.dk/menneskets-forhold-naturen

Husted, M., Gjøtterud, S., and Olin, A. (2020). Tema: Forskning for Bæredygtig Udvikling, *Forskning & Forandring* 3(2):1–5.

Ibimilua, F. O. (2011). Linkages between Poverty and Environmental Degradation. *African Research Review* 5(1):475–484. https://www.ajol.info/index.php/afrrev/article/view/64545

Kandemir, O. (2021). Dünya Ülkelerinde Sosyal Eşitsizliklerin Mutluluk Düzeyine Etkisi: Lojistik Regresyon Analizi. *International Journal of Eurasia Social Sciences* 12(45):612–625.

Karacan, A. R. (2007). *Çevre Ekonomisi ve Politikası: Ekonomi, Politika, Uluslararası ve Ulusal Çevre Koruma Girişimleri.* İzmir: Ege Üniversitesi Yayınları İktisadi ve İdari Bilimler Fakültesi Yayın No. 6.

Kılıç, S. (2006). Yeni Toplumsal ve Ekonomik Arayışlar Sürecinde Sürdürülebilir Kalkınma, *Gazi Üniversitesi İktisadi ve İdari Bilimler Fakültesi Dergisi* 8(2):81–101.

Kopnina, H., and Shoreman-Ouimet, E. (Eds.). (2015). *Sustainability: Key Issues.* Routledge.

Li, B., and Haneklaus, N. (2022). Reducing CO_2 Emissions in G7 Countries: The Role of Clean Energy Consumption, Trade Openness and Urbanization. *Energy Reports* 8(Supplement 4):704–713.

Nystad, Ø., Jaminon, J., and Jakobsen, O. (2008). Er Målsetningen Om Økonomisk Vekst Forenlig Med Kravet Om Bærekraftig Utvikling? *Magma—Tidsskrift for Økonomi og Ledelse* 4:66–76.

OECD. (2008). Bæredygtig Udvikling: Sammenkædning Af Økonomi, Samfund, Miljø. OECD Insights—Sustainable Development: Linking Economy, Society, Environment.

Olanrewaju, V. O., Irfan, M., Altuntaş, M., Agyekum, E. B., Kamel, S., and El-Naggar, M. F. (2022). Towards Sustainable Environment in G7 Nations: The Role of Renewable Energy Consumption, Eco-innovation and Trade Openness. *Frontiers in Environmental Science* 10:925822, 1–9.

Pata, U. K., and Aydın, M. (2023). Persistence of CO_2 Emissions in G7 Countries: A Different Outlook from Wavelet-based Linear and Nonlinear Unit Root Tests. *Environmental Science and Pollution Research* 30:15267–15281. https://doi.org/10.1007/s11356-022-23284-2

Porsmose, E. (1992). Menneske og Natur—Nogle Perspektiver. *Forskningscenter Menneske og Natur* 8(1):37–47.

Rosiek, J. (2016). Determinants of the EU Sustainable Development Policy Effectiveness: DEA Approach. *Economic and Environmental Studies* 16(4):551–576.

Sağır, H. (2020). Çevresel Sürdürülebilirlik Bağlamında Konya Kapalı Havzası Üzerine Bir Değerlendirme. *Çağdaş Yerel Yönetimler Dergisi* 29(4):73–118.

Şanlı, B., Bayrakdar, S., and İncekara, B. (2017). Küresel İklim Değişikliğinin Etkileri ve Bu Etkileri Önlemeye Yönelik Uluslararası Girişimler. *Süleyman Demirel Üniversitesi İktisadi ve İdari Bilimler Fakültesi Dergisi* 22(1):201–212.

Statista. (2023). Annual Carbon Dioxide (CO_2) Emissions Worldwide from 1940 to 2023 (in billion metric tons). Accessed March 20, 2023. https://www.statista.com/statistics/276629/global-co2-emissions

Tıraş, H. H. (2012). Sürdürülebilir Kalkınma ve Çevre: Teorik Bir İnceleme. *Kahramanmaraş Sütçü İmam Üniversitesi İktisadi ve İdari Bilimler Fakültesi Dergisi* 2(2):57–73.

UNDP. (2023). What are the Sustainable Development Goals? United Nations Development Programme. Accessed May 9, 2023. https://www.undp.org/sustainable-development-goals

UNESCO. (2021). Bildung für nachhaltige Entwicklung: Eine Roadmap, Deutschland.

United Nations. (2023). World Summit for Social Development 1995. Retrieved from: https://www.un.org/development/desa/dspd/world-summit-for-social-development-1995.html (Accessed: 25.03.2023).

United Nations Climate Change. (2023). The Paris Agreement. Accessed March 31, 2023. https://unfccc.int/process-and-meetings/the-paris-agreement

Uysal, Ö. (2013). Sürdürülebilir Büyüme Kavramının Çevre ve Ekonomik Boyutlarının Ayrıştırılması. *Uluslararası Alanya İşletme Fakültesi Dergisi* 5(2):111–118.

Voumik, L. C., Islam, M. A., Ray, S., Mohamed Yusop, N. Y., and Ridzuan, A. R. (2023). CO_2 Emissions from Renewable and Non-Renewable Electricity Generation Sources in the G7 Countries: Static and Dynamic Panel Assessment. *Energies* 16(3):1044, 1–14.

Wolf, M. J., Emerson, J. W., Esty, D. C., de Sherbinin, A., Wendling, Z. A., et al. (2022). 2022 Environmental Performance Index. New Haven, CT: Yale Center for Environmental Law & Policy. https://epi.yale.edu/

World Bank. (2023). World Bank Open Data. Accessed March 28, 2023. https://data .worldbank.org

———. Accessed March 23, 2023. https://bu.dk/introduktion/baeredygtig-udviklings -historie/1987-brundtland-rapporten

———. Accessed March 26, 2023. https://www.globalis.dk/om-fn/konventioner/ miljoe-og-klima/kyoto-protokollen

———. Accessed March 26, 2023. https://www.mfa.gov.tr/surdurulebilir-kalkinma .tr.mfa

———. Accessed March 31, 2023. https://ocean-energyresources.com/2021/06/02/ g7-countries-among-the-most-polluting-in-the-world

———. Accessed September 10, 2022. https://www.activesustainability.com/sustain- able-development/g7-countries-toward-2030-agenda-sdgs/?_adin=0896481732

Yaşaroğlu, C. (Ed.). (2020). *Çevre Psikolojisine Giriş*, 1. Basım, Ankara: Nobel Yayıncılık.

Yeni, O. (2014). Sürdürülebilirlik ve Sürdürülebilir Kalkınma: Bir Yazın Taraması. *Gazi Üniversitesi İktisadi ve İdari Bilimler Fakültesi Dergisi* 16(3):181–208.

Yıldırım, O., and Nuri, F. İ. (2018). Tarihsel Gelişim Süreci Çerçevesinde Sürdürül- ebilir Kalkınma, Econworld, 23–25 January 2018, Lisbon, Portugal, 1–21.

Yücel, G., and Kurnaz, L. (2021). *Yeni Gerçeğimiz Sürdürülebilirlik,* 1. Baskı, İstanbul: Yeni İnsan Yayınevi.

Yurtsal, K. (2019). Türkiye'de Sürdürülebilir Turizm. *Sivas Interdisipliner Turizm Araştırmaları Dergisi* 4:61–70.

9

Considerations on Global Governance in the Context of Sustainable Development

İbrahim Tanju Akyol

INTRODUCTION

Globalisation, which gained momentum after the 1980s, has brought significant transformations in national and international systems. With globalisation, social, economic, cultural, and political interactions among people have increased, leading to both positive and negative outcomes. Globalisation has boosted foreign trade, technology transfer, and cultural exchange, but it has also resulted in social inequalities, increased economic dependencies among countries, and a diversification of environmental problems, such as climate change, global warming, and the decline of biodiversity. These global issues, including climate change, have necessitated finding common ground rather than being merely a preference for achieving sustainable development.

Sustainability concerns rank among the most focused global issues for countries. Ensuring the needs of future generations, protecting the environment, building social justice, and maintaining economic stability are fundamental components of the sustainability concept. In this context, countries seek solutions to global problems, such as escalating and life-threatening global warming, climate change, forest fires, rapid population growth, and depletion of natural resources. It is widely agreed that minimising the negative externalities associated with these issues is crucial for achieving sustainable development. Consequently, international actors have organised various initiatives, set targets, and reached agreements on the reconstruction of a liveable environment within the framework of development.

The complexity of the process has arisen from the necessity of considering environmental and social factors alongside economic factors in development. Although the integration of these three pillars is acknowledged as a fundamental indicator of sustainable development, theoretical realities have not always found sufficient practical responses. Nevertheless, it is acknowledged that reaching common ground in policies and actions and identifying and remedying shortcomings in existing policies are essential for the success of global governance initiatives. With the assumption that global problems can be solved on a global scale, the involvement of governance actors at all levels and their collaboration in fulfilling their responsibilities are highlighted as key elements for the success of the process.

To achieve sustainability goals, there must be an understanding where all actors are involved in the process, have a place in decision-making mechanisms, and reach decisions as a product of "collective wisdom." In this context, the United Nations (UN) has set sustainable development goals and identified 2030 as the target year for a more liveable future.

This study aims to present, through scientific research, the level of implementation of sustainable development goals that have been proposed and, in many cases, ratified by international actors. The research primarily focuses on two questions: 1) What do international actors do to achieve sustainable development? 2) What are the obstacles to the success of the sustainable development process? In this regard, given the interdependency of UN sustainable development goals, identifying these dilemmas is of paramount importance. To achieve this, data has been collected through a literature review, and secondary data has also been considered. The data has been evaluated within the themes generated by the descriptive analysis technique. The study first discusses the concepts of sustainable development and global governance. Second, it elaborates on the efforts of global actors at the international level to achieve sustainable development. Finally, the study reveals the obstacles to implementing global governance for sustainable development, as identified through the conducted research.

CONCEPTUAL BACKGROUND: ON SUSTAINABLE DEVELOPMENT AND GLOBAL GOVERNANCE

Advancements in information communication technologies and the differentiation of market mechanisms have led to the questioning of conventional patterns in governance processes. National and international politics have been taken to a different dimension, necessitating regulation beyond the nation-state and focusing on global issues (Ronit and Schneider, 1999, 243). With globalisation, the problem of governance has often been evaluated similarly. The classical understanding of governance, which considers the state as the fundamental unit, has faced challenges in addressing the problems arising from the increasing global networks of relationships (Koenig-Archibugi, 2011).

One of the significant goals of global governance is development. Global governance is examined in the context of fundamental components such as global economic governance, global security governance, global environmental governance, or global governance for development. International actors like the United Nations have advantages in establishing a close relationship between global governance and development. The capacity of developed and developing countries to act collectively in areas such as security, economy, and environment is crucial for achieving development. In this context, considering the needs and capacities of developing countries and acting accordingly is of vital importance for global governance (Qoraboyev, 2021). The relationship between countries in the process of sustainable development will not only increase global interaction but also contribute to the efficient use of resources, the transfer of technology, and the strengthening of international cooperation. Moreover, there is a need for a system that will encompass various components like technological advancements, environment, and migration (UN, 2020, 14). In this regard, global governance reflects a different unity from centralised, authority-based understandings. Global governance reflects the capacity of international, national, regional, and local actors to work together based on mutual interdependence and shared goals and values (Qoraboyev, 2021).

Global governance aims to develop international standards that will serve the interests of all countries (Mayntz, 2002). However, organisations, where national governments come together to address global issues, tend to adopt an approach of evaluating problems in a fragmented manner rather than comprehensively and effectively. For example, organisations such as the World Trade Organization (WTO), World Health Organization (WHO), UN Security Council (UNSC), World Bank (WB), regional development banks, and International Monetary Fund (IMF) deal with issues in their respective areas of expertise. Although cooperation among these organisations exists, they continue to act independently in their fields (Boughton and Bradford, 2007, 11). As a result, comprehensive approaches to global issues cannot be developed, and the solutions created may conflict with each other, decisions that include all societies cannot be made, and coordination problems arise. In other words, the failure to achieve global governance makes it difficult to solve global problems.

The rise of the concept of sustainable development coincided with the rise of market liberalisation. The neoliberal political approach advocates the liberalisation of the market and the reduction of public affairs. This understanding necessitates the privatisation of public affairs and requires global conformity of goods and services markets. The emergence of cost-benefit analyses in the production of public and semi-public goods and services has also led to the commodification of natural resources. Sustainable development aims to ensure the protection of the environment, including nature, humans, and social life while using natural resources. In other words, it aims to promote harmony between humans and nature (UN, 1987). Sustainable development demonstrates a comprehensive and integrated approach to economic, social, and political processes. Economic development aims to achieve outcomes while ensuring that the needs of future generations are fairly taken into account. In this context, the basic components of the sustainable development paradigm include environmental sustainability, intergenerational equity, strong political participation, and a sense of intergenerational responsibility (Kysar, 2005, 2115–2116).

The continuity of the understanding of sustainable development is directly related to the success of global governance. The realisation of common policies, the establishment of inclusive legal regulations, the efficient and effective use of scarce natural resources, and the elimination of economic and social injustices are closely related to the coordination and collaboration of stakeholders at the global level. In this regard, various stakeholders, especially the United Nations, have organised conferences and produced various agreements to gain acceptance for the understanding of sustainable development.

EFFORTS OF INTERNATIONAL ACTORS IN THE PURSUIT OF SUSTAINABLE DEVELOPMENT

Population growth, development necessities, and depleting natural resources have driven countries to seek solutions not only individually but also on a global level. Considering the rapid increase in world population, especially in developing countries, the demand for food, water, energy, and employment has surged, making it challenging for governments to find solutions to these issues. In the short term, countries have attempted to find temporary and expedient solutions to these problems, leading to even greater issues such as the rapid depletion of natural resources, increased environmental pollution, and the disappearance of natural habitats. If governments fail to provide swift and effective solutions to these global-scale problems, the future outlook does not appear promising for the next generations. In this context, stakeholders today, including governments, international organisations, civil society organisations, and the private sector, are trying to collaborate in overcoming sustainability challenges.

The United Nations' concerns about sustainability are not new. The "1972 United Nations Conference on the Human Environment" (Stockholm Conference) was significant as the first conference to address environmental issues as a problem. It contributed to placing the relationship between environment and sustainability on the global agenda. In other words, it played a role in shaping international awareness and environmental policies. The conference considered social justice, economic growth, and environmental sustainability as fundamental components and emphasised their interdependence. Additionally, the conference led to the establishment of the "United Nations Environment Programme" (UNEP) (UN, 1972). In 1983, the United Nations convened the "World Commission on Environment and Development" (Brundtland Commission). In its report "Our Common Future," published in 1987, the commission addressed the concept of sustainability based on the degradation of the environment and the rapid depletion of natural resources. The report emphasised the obligation to meet the needs of the present without compromising the ability of future generations to meet their own needs (UN, 1987).

The "United Nations Conference on Environment and Development" (UNCED), held in Rio de Janeiro in 1992, addressed sustainable development from a human-centred perspective. Emphasising the need to change production and consumption patterns to improve human living standards, the conference also recognised environmental protection, poverty eradication, and women's participation as crucial components of sustainable development. One of the key topics extensively discussed during the conference was the importance of partnerships and collaboration among various actors. It was noted that developed countries should take responsibility for global environmental issues, and there were calls for promoting the international economic system. Furthermore, the conference highlighted the necessity of governance for the preservation and restoration of the global ecosystem. In this context, global consensus was seen as essential for resolving global challenges (UN, 1992b). The "United Nations Framework Convention on Climate Change" (UNFCCC), established to combat climate change and mitigate its adverse effects, aimed to identify the factors contributing to climate change and implement measures to reduce its impacts. Additionally, it emphasised the need for policy changes to protect the climate system from human-induced influences, and it encouraged participating states to develop policies tailored to their specific conditions to support sustainable development (UN, 1992a; Shevenell, 2013, 392–393). The "Kyoto Protocol," signed in 1997, focused on global warming, outlining policies to reduce greenhouse gas and methane emissions. Deforestation was also discussed as a matter that needed to be addressed, with an emphasis on promoting afforestation. The protocol committed to enhancing energy efficiency, implementing sustainable agricultural methods, and preferring renewable energy and environmentally friendly technologies (UN, 1998).

In 2000, the "Millennium Development Goals" (MDGs) were proclaimed to contribute to international development. The MDGs targeted eliminating extreme poverty and hunger, achieving universal primary education, promoting gender equality and empowering women, reducing child mortality and improving maternal health, combating infectious diseases, ensuring environmental sustainability, and developing global partnerships (UN, 2005). The "2002 World Summit on Sustainable Development" (Johannesburg Summit) aimed to assess the progress made since the "1992 Rio Conference" and establish a new global agreement on sustainable development. It discussed different decisions compared to the 1992 conference and debated the implementation level of existing regulations (von Schirnding, 2005). The summit sought to achieve sustainable production and consumption and address climate change. Other topics discussed included water and sanitation, energy, and biodiversity. The meeting involved government representatives, environmental NGOs, and participants from the business sector. The importance of national and global governance for sustainable development was emphasised, promoting multi-stakeholder arrangements (UN, 2002).

The "2012 Rio+20 Summit," held in Rio de Janeiro, laid the foundation for the "2030 Sustainable Development Goals" (SDGs) aimed at achieving sustainable development. During the conference, discussions revolved around preserving the environment, reducing environmental risks, alleviating poverty, decreasing greenhouse gas emissions, preventing deforestation, conserving biodiversity, constructing sustainable cities, and establishing mechanisms to promote renewable energy (UN, 2012). In 2015, the "Sustainable Development Summit" was organised in New York after the "Millennium Development Goals" (MDGs) expired. The implementation of the sustainable development goals, which came into effect in 2016, necessitates the collaboration of governments, the private sector, civil society, and international actors to define, identify, and develop solutions for various issues. The SDGs propose innovative means of mobilising, allocating, and managing funds in global health, environment, and climate domains (Kloke-Lesch, 2021). Within this context, the United Nations comprehensively addressed economic, social, and environmental aspects of development by formulating 17 main goals and 169 subgoals in the "2030 Sustainable Development Goals." These goals encompass tackling poverty and hunger; ensuring a healthy and good life; providing quality education; promoting gender equality; ensuring clean water and sanitation, accessible and clean energy, decent work and economic growth, industry and innovation; reducing inequalities; building sustainable cities and communities, sustainable production and consumption; taking climate action; protecting life below water and life on land; promoting peace, justice, and strong institutions; and establishing global partnerships (UN, 2015).

The subject of sustainable development, one of today's most debated topics, has continuously been on the agenda of global actors throughout history.

However, over time, the conferences and agreements on the subject have only produced solutions on paper, as the problems continue to grow in the present day. Commitments made to addressing issues such as global warming, forest fires, food problems, water and energy crises, and poverty have not been adequately met, and the parties responsible for these problems are not subjected to binding sanctions. In academic literature, it is frequently emphasised that global governance is not functioning as it should. Though thinkers who address sustainable development touch upon different aspects of the problem, their general conclusions are often the same. Failure of theoretical arrangements to find sufficient implementation, sacrificing natural resources for the sake of development, and "robbing the future" of generations to come can easily be observed. The primary argument underlying these issues is considered to be the free-market economy. In this context, it is foreseeable that the addressed problems will branch out if the current state of global functioning persists. Therefore, it is necessary to consider the perspectives of thinkers who address the issue on the international stage.

DEBATES REGARDING GLOBAL GOVERNANCE ACTORS IN ACHIEVING SUSTAINABLE DEVELOPMENT

In the present day, an important network has been established at the international level and among institutions to achieve sustainable development. The actors involved in the sustainable development process have prepared action plans, set goals, and outlined strategies related to the topic. One of the most significant elements of these efforts is the Sustainable Development Goals (SDGs), which came into effect in 2016, and they promise important achievements in theory for attaining sustainability. The existence of a sincere effort from various actors, primarily states, is necessary for achieving sustainability. The scarcity of natural resources necessitates global partnerships. Issues such as global warming, air pollution, and climate change are known to not affect just one or a few states but have global implications.

Thinkers who take a global perspective on sustainable development often approach the topic critically, emphasising that global governance is not occurring at a sufficient level. Kloke-Lesch (2021) asserts that the first step toward developing global governance is ensuring the true implementation of the 2030 Agenda and the Paris Agreement. According to the author, creating new mechanisms for cooperation among actors at this level will help reduce implementation-related issues. Additionally, the thinker links sustainability to the functioning of markets. The main obstacles to the success of the global governance approach are the rise of populist and nationalist ideologies and an increase in geopolitical disputes. Policies developed within the context of sustainable development should involve multi-stakeholder processes, including governments, international organisations, the private sector, universities, and citizens. Another barrier to global governance is the narrow interpretation of the role of the state and the relationships between states. Kysar (2005, 2114) states that there is a normative and empirical mismatch between sustainable development and market liberalisation, which hinders the realisation of the paradigm's objectives, as market liberalisation directs the political and economic trends of global markets. Bruzos (2020, 6) attributes the weakening of global governance principles and institutions to countries' failures in predicting international problems. According to him, national governments tend to remain within their nation-state boundaries, particularly when dealing with rapidly emerging issues, and move away from global cooperation.

One of the most debated topics is the insufficient functionality of governance mechanisms arising from international cooperation. In this context, the United Nations, as one of the key actors in global governance, emphasises that the process is not functioning effectively. The global governance system is not designed to manage integration and interdependence among countries. The lack of regulations is apparent in dealing with numerous sustainability issues, such as the regulation of greenhouse gas emissions and the reduction of biodiversity loss. The ambiguity of rules that developing countries are required to follow implies the continuation of a model with problems related to inclusivity, representation, and accountability. Furthermore, even though these countries are stakeholders in sustainability issues, they approach the presented "common interest" with caution (UNCDP, 2014).

The topic of interactor coordination, which is an essential argument for achieving sustainable development, has also found its place in academic literature. In this context, Held (2017, 7) states that efforts to combat global problems through international cooperation take place within an intense "institutional ecosystem." The new form of global governance is shaped by both multilateral and transnational organisations. As a result, the process of global governance has given rise to a complex, multilevel, and multi-actor system. In other words, it has created an understanding where powers conflict within the network of institutions, coordination is inadequate, and competition occurs. Shevenell (2013, 394–395), who shares similar thoughts, emphasises the weakness of coordination among institutions involved in sustainable development. According to her, the autonomy of institutions in different cities leads to differentiation in agendas, inefficient use of resources, and inconsistency in norms related to the issue, which reduces the effectiveness of global governance in pursuit of sustainability. She points out that institutions such as the World Trade Organization and the World Bank make decisions on sustainable development issues, but they remain largely outside the debates on the global governance of sustainability. In this context, Mayntz (2002) draws attention to the necessity of hierarchical authority. According to the scholar, global governance can only be achieved with the existence of hierarchical authority, which is currently lacking. Even in the United Nations Security Council, decisions are subject to debate and are approved by a majority vote. Held (2017, 5–9) identifies the barriers to global governance necessary to address global issues. He argues that the increase in the number of states has led to a multipolar structure. Additionally, some problems are relatively easier to address and evaluate for developed countries because they concern specific countries. For instance, it can be argued that an underdeveloped country would not become a party to a treaty aimed at reducing damage to the ozone layer. However, comprehensive solutions are required for global issues such as global warming and climate change. Moreover, the privileges of key actors in the global system have been considered another obstacle to global governance. It is also noted that institutional fragmentation particularly causes coordination deficiencies in urgent humanitarian crises.

Following the COVID-19 pandemic, the importance of financial support in achieving sustainable development goals has increased even further. The necessity of effectively managing global funds in line with development objectives is evident (Kloke-Lesch, 2021). Similarly, Najam and others (2006, 15–16) argue that the actors of global governance collectively possess sufficient resources. However, the inadequate development of coordination among institutions can hinder the effective utilisation of these resources. Greco (2020, 13) highlights the structural weaknesses in the global governance system. According to him, the COVID-19 pandemic has exposed coordination and disparities in the health sector. In this context, developed countries need to take a more active role in health and global problem-solving. Boughton and Bradford (2007, 12) suggest that actors dealing with global issues, starting from the local level to international organisations, need to act with coordination and a comprehensive vision. Otherwise, effective solutions for issues such as poverty, climate change, the development of renewable energy capacity, and the elimination of health risks seem unattainable. The developments observed during the COVID-19 pandemic have actually demonstrated to the entire world that the existence of global governance is not merely theoretical. Therefore, the realisation of the 2030 sustainable development goals is closely linked to the construction of a functional governance system.

CONCLUSION

The twenty-first century continues to be the century of global challenges. Throughout this century, the number and severity of global problems, including climate change, water scarcity, poverty, diseases and pandemics, environmental pollution, and migration, have continued to increase. National and international actors have organised various meetings to combat global issues. The topic of sustainable development has also been discussed in these meetings, leading to the formulation of various decisions and policies. However, the efforts towards achieving sustainable development throughout history have not yielded the desired outcomes, and existing problems have continued to escalate. There is a consensus on the need for international cooperation to achieve development sustainable. In this context, it is well-known that global governance will play a facilitating role in ensuring sustainable development.

There are challenges and obstacles in implementing global governance. Despite decades of emphasis on the need for establishing new and fair partnerships, theoretical realities have not found practical implementation. Indeed, the interests of developed countries and dominant structures within international organisations have negatively affected the fight against global problems. The increasing intensity of debates on the 2030 Sustainable Development Goals in today's world should be seen as a manifestation of this institutional functioning.

In the context of sustainability, it is essential for policies developed or to be developed to first be implemented at the local level. In fact, some local-level issues taken on by national governments may lead to delays in fulfilling responsibilities at the global level. Therefore, focusing on problems within the framework of the principle of local service and considering the scale not only reduces the problems that national governments need to address but also enhances their capacity to combat these issues.

The effective realisation of global governance is closely related to interactor coordination and information sharing in achieving sustainable development. In a process where reliable data flow is lacking and actors perceive each other as "rivals" rather than "partners" in the governance approach, achieving sustainable development goals does not appear to be an easy task. In other words, in achieving sustainable development, governance must be a necessity rather than a mere requirement to represent the world. It is challenging to claim that a non-inclusive governance mechanism can be just, accountable, transparent, participatory, and thus democratic. Such a governance process would not truly qualify as governance.

One of the most significant obstacles to the success of the sustainable development process is that the support provided for it takes place at a single level. Looking at today's perspective, it is quite understandable that monetary investments, technical assistance, and gains such as raising awareness alone do not hold much meaning. Efforts toward sustainable development have not yielded tangible results for decades, which is why these issues are still being discussed. While the mentioned components are essential in achieving sustainable development, governments also need to consider their global counterparts in policy-making processes and legal regulations to align their actions accordingly. Additionally, even though various objectives are set for achieving sustainable development, the adequacy of policies aimed at strengthening global governance is still subject to debate.

To achieve sustainable development, it is essential to involve developing countries as stakeholders and enhance their negotiation capacity. The issue of sustainable development can only be solved by including all countries in the process and allowing them to participate in decisions. Solutions that address sustainability challenges and lead to achieving sustainable development goals must involve all actors serving sustainability, not just specific countries. In this regard, organisations with international recognition, such as the United Nations and the World Bank, need to strengthen global governance mechanisms, improve interactor communication networks, enhance democratic values, and reinforce monitoring and tracking mechanisms required for sustainability.

Practices that hinder the functioning of the sustainable development process should be subject to binding decisions and sanctions. At this point, the process needs common norms to be successful. Additionally, developed countries need to support sustainable development by sharing their technologies and experiences. Only through such efforts can the world become a more liveable place for humanity.

REFERENCES

Boughton, James M., and Colin I. Bradford Jr. (2007). Global Governance: New Players, New Rules. *Finance & Development* 44(4):10–14.

Bruzos, Lars. (2020). The Difficulty of Anticipating Global Challenges: The Lessons of COVID-19. *Challenges of Global Governance Amid the COVID-19 Pandemic* (pp. 6–9). New York: Council on Foreign Relations.

Greco, Ettore. (2020). G20 in the Spotlight: The Fight Against COVID-19. *Challenges of Global Governance Amid the COVID-19 Pandemic* (pp. 13–15). New York: Council on Foreign Relations.

Held, David. (2017). Elements of a Theory of Global Governance. *Glocalism: Journal of Culture, Politics and Innovation* 2. https://glocalismjournal.org/elements-of-a-theory-of-global-governance/

Kloke-Lesch, Adolf. (2021). Global Governance Needs Reshaping if We're to Achieve the SDGs. SDG Action. https://sdg-action.org/global-governance-needs-reshaping-if-were-to-achieve-the-sdgs/

Koenig-Archibugi, Mathias. (2011). Global Governance. In Jonathan Michie (ed.), *The Handbook of Globalisation* (pp. 393–406). Cheltenham: Edward Elgar. ISBN 978-1-84980-369-4.

Kysar, Douglas A. (2005). Sustainable Development and Private Global Governance. *Cornell Law Faculty Publications.* Paper 31, 2109–2166. http://scholarship.law.cornell.edu/lsrp_papers/31

Mayntz, Renate. (2002). National States and Global Governance. VII Inter-American Congress of CLAD on State and Public Administration Reform. October 8–11, Lisbon, Portugal.

Najam, Adil, Mihaela Papa, and Nadaa Taiyab. (2006). Global Environmental Governance: A Reform Agenda. International Institute for Sustainable Development (IISD). https://www.iisd.org/system/files/publications/geg.pdf

Ronit, Karsten, and Volker Schneider. (1999). Global Governance through Private Organizations. *International Journal of Policy and Administration* 12(3):243–266.

Shevenell, Lisa. (2013). Global Governance. In *Achieving Sustainability: Visions, Principles, and Practices* (pp. 391–398). Boston: Cengage Learning.

Qoraboyev, Ikboljon. (2021). Global Governance. In K. De Feyter, G. E. Turkeli, and S. De Moerloose (eds.), *Law and Development Encyclopedia* (pp. 99–103). Edward Elgar. ISBN: 978-1-78811-796-8.

UN. (2020). The 2030 Agenda for Sustainable Development in the New Global and Regional Context: Scenarios and Projections in the Current Crisis. Economic Commission for Latin America and the Caribbean (ECLAC) (LC/PUB.2020/5). Santiago: United Nations Publications.

———. (2015). Transforming Our World: The 2030 Agenda for Sustainable Development. https://sustainabledevelopment.un.org/content/documents/21252030%20Agenda%20for%20Sustainable%20Development%20web.pdf

———. (2012). Report of the United Nations Conference on Sustainable Development. Rio de Janeiro, Brazil, 20–22 June 2012. https://digitallibrary.un.org/record/737074#record-files-collapse-header

———. (2005). The Millennium Development Goals Report 2005. Santiago, Chile: United Nations Publications.

———. (2002). Report of the World Summit on Sustainable Development. Johannesburg, South Africa, 26 August–4 September 2002. https://www.un.org/en/conferences/environment/johannesburg2002

———. (1998). Kyoto Protocol to the United Nations Framework Convention on Climate Change. https://unfccc.int/resource/docs/convkp/kpeng.pdf

———. (1992a). United Nations Framework Convention on Climate Change. https://unfccc.int/resource/docs/convkp/conveng.pdf

———. (1992b). Report of the United Nations Conference on Environment and Development. Rio de Janeiro, 3–14 June 1992. https://www.un.org/en/development/desa/population/migration/generalassembly/docs/globalcompact/A_CONF.151_26_Vol.I_Declaration.pdf

———. (1987). Report of the World Commission on Environment and Development: Our Common Future. https://sustainabledevelopment.un.org/content/documents/5987our-common-future.pdf

———. (1972). Report of the United Nations Conference on the Human Environment. Stockholm, 5–16 June 1972. https://digitallibrary.un.org/record/523249?ln=en

UNCDP. (2014). Global Governance and Global Rules for Development in the Post-2015 Era. Committee for Development Policy (CDP). https://www.un.org/development/desa/dpad/publication/cdp-policy-note-2014/

von Schirnding, Yasmin (2005). The World Summit on Sustainable Development: Reaffirming the Centrality of Health. *Globalization and Health* 1:8. https://doi.org /10.1186/1744-8603-1-8

10

The Impact of Green Parties on European Politics

Alper Çakmak and M. İnanç Özekmekçi

INTRODUCTION

In the midst of our present day, marked by a multitude of environmental issues and catastrophes, foremost among them the climate crisis, nearly all political actors endeavour to interpret life beyond the realm of conspiracy theories and, in doing so, tend to incorporate varying degrees of "greening" into their respective political agendas. When examined comprehensively, the term "green politics" encompasses a wide spectrum. This inclusive scope spans from modest appeals for environmental preservation to the in-depth analysis of the relationship between humanity and nature, ultimately culminating in a demand for a profound transformation (Vincent, 1993). At this juncture, a discernment between environmentalism and ecologism becomes imperative. Environmentalism, while encapsulating a cognisance of environmental concerns and the safeguarding of the environment, predominantly directs its attention towards pragmatic solutions and is not predicated upon well-defined theoretical postulations or systematic interrogations. In contrast, ecologism, underpinned by a more distinctly delineated political posture, encompasses a precisely formulated and logically interconnected array of ideas, thereby rendering it eligible for classification as a discernible political ideology (Dobson, 2007). In this context, green politics represents a departure from conventional political paradigms characterised solely by heightened awareness of environmental issues. Conversely, the assertion of a distinctly unique ecological political theory underscores that the mere integration of environmental concern into one's political stance falls short of meeting the criteria for a truly "green" political orientation.

The majority of analyses pertaining to green ideology concur on the premise that its fundamental hallmark revolves around a pronounced centrality to nature. This emphasis extends particularly to the conditions governing the very survival of Earth's ecosystem and, by extension, the perpetuation of human existence. This, in turn, necessitates a profound reevaluation of the interconnectedness between humanity and the natural world. Consequently, the primary objective of green ideology lies in the comprehensive restructuring of societal, political, and economic frameworks, with an overarching emphasis on ecological equilibrium. Therefore, the focal point on delineating the correlation between human beings and the natural environment as a means to formulate political, social, and economic tenets is believed to constitute the pivotal element that both distinguishes green political thought and sets it apart from alternative ideological orientations. Therefore, the concept of green politics, within this framework, encompasses a more specific connotation that extends beyond the mere incorporation of environmental issues into the political agenda. It embodies an ideology derived from theories concerning the human-nature relationship, and this ideology is embraced by Green parties that seek to establish their social and political objectives. Green parties across Europe have undergone a significant transformation, progressing from their origins as protest-oriented entities to becoming integrated participants assuming significant roles within the institutional frameworks of mainstream political arenas. As a result, they have evolved into prominent political actors on a European scale today. Currently, the Greens are still part of the coalition government in some EU countries, including Germany, Belgium, Austria, Luxembourg, and Ireland. Additionally, the European Greens also hold significant influence as a bloc movement in the European Parliament. However, the tension between theory and practice raises questions about the credibility and legitimacy of the Greens in the eyes of the public regarding the compatibility and sustainability of their proposed policies at the national level, especially when confronted with realpolitik. Such contradictions are often observed when political parties have to strike a balance between their ideals and the practical implementation of policies. This can influence the public's trust in political parties and the level of acceptance of their policies for the future.

THE "GREENING" OF POLITICAL SPHERE

While traces of notable awareness regarding "environment and environmental issues" can be retrogressively traced to premodern eras within the annals of intellectual history, its emergence as a political stance coincides with the epoch labelled as the age of ideologies, concomitant with the nineteenth century. Nevertheless, environmental concerns during this period are generally products of a cognitive reaction specifically directed towards the ramifications of modernity, and more specifically, rapid industrialisation and urbanisation. Nevertheless, the accomplishment of industrialisation in enhancing the quality of life in the developed world has resulted in these kinds of critiques being categorised as nostalgic and irrational, thereby impeding their transition into a political movement with widespread appeal.

The inception of a distinct political movement encapsulating green politics, culminating with the emergence of parties referred to as "Greens," finds its roots in the thought of ecologism, which mobilised various societal strata into action. This evolution has occurred within a relatively proximate timeframe. One of the two processes that shapes contemporary Green parties is the emergence of new social movements starting from the mid-1960s, while the other involves the expansion of eco-philosophy and the emergence of a new wave of green political thought, which also brings a novel understanding of politics (Burchell, 2002).

The Legacy of New Social Movements

The "New Social Movements"—encompassing movements such as those focused on students, peace, antinuclear efforts, feminism, and the environment—emerged as prominent leaders challenging the conventional materialist-oriented value system and the resulting lifestyles that were prevalent in late 1960s Western Europe. These movements also took on the role of safeguarding civil society against the interventionist policies of the state (Carter, 2007). When examined through the lens of new social movements, the emergence of green politics is commonly attributed to a specific intersection of historical movements and incidents that coalesced during the late 1960s and early 1970s, primarily within industrialised Western Europe.

During its early stages, the realm of green politics in Western Europe exhibited a relatively restrained reaction to the increasing public apprehension regarding the "ecological crisis" that gained prominence in the mid-1960s. It was a response to the negative consequences of economic growth, especially to environmental issues that affected both human health and the health of the world, such as pollution, deforestation, and biodiversity loss. This period in industrialised Western countries, where environmental issues and risks became politicised at the local level, was also the time of the Cold War and nuclear competition. In this political atmosphere, concerns related to the environment and peace, especially in the context of nuclear armament and nuclear energy technology, had a fundamental impact on the ideologies and policy priorities of these movements that would later become political parties at the national level. Certainly, it is necessary to incorporate feminism and the 1968 youth movements into these emerging new social movements, along with the demands of the sexual revolution during that period. The green movement benefited from both the existence and the accumulation of these reactionary movements, and in a way, it evolved intertwined with them. As a legacy of this, the origins of many Green parties consisted of various groups such as peace activists, antinuclear advocates, feminists, development activists, and radical-left factions (Newell, 2019).

These new social movements, mostly initiated as citizen initiatives at the local level through local civil society networks, have attempted to influence "establishment parties" in government or opposition through various forms of noninstitutional political activism concerning environmental issues (Bomberg, 1998; Müller-Rommel, 1985; O'Neill, 2019). Throughout the process, new social movements sought support from established leftist parties, particularly in their opposition to unrestricted economic growth, environmental degradation, and nuclear armament. However, these movements were unable to secure the anticipated backing (Müller-Rommel, 2019). This circumstance has prompted an interrogation not only of existing political institutions, organisational structures, and the nature of politics itself but also of the styles of political engagement. Consequently, this political climate has set the stage for the conceptualisation of the "new politics," in which Green parties emerge as significant actors. In this context, environmental issues have prompted inquiries into the dynamics of community-building and the intricacies of collective decision-making processes (Dyer, 2017).

The Eco-Philosophy and New Politics

The Green movements stood apart from conventional political factions due to their inherent ecological orientation, characterised by an aversion to professionalisation, a commitment to participatory and decentralised party structures, and a strong affiliation with the emerging social movements of the 1960s and 1970s. This new understanding of politics fundamentally challenges the established ideologies of parties and movements associated with the Left and the Right, allowing the green movement rooted in eco-philosophy to manifest itself as a distinct ideology. In this context, it is imperative to acknowledge the substantial heterogeneity inherent within the realm of green ideology. Within the overarching framework of this ideology, a spectrum of perspectives emerges, encompassing eco-capitalists, eco-liberals, eco-conservatives, eco-socialists, eco-anarchists, and ecofeminists. Each subgroup attributes the degradation of the natural world to distinct factors. Furthermore, within the contours of green ideology, certain ecological thinkers hold divergent viewpoints regarding the resolution of environmental challenges, as evidenced by the juxtaposition of shallow ecologists and deep ecologists. Consequently, the spectrum encompasses moderate elements, exemplified by shallow ecologists, who endeavour to reconcile the evolution of the green ideology with the tenets of the capitalist system. In contrast, radical factions represented by deep ecologists advocate for the construction of a postindustrial society characterised by small, agrarian communities centred on artisanal skills. This multiplicity engenders the emergence of theorists who cast doubt upon the categorisation of green ideology as a conventional ideological framework. However, prevailing within the realm of political science is the perspective that diversity is not exclusive to the green ideology, and that despite its intricate nature, it presents a coherent yet multifaceted political landscape (Humphrey, 2013).

Whether they lean towards shallow or deep ecology, the green movement fundamentally converges on challenging the paradigm of unrestricted economic growth underpinned by an anthropocentric worldview promoted by established parties. According to green thought, which criticises anthropocentrism based on the belief that human needs and interests hold morally and philosophically superior importance, thus viewing the natural world as a resource solely available for fulfilling human needs, humans are merely a small component within the entirety of natural systems and hold no greater or lesser significance than other components of nature. The philosophy they present, known as an eco-centric perspective, strives to align the needs of the planet with the needs of the individual and equate the rights of the individual with the rights of the planet (Richardson, 2005).

Ecologism certainly forms the foundation of the green movement, albeit representing only one of the components of the new political paradigm. The concept of the four pillars, embraced by the German Greens in 1980 and later adopted by the European Federation of Green Parties, provides a succinct overview of the thematic underpinnings of the new political ideology emerging within the European green movement. Within this framework, European Greens are recognised to be grounded in not only ecologism but also the principles of social responsibility, grassroots democracy, and nonviolence. Social responsibility, among these pillars, is predicated on the green approach's assertion that socioeconomic and ecological realms are inextricably interlinked. This implies that in the pursuit of societal restructuring based on ecological principles, there should be no detriment to impoverished segments and the working class. Another pillar, grassroots democracy, underscores the desire within the new green political ideology for novelty not only in terms of political content but also in the organisational structure and mode of operation. Indeed, Poguntke (1993), who regards grassroots democracy as the fundamental concept of the new politics, points out distinctive features of emerging Green parties, such as collective and amateur leadership in lieu of professional leadership, imperative mandates, the separation of party functions from parliamentary duties, rotation, open access to meetings, the primacy of the lowest organisational unit, and gender parity for all party roles. Lastly, the principle of nonviolence serves as a manifestation of resistance against both individual acts of violence and violence perpetrated by states and institutions, underscoring a commitment to peaceful means of conflict resolution.

THE GREEN PARTIES IN EUROPE

Van Haute's study (2020), summarising the development of Green parties across Europe and their adaptation to changing political and social contexts, notes that the 1970s witnessed the emergence of Green parties in response to new political challenges such as nuclear energy opposition, pacifism, human rights, and radical democracy. Although these issues were initially raised by environmental movements, existing political parties were unable to address them adequately, thus creating a political space for the formation of Green parties. The process of how these groups or movements transformed into political parties has often been a subject of debate and sometimes a tense one. The emergence of these parties was often triggered by resistance to dominant political systems and ecological concerns. These parties' emergence was frequently driven by resistance to the dominant political system as well as ecological concerns. The New Zealand Values Party (1972), although not in the European Union, is noteworthy as the first Green party in history and represents a significant turning point in the development of Green parties. Similar movements followed across Europe as a result of it. The Ecology Party of the United Kingdom, which is regarded as one of the first Green parties in Europe, was founded in 1973. It eventually changed its name to the Green Party of England and Wales. One of the most significant Green parties in Europe, Germany's *Die Grünen* (The Greens) (1980) was created via the union of numerous grassroots environmental and peace organisations. To promote collaboration and coordination among Green parties across Europe, the European Federation of Green Parties (EFGP) was founded in 1984.

By the late 1980s, Green parties, known as "The Greens," had organised in almost every country in Western and Northern Europe. The transition from a social movement to a political party has always been a contentious issue, particularly concerning whether to hold influential positions within the political arena. This dilemma, which applies to all movements evolving into political parties, took on a specific meaning within the context of the Green movement: Parliamentary representation could provide a suitable platform for disseminating green ideas and demands to a broader audience. However, engaging within the existing political system as a party and aiming to convince large voter bases, essentially transitioning from theory to practice, would inevitably entail political compromises and undermine the movement's antiestablishment nature (Poguntke, 2002).

The first green parliamentarian to be elected to a national legislature was Daniel Brélaz from Switzerland in 1979. In Europe, we can chronologically list the first Green parties and alternative lists to surpass electoral thresholds and enter national parliaments as follows: Belgium in 1981; Switzerland, Finland, Germany in 1983; Luxembourg in 1984; Austria in 1986; Italy in 1987; Sweden in 1988; Ireland, the Netherlands, Greece in 1989. Although they were not the "first" Green party to achieve success in national elections, the German Green Party gained global attention. Their entry into the traditionally three-party Bundestag in 1983 with 28 seats as the fourth-largest party significantly altered the course of both the green movement and the established political system.

In the 1990s, the disintegration of communism and the evident intellectual and practical shortcomings of socialism further solidified the political aspect of the ecological movement. In this period, the intensifying significance of environmental matters in political debates provided a prospect for Green parties to gain prominence and backing. As Kriesi et al. (2008) propose, the customary concentration of political discourse on the economy has been marginalised or reinterpreted in the context of cultural concerns such as extensive immigration and opposition to European integration. This alteration has enabled Green parties to position themselves as proponents of environmental preservation and sustainable advancement. The influence of the Green Party on the political and societal landscape of Germany during the years subsequent to its inception presents a multifaceted issue. Despite its inability to profoundly alter democratic establishments or provoke the destabilisation of West German democracy, the party's subtle and enduring effect on the demeanour and objectives of politics triggers contemplation regarding the extent of these transformative stimuli. The enduring repercussions of the Greens' environmental concerns, feminist principles, and promotion of tranquillity and nonaggression have left an indelible mark on German politics and society, prompting modifications in policies and societal conventions (Milder and Jarausch, 2015, 14). In a similar vein, the consequences of globalisation and denationalisation have engendered a schism between "victors" and "losers" in Western Europe (Kriesi et al., 2008). This has stimulated the rise of a tripartite configuration of political authority, encompassing the left, the moderate right, and the novel populist right. Green parties have been capable of capitalising on this division by concentrating on environmental issues and garnering backing from voters who prioritise sustainability and ecological concerns.

After a gradual process of gaining parliamentary representation, Green parties have become established political actors throughout Europe, solidifying their presence over time. This does not imply that the Greens have been able to organise or secure voter support to the same extent in all of these European countries. Robust green political parties have gained prominence in several European nations, including but not limited to Germany, Austria, Switzerland, Belgium, the Netherlands, Finland, Sweden, Latvia, Lithuania, Ireland, and Croatia. Over the past decade, these political parties have increasingly emerged as appealing alternatives for disillusioned citizens who have grown disenchanted with conventional political entities and are apprehensive about the ascent of far-right movements.

The ascension of Green parties as a formidable force and "challenger parties" in European politics marks a substantial advancement in recent epochs (De Vries and Hobolt, 2020, 15). These challenger parties gained momentum from a political spectrum that could be defined as peripheral or marginal, focusing on ecological concerns and advocating sustainable policies, first trying to influence centrist parties and then greening centrist or mainstream policies. The genesis of Green parties can be ascribed to an array of elements, encompassing the repercussions of globalisation and denationalisation, along with the tactical realignment of political parties. Green parties have achieved a triumph in amassing backing by underscoring cultural matters such as widespread migration and opposition to European integration and deepening in EU policies (Kriesi et al., 2008). Green-Pedersen and Mortensen (2010) deliberate on the model of issue competition, which underscores the interplay between governmental and opposition factions within the framework of the party-system agenda. This model proposes that opposition parties have greater latitude to centre on issues advantageous to them, whereas governing parties are more frequently compelled to react to issues raised within the party-system agenda. This could elucidate why Green parties, functioning as opposition entities, have been consistently capable of directing their focus toward ecological issues and garnering voter support.

Despite the presence of Green parties that have provided parliamentary representation in various countries for many years, none of these Green parties has been able to achieve governance or secure the highest number of parliamentary seats by obtaining an overall majority of votes in a national election. While Green parties have occasionally served as auxiliary members within government coalitions and, on rare occasions, assumed the position of prime minister, it cannot be asserted that they have attained the capacity to formulate comprehensive policies akin to those implemented by traditional governing parties. Nevertheless, this does not imply that Green parties, whether in opposition or as coalition partners, have been merely ineffective entities. Regarding their function in governance and governing bodies, Green parties have experienced differing levels of achievement. In certain states, like Germany, Green parties have succeeded in forging coalition governments and have wielded a substantial influence on policy formulation (Kwidziński, 2020). Nonetheless, in other countries, Green parties have encountered difficulties in securing notable political authority and have persevered on the periphery of the political panorama (Kwiatkowska, 2019).

With achievements in elections, Green parties have encountered diverse degrees of backing throughout distinct European nations. In particular countries like Austria and Belgium, Green parties have consistently attained triumph over spans exceeding two decades (Carter, 2015). Nevertheless, the prosperity of Green parties in electoral contests isn't solely dictated by their stance on ecological matters or European unification. Other factors, such as the performance of ruling factions and the all-encompassing political climate, also exert substantial influence (Hix and Marsh, 2007). In a similar vein, Hix and Marsh (2007) underline that anti-EU parties and Green parties tend to fare better in European Parliament elections in contrast to domestic elections. However, they additionally observe that a party's stance on Europe scarcely impacts its performance. This implies that while European Parliament elections offer a stage for Green parties to exhibit their environmental program, their success is not exclusively hinged on their stance on European integration. The surge of these parties can be attributed to an assortment of elements, including the shifting political panorama and the growing significance of environmental concerns. In their investigation of the transformation of party-political systems in six nations (Austria, France, Germany, the Netherlands, Switzerland, and the United Kingdom), Kriesi et al. (2008) establish that Green parties have encountered assorted levels of triumph in distinct countries. For instance, the Green Party in Germany has attained a pivotal triumph, consistently securing seats in the Bundestag and even participating in coalition governments. In contrast, the Green Party in the United Kingdom has encountered greater obstacles and has not attained an analogous degree of electoral accomplishment. The success of Green parties in elections can also be attributed to their aptitude in rallying support via grassroots movements and activism. Kriesi et al. (2008) underline the significance of the supply-side aspect of electoral politics, where Green parties have effectively conveyed their environmental plan and rallied voters concerned about climate change and sustainability.

GREENS AT THE EUROPEAN PARLIAMENT

The rise of Green parties in the 1990s coincides with a period in which the European Union was also institutionalising within its integration strategy. Many Green parties have lent their support to this process. Amidst this process, the rapid advancement of the European Union's integration journey has facilitated the expansion of the movement's political presence beyond national realms, transitioning into a multilayered dimension. As a result, the impact of Green party politics transcends the confines of the national sphere, encompassing local, regional, and global dimensions. Notably, Green parties have secured representation not only at local and regional levels in diverse European nations but have also constituted a significant parliamentary bloc within the European Parliament since 1989, known as the Green Group in the European Parliament. In the most recent European Parliament elections held in May 2019, the Greens garnered approximately 10 percent of the votes, leading to the Greens/European Free Alliance group becoming the fourth-largest party bloc in the European Parliament.

Regarding the European Parliament's role in addressing environmental matters, its powers mainly pertain to the regulation of the single market, encompassing environmental standards. The primary source of conflict in the European Parliament is the left-right division, with disparities in national party policies on European integration primarily elucidated by different party families' preferences on socioeconomic matters (Hix and Marsh, 2007). Moreover, the increasing fragmentation of party clusters in the European Parliament has presented an opportunity for Green parties to rally support for their environmental agenda. As the European Parliament has grown more diverse, progressive party clusters like the Greens have been able to forge alliances and build coalitions to advance their climate policy objectives (Hix et al., 2005). This has resulted in the European Parliament's ability to legislate in ways that address climate change and advance sustainable energy. Nonetheless, the stance a party adopts on Europe or environmental issues does not exert a significant impact on electoral outcomes. European Parliament elections are often viewed as midterm contests to penalise governing parties, rather than as a platform for expressing views on EU politics and policies (Hix and Marsh, 2007). The ascent of European Green parties necessitates contextualisation within the broader transition from predominant catch-all political parties to more specialised and compact party entities across the European landscape. The Green parties, distinguished by their emphasis on post-materialist principles encompassing environmentalism, anti-militarism, antidiscrimination, and social equity, stand in stark ideological contrast to the right-wing populist factions that likewise witnessed an upsurge in their representation during the 2019 European Parliament elections. Paradoxically, these divergent party collectives both advocate for niche agendas—be it environmental concerns or immigration—that conventional mainstream parties have struggled to effectively address (Berman, 2019).

The imprint of Green parties, particularly the German Green Party, has contributed to the adoption of ambitious energy and climate regulations (Kaza and Smith, 2023; Buzogány and Ćetković, 2021). However, discussions and contention surrounding climate policies underscore the complexity of addressing environmental issues at the European Parliament level

(Bäckstrand and Lövbrand, 2006). The Green parties' influence on the European Parliament's agenda can also be understood through the lens of issue rivalry and agenda-setting (Cuyvers, 2017). Research has demonstrated that opposition parties, such as the Greens, can shape the agenda by bringing attention to specific issues and compelling the government to respond (Green-Pedersen and Mortensen, 2010). The Green parties' emphasis on carbon emissions and environmental sustainability has prompted other political actors to address these issues and incorporate them into their policy platforms. Their stress on environmental matters, advocacy for sustainable development, and strategic positioning within the political landscape have influenced the European Parliament's agenda and led to the adoption of more ambitious energy and climate regulations.

The Green parties have played a significant role in making the carbon emission issue a focal point for the European Parliament. Their emphasis on environmental matters and sustainability has garnered attention towards the urgent requirement to tackle climate change at the European Parliament level. Through their advocacy and policy propositions, Green parties have effectively impacted the European Parliament's priorities and driven for ambitious energy and climate regulations. The initiation of the carbon emission matter into the European Parliament by Green parties has had a notable influence on environmental governance and climate policy. The German Green Party, in particular, has been influential in championing sustainable development and decreasing carbon dioxide emissions. The party was established in 1979 in response to escalating concerns about the environment and has consistently gained votes in every election. Its success can be attributed to the deeply ingrained culture of environmentalism in Germany, which predates World War II (Kaza and Smith, 2023). The impact of Green parties on the European Parliament has been fortified by the growing fragmentation of party groups. As the European Parliament has become more fragmented, progressive party clusters like the Greens have been able to rally support for ambitious energy and climate regulations. This has resulted in the European Parliament's capability to enact policies that address climate change and champion sustainable energy (Buzogány and Ćetković, 2021).

One specific illustration of the Green parties' influence is their role in shaping the European Union's climate and energy targets. The Green Party in Germany, for instance, has been instrumental in advocating for the nation's transition to renewable energy sources and reducing carbon dioxide emissions. This advocacy has impacted Germany's national policies and has also had a ripple effect on the European Union's climate aspirations. The European Green Deal, a plan to make the EU carbon neutral by 2050, was pledged in the European Parliament by Ursula von der Leyen, President of the European Commission, in July 2019. Greens' expanded representation grants them the power to play kingmakers within the European Parliament and urge climate change legislation (Tagliapietra, 2019). The Green parties' focus on carbon emissions and sustainable development has propelled the concern higher on the European Parliament's agenda, leading to the adoption of more ambitious targets and policies. The introduction of the carbon emission issue by Green parties has also incited discussions and contention within the climate negotiation process. Divergent discourses, such as the win-win discourse of ecological modernisation, the green governance discourse, and the critical civic environmentalism discourse, have moulded the articulation and institutionalisation of climate policies. These discourses mirror conflicting and overlapping perspectives on forest plantation projects and their effectiveness in mitigating climate change (Bäckstrand and Lövbrand, 2006).

CONCLUSION

It is evident that contemporary green thought and social movements exert a broad spectrum of influence, ranging from the alteration of government policies and laws at the national level to the signing of multilateral international agreements on environmental protection, as well as the reshaping of corporate and consumer behaviours. With the increasing public awareness of environmental concerns, Green parties have been achieving significant success in both national and EU parliamentary elections for some time now. Green parties have established a notable presence across most Western industrialised societies. However, the extent of their engagement varies significantly at the national level and across different levels of governance within individual nations. What sets these parties apart is their transnational dimension, marked by a relatively consistent organisational structure and policy orientation that spans the European continent. Parties of this kind possess a significant capacity to exert influence in various political domains.

Firstly, the impact of Green parties has led to well-established and major political parties in Western Europe revisiting their policy decisions as a result of the activism of Green parties. Therefore, Green parties have begun to play a key role in shaping the political agenda and policy discourse, especially in Western Europe. In this context, Green parties can be described as issue entrepreneurs. The distinctive characteristics of Green parties and the strategies they employ, as well as the responses of other parties in the political arena to these strategies, will continue to significantly influence European political life in the future. However, the reactions of other parties to the issue mobilisation undertaken by Green parties are contingent upon the electoral threat posed by the Green party and the prevailing political and economic conditions that render green issues potentially appealing to voters (Spoon et al., 2013).

Connected to the impact mentioned above, the second potential effect of Green parties in the European political landscape pertains to national party systems. It is difficult to predict to what extent Green parties positioning themselves outside of the established mainstream parties will be accepted within the societal context. Van Haute (2020) points out that the Green parties have roots outside of parliament and that, in the majority of countries, the process by which these organisations or movements became political parties was contentious and led to some difficulties. Throughout history, there have been several obstacles for Green parties and the Green movement, including maintaining unity; as the Green movement grew, ideological differences among Green parties sometimes led to divisions and splinter groups. Another aspect is the electoral systems. First-past-the-post electoral systems in some EU countries posed challenges for Green parties in gaining proportional representation. The next one is political integration, since Green parties need to balance their commitment to environmental issues with broader political agendas and coalition politics. Furthermore, it should be noted at this point that Green parties in Europe, over the course of approximately forty years during which they evolved from a social movement into significant political actors, have not remained static. The transformation from a social movement to a political party, for the Greens, primarily necessitated a shift towards the centre, enabling them to reach broader voter bases across the countries where they operate, rather than catering primarily to the supporters of a movement.

Despite these challenges, the Green movement and Green parties have achieved notable successes, including: increased awareness, policy influence, and international cooperation. The Green movement significantly raised public awareness about environmental issues and the need for sustainable practices. Green parties influenced the development of environmental policies at both national and EU levels. They collaborated with other environmental organisations and social movements to foster international cooperation on global environmental challenges. Finally, As Van Haute (2020) underlines, Green parties can aid in the creation of a European public sphere by having common traits, fundamentally similar ideologies, a certain organisational structure, and a strong group within the European Parliament. With an emphasis on environmental preservation, sustainability, renewable energy, and climate change, Green parties have played an increasingly prominent role in formulating EU policies throughout time.

REFERENCES

Bäckstrand, K., and Lövbrand, E. (2006). Planting Trees to Mitigate Climate Change: Contested Discourses of Ecological Modernization, Green Governmentality and

Civic Environmentalism. *Global Environmental Politics* 6(1):50–75. https://doi.org/10.1162/glep.2006.6.1.50

Berman, S. (2019, June 3). Populists, Greens and the New Map of European Politics. *Social Europe*. Retrieved November 10, 2019, from https://www.socialeurope.eu/populists-greens-new-political-map

Bomberg, E. (1998). *Green Parties and Politics in the European Union*. London: Routledge.

Burchell, J. (2014). *The Evolution of Green Politics: Development and Change within European Green Parties*. Routledge.

Buzogány, A., and Ćetković, S. (2021). Fractionalized but Ambitious? Voting on Energy and Climate Policy in the European Parliament. *Journal of European Public Policy* 28(7):1038–1056. https://doi.org/10.1080/13501763.2021.1918220

Carter, N. (2015). Green Parties. In *International Encyclopedia of the Social & Behavioral Sciences*, edited by J. Wright (pp. 379–384). Oxford: Elsevier. https://pure.york.ac.uk/portal/en/publications/green-parties

———. (2007). *The Politics of the Environment: Ideas, Activism, Policy*. Cambridge: Cambridge University Press.

Cuyvers, A. (2017). The Road to European Integration. In *East African Community Law: Institutional, Substantive and Comparative EU Aspects*, edited by A. Cuyvers, E. Ugirashebuja, J. E. Ruhangisa, and T. Ottervanger (pp. 22–42). Brill. http://www.jstor.org/stable/10.1163/j.ctt1w76vj2

Dalton, R. J., and Kuechler, M. (Eds.). *Challenging the Political Order: New Social and Political Movements in Western Democracies*. Oxford: Oxford University Press.

De Vries, C. E., and Hobolt, S. B. (2020). The Rise of Challenger Parties. In *Political Entrepreneurs: The Rise of Challenger Parties in Europe* (pp. 15–39). Princeton University Press. https://doi.org/10.2307/j.ctvt9k3d3.5

Dobson, A. (2007). *Green Political Thought*. Routledge.

Dolenec, D., and Širinić, D. (2017). Green Flash in the Croatian Pan: Green Party Survival in Post-socialist Europe. *East European Politics and Societies and Cultures* 31(4):840–862. https://doi.org/10.1177/0888325417720489

Dyer, H. C. (2017). Green Theory, International Relations Theory. In *International Relations Theory: E-International Relations*, edited by S. McGlinchey, R. Walters, and C. Scheinpflug (pp. 84–91). Bristol: Creative Commons.

European Parliament. (n.d.). Retrieved from https://www.europarl.europa.eu/

Green Party Germany. (n.d.). Retrieved from https://www.gruene.de/

Green-Pedersen, C., and Mortensen, P. (2010). Who Sets the Agenda and Who Responds to It in the Danish Parliament? A New Model of Issue Competition and Agenda-Setting. *European Journal of Political Research* 49(2):257–281. https://doi.org/10.1111/j.1475-6765.2009.01897.x

Hix, S., and Marsh, M. (2007). Punishment or Protest? Understanding European Parliament Elections. *Journal of Politics* 69(2):495–510. https://www.journals.uchicago.edu/doi/10.1111/j.1468-2508.2007.00546.x

Hix, S., Noury, A., and Roland, G. (2005). Power to the Parties: Cohesion and Competition in the European Parliament 1979–2001. *British Journal of Political Science* 35(2):209–234. http://www.jstor.org/stable/4092349

Hülsberg, W. (1988). *The German Greens: A Social and Political Profile*. London: Verso.

Humphrey, M. (2013). Green Ideology. In *The Oxford Handbook of Political Ideologies*, edited by M. Freeden and M. Stears (pp. 422–438). Oxford: Oxford University Press.

Kaza, N., and Smith, A. (2023). The Green Party and Germany's Environment: Integration, Influence, and Comparisons. *Journal of Student Research* 10(4). https://doi.org/10.47611/jsrhs.v10i4.2108

Kitschelt, H. (2019). *The Logics of Party Formation: Ecological Politics in Belgium and West Germany*. Cornell University Press.

Kitschelt, H., and Hellemans, S. (1990). *Beyond the European Left: Ideology and Political Action in the Belgian Ecology Parties*. Duke University Press.

Kolinsky, E. (Ed.). (1989). *The Greens in West Germany: Organization and Policy Making*. Oxford: Berg.

Kriesi, H., Grande, E., Lachat, R., Dolezal, M., Bornschier, S., and Frey, T. (2008). *West European Politics in the Age of Globalization*. https://doi.org/10.1017/cbo9780511790720

Kwiatkowska, A. (2019). Institutionalisation Without Voters: The Green Party in Poland in Comparative Perspective. *Zeitschrift für Vergleichende Politikwissenschaft* 13(2):273–294. https://doi.org/10.1007/s12286-019-00424-6

Kwidziński, E. (2020). German Green Party: The Evolution of Political Agenda. *Journal of Geography Politics and Society* 10(2). https://doi.org/10.26881/jpgs.2020.2.06

McBride, J. (2022). How Green-Party Success Is Reshaping Global Politics. Council on Foreign Relations. Accessed August 21, 2023. https://www.cfr.org/backgrounder/how-green-party-success-reshaping-global-politics

Milder, S., and Jarausch, K. H. (2015). Introduction: Renewing Democracy: The Rise of Green Politics in West Germany. *German Politics & Society* 33(4)(117):3–24. http://www.jstor.org/stable/43917548

Müller-Rommel, F. (1985). The Greens in Western Europe: Similar But Different. *International Political Science Review* 6(4):483–498.

———. (Ed.). (2019). *New Politics in Western Europe: The Rise and Success of Green Parties and Alternative Lists*. Routledge.

Newell, P. (2019). What is Green Politics? In *Global Green Politics* (pp. 21–48). Cambridge: Cambridge University Press.

O'Neill, M. (2019). *Green Parties and Political Change in Contemporary Europe: New Politics, Old Predicaments*. Routledge.

Poguntke, T. (1993). *Alternative Politics: The German Green Party*. Edinburgh University Press.

———. (2002). Green Parties in National Governments: From Protest to Acquiescence? *Environmental Politics* 11(1):133–145. https://doi.org/10.1080/714000585

Richardson, D. (2005). The Green Challenge: Philosophical, Programmatic and Electoral Considerations. In *The Green Challenge: The Development of Green Parties in Europe*, edited by D. Richardson and C. Rootes (pp. 8–16). New York and London: Routledge.

Tagliapietra, S. (2019). The impact of the global energy transition on MENA oil and gas producers. *Energy Strategy Reviews* 26:100397.

Rootes, C. (2002). It's Not Easy Being Green: Green Parties: From Protest to Power. *Harvard International Review* 23(4):78–82. http://www.jstor.org/stable/42762767

van Haute, E. (2020). The Development of Green Parties in Europe: Obstacles and Opportunities 1970–2015. In *The Environment and the European Public Sphere: Perceptions, Actions, Policies*, edited by C. Wenkel, E. Bussière, A. Grisoni, and H. Miard-Delacroix (pp. 165–180). White Horse Press. http://www.jstor.org/stable /j.ctv289dvb9.14

Vincent, A. (1993) The Character of Ecology, *Environmental Politics* 2(2):248–276.

11

How Can/Will the European Union Succeed in Its Green Policies in the Course of the Existing Energy Crisis?

Sina Kısacık and Arzu Alvan

INTRODUCTION

The European continent, devastated after two world wars within the first fifty years of the past century, has favoured the handing over of control of coal and steel, seen as the raw materials and the motives for these two wars. Energy resources have remained the start of that integration movement prompted by the German-French Great Compromise. Subsequent to the 1950 Robert Schuman Declaration, the 1951 Paris and 1957 Rome Treaties, and the creation of the European Coal and Steel Community (ECSC), the integration process has accelerated. Since then, the European Community, developing legal arrangements including other parts of modern life, has progressively expanded integration to become the European Union (EU) with twenty-seven members. Principally as an expected consequence of this enlargement and deepening processes, the Union has met with growing energy usage annually in order to withstand its economic progress and also its existing welfare. Insufficiency of primarily hydrocarbons along with declining production of these energy resources has required EU member countries to prioritize the broadening use of gas providers, because of the snowballing of gas consumption in the Union owing to its ecologically approachable feature.

At this point, it is necessary to underscore the impact of the population growth that occurred following the incorporation of former Soviet Union states into the European Union in the post-1990 period, as well as the need to seek answers to the ever-growing dependency of not only these states but also the Union generally on Russian gas imports. Gas price confrontations between Russia and Ukraine materialized in 2006, 2009, and 2013, with disruptions that obliged the European Union to search for fresh providers.

Since the onset of the February 2022 war between Russia and Ukraine, Europe has once more been confronted with gas cut-offs by Russia as an answer to Western sanctions against it. Additionally, when winter terms approach, panicky situations regarding the likelihood of natural gas disruptions originated by Moscow present grave concerns for EU member countries. Thus, serious questions remain with regard to energy security as well as interdependence amid energy sellers and clients in the twenty-first century.

While the abovementioned crises are ongoing, since 2019 the European Union has also been increasing its efforts to decrease its dependence on Russian gas and transition to a greener economy by focusing on carbon-decreasing energy technologies with the European Green Deal. It remains to be seen whether or not this policy will be successful under war conditions; possible developments on this issue will be determinants in that case.

By considering the abovementioned factors, this paper will try to examine whether or not the European Union will succeed in realising its green policies under the new energy crisis caused by 2022 Russian-Ukrainian crisis. Therefore, the paper will firstly discuss the fundamentals of European energy security since the 1990s. Secondly, the paper will analyse an outlook concerning Green New Deal and the EU Energy Crisis. Finally, the authors will share their joint analyses on the researched topic.

THE CHIEF COMPONENTS OF EUROPEAN ENERGY POLICIES SINCE THE 1950S

Nowadays, the transformation within the context of energy in the international sense is interpreted as one of the necessities of climate change in the wider context. From the beginning of human history until now, the transitions from wood to coal, and from coal to oil and natural gas have been shaped on the basis of availability, low cost, and the advantages of new energy resources. For now, the transition to new energy types includes sources of renewable energy such as solar, wind, water, bioenergy, and geothermal, and the main aim within this context is to decrease the use of carbon energy as well as to diversify and to develop energy efficiency and production. Simultaneously, it is intended to lessen the consumption of fossil fuels in terms of their environmental and social aspects. The objective is to reach the lowest level of energy dependency. Global energy transitions basically are illustrations of the search for modern energy solutions—in other words, clean energy (Gielen et al., 2019, 38–50). Moreover, technological advancements are among the most important reasons causing energy transitions (Kısacık and Yorulmaz, 2022, 264).

The European Commission (EC) describes energy security as a "continuous corporal accessibility of energy products within the market, at affordable prices for all end-users including private and industrial ones." Commonly, energy security stands guaranteed wherever it stays acceptable, affordable, and consistent. The accessibility of supply, fee steadiness together with affordability, effectiveness, as well as differentiation of supply resources are generally accepted as the most communal elements of energy security in the modern world. Multiplicity of energy supply remains among the foremost pointers of energy security because "energy systems that stand varied stay more robust and adjustable to shockwaves in terms of energy transfers" and also decreases the influence of energy supply cut-off via extended substitutions. It ought to be underscored that an unexpected and unmanageable energy shift (Perez et al., 2019) has been established as unproductive. More exactly, due to the fact that the European Union stands as the principal energy buyer in the world and in order to ensure a "strong energy union," the implementation of an all-inclusive energy shift strategy seems to remain practical. As of 2015, the European Union approved a Framework Strategy for a Resilient Energy Union (European Commission, 2015) for guaranteeing the Union's energy security and also to link the members via energy substructure, among others. Moscow's incursion into Kyiv in February 2022 (Verma and Düben, 2023, 75–92) has revealed operational complications for European energy security and has demonstrated the necessity to guarantee nuclear energy as an imperative substance when compared with the near past. The war has impacted universal energy security and countrywide strategies in many-sided ways. The World Economic Forum in 2022 distinguished six areas where the war has impacted the energy field across the world: a shockwave to the organisation, interruption in terms of the supply chain, energy strategy deviations, outcome over universal trade, influence over CO_2 emissions, and also a push towards renewables (Teshome, 2023, 21–22).

The universal objectives of energy strategy being inexpensive, steadfast, and reachable display parallels not only in local but also within the milieu of Union stages. Nonetheless, the EU Energy Policy (EUEP) essentially focuses on the formation of a sole energy market accompanied by the ecological features of energy. At the beginning phases of the European integration, in conjunction with the 1951 Paris Treaty for the European Coal and Steel Community (ECSC) together with the formation of the European Atomic Energy Agency in 1957, coal and nuclear energy further came to the fore. Essentially, the ECSC remained a political plan intended for the international control/ management of coal realised as a cause of war. Subsequent to its functioning as a social instrument, economically backing up the Western European coal mining industry and steel production for fifty years, the ECSC was ended in 2002.

In order to be a member of the International Energy Agency, membership of a state in the Organisation for Economic Co-operation and Development is a must. But, since not all EU members are standing members of this organisation, trouble with the establishment of a joint EUEP is simple to comprehend. The economic effect of energy has further come to the fore, principally with the 1986 Single European Act and the setting forth of the objective of a Single Market in line with this document. Centred on free market and anti-monopoly articles in the founding treaties, the European Commission has established regulations for the liberalisation/deregulation of electricity and gas markets. In this field, when the rules concentrating on transborder constant grids and dominant dealers are considered, the slight measurement of EUEP can straightforwardly be detected (Kısacık and Güçyetmez, 2022, 102–104).

In the meantime, papers examining the Maastricht and Lisbon Treaties set by EUEP regarding energy have highlighted three key areas of focus:

1) Sustainability: (i) the growth of modest, renewable energy forms along with additional carbonless (less carbon) energy resources besides transporters (predominantly the substitute transportation energy resources; (ii) reducing European energy need as well as; (iii) being the leader of the international initiatives for the race against climate change and to safeguard air quality.

2) Competitiveness: (i) allowing the appearance of liberalisation within the energy market for both end-users and economics generally while reassuring investments in clean energy and energy effectiveness; (ii) decreasing the outcome of developed, worldwide energy expenses on EU economic system and peoples to a sensible level; and (iii) defending Europe in terms of forthcoming probable energy expertise.

3) Security of supply: (i) reducing the growing energy import reliance of the Union through decreasing need; differentiating the Union's energy mix by benefitting from viable, numerous, and renewable energy resources; guaranteeing the route, variety, and also diversity in imported energy supply resources; (ii) creating an atmosphere that will generate essential funds for meeting the snowballing energy need; (iii) better preparing the European Union to adapt to emergency circumstances; (iv) guiding European countries seeking to tap into global resources as well as; (v) ensuring easy access for all citizens and firms to energy sources (Kısacık and Güçyetmez, 2022, 104–105).

To provide background information on this issue, in 2005, after the 2004 Orange Revolution, Kyiv had begun to distance itself from Moscow. Ukraine persevered for the next ten years; nonetheless, that period was sufficient to cause the initial stage of an energy predicament that recognised strategies when benefiting from energy as a political force against its clients is applying diverse tariffs to friends and adversaries. Utilising recognised strategies, Russia benefitted from using energy as a political force to influence its customers, applying diverse energy rates to its associates and adversaries. Primarily former Soviet nations, those that followed strategies in favour of Moscow were able to buy natural gas under more approving tariffs and clauses, while the other remaining states were obliged to purchase pursuant to the conditions of market charges aligned to the Western world and when Ukrainian government was futile to recompense unpaid bills gas from raised prices. Once Kyiv was unable to meet the debt of unpaid gas bills caused by higher fees, Gazprom ultimately decided to halt gas supplies to the country. A remote occurrence, it nevertheless alerted Ukraine, and the presence of a transit state did meet its demands from the gas delivered towards Europe, by way of a preceding option. Henceforth streams into Europe were broken up twice in 2006 and 2009. Albeit this provisional disruption did not result in key economic interruptions and the problem was settled in a short period of time, both culminations of the contract held significant lessons and European countries commenced to pursue their individual plans to eradicate the likelihood of a recurrence of an equivalent state of affairs (Kaynak, 2022, 443).

For Laura Rodriguez-Fernandez and J. Garcia Verdugo, considering EU gas supply security, there are some issues that need to be addressed. Key dangers stand defined with five scopes that might cause supply disruptions: economics, energy-linked, political, societal, as well as methodological (i.e., economic and population growing, energy reserves, political rule, worldwide political grouping, ordinary catastrophes, accidents). Minor dangers are able to bear three results: power disruptions, ecological hazards, and hazards to social well-being as well as property. The energy security column has factually stayed associated with outward measurement of energy dangers in terms of the European energy policy. The outward measurement associated with these dangers encompasses all features connected to dependency on energy importations, geopolitical circumstances, worldwide passage, and mechanical matters. This measurement remains more important for the European Union because of its high energy dependency. Yet as the Union encounters inner and exterior energy security dangers, the inner measurement of the gas sector should be noted. Also, this latter measurement stands related to the EU market and the industry's deregulation; outside measurement is totally associated with a rising need for importations. The external causes of risks—geopolitics, vulnerability, and impact on society—emerge as the key dimensions of energy supply security. For the EC Statistics Office, energy dependency stands as the mark wherein an economy counts on importations for handling its energy requirements. It can be inferred that the more reliant a country is on imported energy, the less supply security it will possess (Rodríguez-Fernandez et al., 2020: 3).

Hence, European countries have begun to implement a counter policy to decrease their reliance on Russia's energy resources comprising strengthening dependence on renewable energy resources, safeguarding original energy suppliers, storing as a means to meet possible supply interruptions, developing balanced energy usage strategies, and also reducing destructive emissions. Numerous issues affect the potential for success or failure with regard to the implementation of European guidelines and measures in safeguarding satisfactory stages of energy security. They can be classified as: the heightened struggle between the foremost global powers in transferring energy resources to Europe, specifically competition between the USA and Russia; political steadiness or uncertainty within the transfer countries; and price instabilities in terms of energy bills. The Energy Security Strategy for the European Union accordingly advances a set of palpable procedures for strengthening the European continent's resistance as well as cut its reliance on energy imports. The European Union stands committed to the 2030 agenda for environment and energy established by the European Council. The progress towards a modest, low-carbon (carbonless/less carbon) economy is going to decrease the amount of trade in energy resources via adapting energy requests as well as benefitting from renewable and supplementary domestic energy resources (European Commission, European Energy Security Strategy, 2014, 1–24).

According to Moscow, reliance on Ukraine as a transit route has been a life-threatening and irresponsible policy. Constructive estimates on its standing as a component of stock chain distribution in the international energy business has not been sufficient in anchoring Kiev to Moscow politically. From Moscow's perspective, it ought not to be included within the fresh energy balance. While this policy has necessitated considerable substructure investments at the beginning, it has nonetheless been economically achievable. Controlling nonstop access into the major natural gas importation place in the world that supports Europe, Russia possibly will pledge money movements which may well rationalise primary expenses over substructure. Nevertheless, new methods ought to favour prudence to prevent repetition of the condition that occurred within Kyiv. Outmoded resentment of Poland prevented entry through it into Europe, so use of a safer, nevertheless much more forceful pathway from a practical standpoint, was commenced. The Nord Stream pipeline has been linking Russia directly with Germany, passing beneath the Baltic Sea. The deepness of the subsurface pipeline system as well as the volume transported have been regarded as a chief technological accomplishment; Russian gas has been going to Lubmin, the pipeline's terminal in Germany. The cost has surpassed $10 billion, nonetheless this has permitted transport of a quantity of an overall 55 billion m³ per annum, substituting a noteworthy portion of the natural gas transported via Kyiv (Kaynak, 2022, 443–445).

The Moscow-Kyiv war which started with the military operation of Russia to Ukraine on February 24, 2022 (Šćepanović, 2024, 1–16), has revived concerns regarding European energy security. Even though the wide-ranging sanctions implemented against Russia do not include its energy sector, Moscow has responded to these sanctions by disrupting the natural gas supply to EU countries. Following this, Brussels has begun to seek new supplies bypassing Russia and also to orient towards alternative energy resources. Qatar has been one of the countries coming to the fore. But as stated by the Qatari Energy Minister, neither his country nor any other country has the sufficient capacity to substitute the supply of Russian LNG gas piped gas to Europe. Moreover, the Qatari Energy Minister has underlined that a great portion of Qatari gas is reserved for Asian buyers with long-term contracts. Just 10–15 percent of Qatar's gas capacity might be exported to Europe. He has also stated that Russia supplies 30–40 percent of Europe's need and no country can close this gap. Ursula von der Leyen, the President of the EU Commission, has remarked that the crisis has clearly shown to Europe that the continent is very dependent on Russian gas. European countries must make huge investments on renewable energy as well as focus on supplier diversifications. Russia is responsible for the existing crisis and, for Leyen, it will rapidly complete the sanctions package. Also, as the Euro-Atlantic Bloc, it should take necessary measures to make Russian aggressive policies harder to realise. Leyen has also underlined that the Nord Stream 2 pipeline suspension decision by Germany is a correct one. This pipeline should be evaluated in light of supplying gas to all of Europe. Supply diversification and huge investments in renewable energy sources are strategic initiatives for Europe's energy independence (Kısacık and Yorulmaz, 2022, 285–286).

In these circumstances, Brussels wishes to quicken the transition to renewable energy resources as well as reach the target level of dropping greenhouse gas releases by no less than 55 percent as of 2030. The energy sector remains responsible for more than 75 percent of EU greenhouse gas releases. Snowballing the portion of nonfossil energy transversely, diverse segments of the economic system stand as an important structural bloc for accessing EU energy as well as environment goals to decrease gas releases by a minimum 55 percent (in comparison with 1990) as of 2030, and to become an environmentally friendly continent as of 2050 (European Commission Energy, n.d.). Meeting over 20 percent of this objective by the second decade of the 2000s, the reorganised Renewable Energy Directive 2018/2001/EU has recognised a fresh requisite nonfossil energy goal for the European Union as of 2030 of, at the best, 32 percent, with an article up for probable reconsideration as of

2023 (European Commission Energy, n.d.). In order to fulfil the advanced climate objective as offered within the December 2019 European Green Deal (Panarello and Gatto, 2023, 1–17), more reconsiderations of the instruction remain necessary. The Commission has offered fresh 2030 climate goals for the European continent, including a proposal for amending the Renewable Energy Directive announced on July 14, 2021. It seeks an upgrade to the existing goal towards no less than 40 percent nonfossil energy resources within a general energy mixture for the European Union as of 2030. The Commission has issued the REPowerEU plan that puts forward a set of procedures for speedily decreasing the Union's dependency on oil and natural gas coming from Moscow well before 2030 via quickening the clean energy transition on May 18, 2022. The REPowerEU plan stands centred on storing energy, generating clean energy, and differentiating energy deliveries towards the European Union. An important component of the Union's raising of nonfossil fuels in electricity generation, manufacturing, housing, and transportation, the Commission has planned to upsurge the objective in the regulation to 45 percent as of the third decade of the 2030s. On March 30, 2023, the European Parliament and the Council have reached a provisional agreement to increase the required nonfossil energy objective towards a minimum 42.5 percent in 2030 (World Economic Forum, 2023; IEA, 2022; Interreg Europe, 2023; European Commission, n.d.; Reuters, 2023).

Its short-term emphasis on gas storing, due to the problems in this area in the preceding year, has been essential notwithstanding inadequate safeguarding of sufficient natural gas volumes for the 2022 and 2023 winters. Consequently, the Commission planned an intentional reduction in gas usage, which encountered resistance from some members, as a result of oil sanctions. Hard discussions were involved in reaching a joint resolution backed by all members, with a few countries even discussing an upsurge in usage, but the European Union as a whole settled to cut usage by 15 percent. While the worst possible circumstances have not come to fruition throughout the winter of 2022–2023, this has been partially because of unexpectedly mild weather conditions resulting in less natural gas usage, as well as immediate reserve gas-storing actions, including provisions for households, with LNG deliveries coming from all around the world. Extended resolutions will be required to ensure the Union's future total energy security in addition to guaranteeing that adequate volumes of natural gas with be available for successive winter and cold weather periods. While, by means of the evolution to carbonless energy resources, "Russia's power over EU energy supplies will vanish," the European Union presently requires huge volumes of natural gas resources, part of which are still Russian-originated. Although penalizing Moscow-originated natural gas might, within the short term, address the problematic condition regarding energy markets, this fuelling tension increases Moscow's hostility towards the Union. Terminating the purchase of Moscow-originated natural gas may serve as a powerful illustration (concerning energy as well as foreign policy) of member states' ability to act in harmony and to uphold the ideals upon which the European Union was constructed. Unity remains a critical notion in this process: there are going to be successes and failures of these courses action in both the near- and longer-term periods, and Brussels must remain capable of assisting these efforts. It is likewise significant that costs be maintained at a steady, predictable rate within the milieu chosen. Quality control difficulties, lack of communication, or other failure of the cohesion mandated among EU member states could render continued harmonious functioning of the Union unrealisable (Misík and Nosko, 2023, 2–3).

AN OVERVIEW OF THE GREEN NEW DEAL AND EUROPEAN UNION ENERGY CRISIS

The Green New Deal ushers in a carbon-neutral energy policy, a universal single-payer healthcare system, and a free public education system. Europe has experienced a major energy crisis due to disruptions in supply, particularly the reduction in gas supplies caused by the Russian invasion of Ukraine. At present, Europe faces an energy crisis (Milne, 2022). In addition to the war in Ukraine and its consequences, rising inflation in Europe has also exacerbated the issue (Liadze et al., 2022). The reason for this is largely due to the region's dependence on imported energy resources and its difficulty in replacing them with renewable energy sources. OECD Europe's gas consumption declined by close to 10 percent between January and August 2022, while production in industry was estimated to have decreased by 15 percent. The strategy focuses on measures to reduce gas demand, such as energy efficiency, energy saving, and the benefitting from nonfossil energy resources. Furthermore, the Commission has projected a Gas Security Package for advancing gas supply security. In order to address this complex issue, European leaders must work together to develop a comprehensive plan to reduce energy demand, increase efficiency, and put money into nonfossil energy resources.

The energy security question, however, is a very topical one that creates significant geopolitical sensitivities, especially between countries that are oil-dependent and those that are energy-producing. The war between Russia and Ukraine is the main driver behind the resurfacing of this issue on the world agenda. During the course of this war, the global energy crisis reemerged, which resulted in an increase in inflation on a worldwide scale (Żuk and Żuk, 2022). The equilibrium of power in the international arena has correspondingly been shaken by this war in a very big way. On account of the energy stalemate that currently plagues the European Union following the decision to sanction Russian energy firms, the issue of recycling renewable energy sources, as outlined in the Green New Deal, has been brought to the forefront of the agenda. Energy stands among the utmost imperative mechanisms of the international economic system, and Russia plays a foremost role in it. Moscow remains the world's principal seller of petroleum to international markets and the second chief crude oil seller after Riyadh (Goldman, 2023). Thus, it may be concluded that there has been a significant fluctuation within the framework of the energy markets owing to the combat between Moscow and Kyiv, causing a rapid rise in the price of hydrocarbons. There is no doubt that the existing energy crisis is causing significant economic shocks in countries that rely heavily on energy. As a result, it is likely that the global crisis will deepen as well (Prisecaru, 2022). In addition to using renewable energy sources on a large scale, the aim of the Green New Deal includes developing alternative sources of energy. Thus, the innovation that is being brought with the Green New Deal is key to the ability to reach a zero-emission target so as to be able to accelerate global investments in this field. There have been a number of recommendations made in this regard. There is no denying that the Russian-Ukrainian war has caused an energy crisis in Europe that will only get worse.

In particular, the Green New Deal seeks to address the European energy crisis that reemerged as of 2022 by positioning the continent as a leader in renewable energy, investing in green infrastructure, and providing incentives for businesses to switch to cleaner energy sources. The Green New Deal also calls for the creation of millions of jobs within the context of the nonfossil energy area, the implementation of a universal basic income, and the implementation of regulations on the banking sector to prevent another financial crisis (Panarello and Gatto, 2023).

The natural gas rates that EU countries paid to Russia in 2022 were considerable. It is evident that European countries rely heavily on foreign energy resources. During the energy crisis in 2022, the European Union's natural gas importation fee was nearly four hundred billion euros, with Moscow's portion of the entire natural gas requirement of the Union decreasing from 40 percent within 2021 to under 10 percent. Despite the drop in demand, Russia still saw significant income by reason of the strident natural gas charges (Mbah and Wasum, 2022). Thus, it is very likely that the transition to a zero-emission target, which must be achieved in full by 2050 in accordance with the New Green Deal, will be a very difficult and costly process.

Especially in economies that have started to rebound since the pandemic, the increase in energy demands has caused prices to rise rapidly. Inflation, which was long absent in the economies of developed countries, has reemerged on account of the rapid upsurge in terms of energy prices. The crisis continued in 2022 and 2023. Economic effects are also expected to be quite extensive. There has been significant impact on the economies of energy-dependent countries as a result of fluctuations in energy prices (Gilbert, Bazilian, and Gross, 2021). This is due to the fact that energy demand is less elastic in these countries. Currently, there are no alternative energy sources capable of replacing fossil fuels completely. Even though renewable energies—such as those derived from the sun, water, or air—are anticipated to hold a progressively imperative role in the future, they cannot yet replace fossil fuels.

It is undeniable, however, that Industry 4.0 will contribute to a greener economy in the long run and that this is a definitive trend. The success and sustainability of the Green New Deal is actually dependent on how widespread Industry 4.0 will become in the future. In terms of what Industry 4.0 brings us, the most noticeable things are artificial intelligence and blockchain technology. Industry 4.0 refers to the fourth industrial revolution that stands to reform the methods corporations use to manufacture, expand, and dispense their goods. With the advent of new knowledge and applications—including the Internet of things (IoT), cloud computing, and analytics, as well as artificial intelligence (AI) and machine learning—manufacturers are integrating technologies throughout their production facilities and operations (Nersisyan and Wray, 2021). For example, AI and machine learning can be used to optimize the efficiency of production lines and to develop predictive maintenance tools that allow manufacturers to anticipate and prevent breakdowns.

Thus, as with any other policy, the triumph of the Green Deal depends on several factors, including the level of political commitment and the stage of communal support, together with technological innovation. Industry 4.0 can contribute significantly to the achievement of the European Green Deal's objectives by helping companies reduce their carbon footprint through increased efficiency and reduced waste. Companies can streamline their operations by utilising smart technologies, such as artificial intelligence, data analytics, and the Internet of Things.

CONCLUSION

Energy as the initiator of European integration has been gradually increasing in prominence, its importance accelerating, deepening, and growing as time passes. Since the 1990s, sustainability, competitiveness, and security of supply have been prioritised in terms of EUEP (European Union Energy Policy). Both Europe and Russia have been prioritising alternative routes bypassing Ukraine after the 2006 and 2009 energy crises. Thus far, the Nord Stream, TurkStream, and Southern Gas Corridor stand operative for gas transfer to Europe.

From February 2022, Europe has been confronted with another inordinate test—the Russian attack against Ukraine. Since then, the West has been sanctioning Russia to halt its aggressiveness against Kyiv. Moscow has the sole power to interrupt gas flows to Europe during winters; thus, Europe has been concentrating more on new gas transportation alternatives, principally LNG along pipelines. Correspondingly, Europe is trying to increase the percentage of renewable energy in its energy mix. Europe understands that it cannot abandon its gas dependence on Russia in the midterm or longer term.

By 2050, the European Union intends to become climate-neutral. Currently, it is witnessing an enormous energy crisis by reason of the ongoing Russian-Ukrainian confrontation. Several other factors affect this energy crisis: a low level of hydroelectric generation, low wind speeds, and high demand for natural gas. Sustainability in energy policies is the key element that must be addressed in order to resolve the current energy crisis. Market manipulation is often discussed by politicians in relation to rising energy prices, but the existing energy dependence is rarely mentioned. Furthermore, the European Union has taken steps to reduce its dependence on Russian gas, including investing in renewable energy sources, but much more needs to be done with the purpose of ensuring energy security as well as avoiding the potential for future energy crises. An effort has been made by Brussels to prevent such a situation from occurring by proposing a "Green New Deal," which would involve large-scale investment in nonfossil fuel energy resources, specifically wind and solar power, together with the development of energy-efficient technologies. As has already been demonstrated, the Union has made significant progress towards achieving its climate change objectives. A legally binding target has been set for reducing greenhouse gas emissions from non-Emissions Trading System sectors.

Conversely, critics of the Green New Deal claim that its implementation would be too expensive, and that it would not reduce EU dependency on imported energy. A further contributing factor to the deepening of the crisis has been the current system on the energy market. There can be no doubt that the fragility of a market occurs when marginal optimisation targets are the driving force. We are likely to experience the worst economic downturn in half a century as a result of the Ukraine-Russian war. Thus, a comprehensive program of managed demand reduction is recommended. Brussels might be capable of limiting the growth in energy prices through lessening demand and mitigating negative economic and social consequences by implementing policies that reduce demand.

Finally, the success of the European Green Deal relies on the political will of the governments of Europe, the support of the public, and technological innovation. The European Green Deal can only be successful if member states demonstrate a strong commitment to achieving their nonfossil energy targets and putting money into the new and innovative nonfossil energy systems. In the industries, it is necessary to move towards a production model that can keep pace with technological advances while expanding its scope to make production more environmentally friendly. In addition, a change in the taxation system is necessary. For green investments to be encouraged and fossil fuel usage to be discouraged, the education system must undergo a revolution. In sum, to ensure the success of European governments in achieving zero-carbon emission targets, the Green New Deal must be implemented in a way that affects all segments of society, with reforms that can positively impact all people's lives.

Therefore, historically, European energy security can be named as answering to energy crises. In order for the European Union to create sensible and clear internal/external energy policies now and in the future, its member states need to act and talk in consensus to evade condemnation for "ECONOMIC GREATNESS BUT POLITICAL DWARFISM." If not, its goals of decarbonisation and reducing substantial energy dependency on external suppliers presently and in the future within the framework of Green Energy Deal cannot be achieved.

REFERENCES

European Commission. (2014). Communication from the Commission to the European Parliament and the Council: European Energy Security Strategy. {SWD(2014) 330 final} COM(2014) 330 final. Brussels. https://eur-lex.europa.eu/legal-content/EN/TXT/PDF/?uri=CELEX:52014DC0330.

European Commission. (2015). Energy Union Package: A Framework Strategy for a Resilient Energy Union with a Forward-Looking Climate Change Policy. Brussels. https://eur-lex.europa.eu/resource.html?uri=cellar:1bd46c90-bdd4-11e4-bbe1-01aa75ed71a1.0001.03/DOC_1&format=PDF.

European Commission. (n.d.). Renewable Energy Directive. https://energy.ec.europa.eu/topics/renewable-energy/renewable-energy-directive-targets-and-rules/renewable-energy-directive_en.

European Commission. (2023). Renewable Energy Targets. https://energy.ec.europa.eu/topics/renewable-energy/renewable-energy-directive-targets-and-rules/renewable-energy-targets_en.

Gielen, D., Boshell, F., Saygin, D., Bazilian, M. D., Wagner, N., and Gorini, R. (2019). The Role of Renewable Energy in the Global Energy Transformation. *Energy Strategy Reviews* 24:38–50. https://doi.org/10.1016/j.esr.2019.01.006.

Gilbert, A., Bazilian, M. D., and Gross, S. (2021, December). The Emerging Global Natural Gas Market and the Energy Crisis of 2021–2022. Brookings Research Report.

Goldman, M. I. (2023). *The Enigma of Soviet Petroleum: Half-Full or Half-Empty?* Vol. 7. Taylor & Francis.

Hardt, J. P. (1982). The Enigma of Soviet Petroleum: Half-Full or Half-Empty? By Marshall I. Goldman. London and Boston: George Allen & Unwin, 1980. x, 214 pp. Maps. Tables. 7.95, paper. *Slavic Review* 41(1): 149–150.

International Energy Agency (IEA). (2022). Is the European Union on Track to Meet Its REPowerEU Goals? Accessed May 15, 2023. https://www.iea.org/reports/is-the -european-union-on-track-to-meet-its-repowereu-goals.

Interreg Europe. (2023). More Ambitious EU Renewable Energy Targets Agreed. Accessed on May 15, 2023. https://www.interregeurope.eu/policy-learning-plat-form/news/more-ambitious-eu-renewable-energy-targets-agreed.

Kaynak, A. B. (2022). Energy Security, Armed Conflict and the Limits of Commitment Strategy: EU-Russia Relations and the War in Ukraine. *Journal of Applied and Theoretical Social Sciences* 4(4): 439–453.

Kısacık, S., and Güçyetmez, F. (2022). European Energy Security: Can the Balanced Energy Mix within the European Union be Accomplished in the 21st Century? In *Global Energy and Geopolitical Transformation*, edited by Sina Kısacık and Ferdi Güçyetmez (pp. 93–118). İstanbul: İdeal Kültür Yayıncılık.

Kısacık, S., and Yorulmaz, M. (2022). Küresel Enerji Geçişinin Orta Doğu ve Kuzey Afrika'daki Jeopolitik ve Jeoekonomik Etkileri. In *Orta Doğu Jeopolitiği (Middle East Geopolitics)*, edited by Hasret Çomak, Burak Şakir Şeker, Mehlika Özlem Ultan (pp. 263–292). Ankara: Nobel Akademik Yayıncılık.

Liadze, I., C. Macchiarelli, P. Mortimer-Lee, and P.S. Juanino. 2022. The economic costs of the Russia-Ukraine conflict. NIESR Policy Paper, 32.

Mata Pérez, M. de la E., Scholten, D., and Stegen, K. S. (2019). The Multi-speed Energy Transition in Europe: Opportunities and Challenges for EU Energy Security. *Energy Strategy Reviews* 26: 100415. https://doi.org/10.1016/j.esr.2019 .100415.

Mbah, R. E., and Wasum, D. F. (2022). Russian-Ukraine 2022 War: A Review of the Economic Impact of Russian-Ukraine Crisis on the USA, UK, Canada, and Europe. *Advances in Social Sciences Research Journal* 9(3): 144–153.

Milne, A. (2022). An Economic Narrative for Better Managing the European Energy Crisis. Available at SSRN. https://papers.ssrn.com/sol3/papers.cfm?abstract_id =4202887.

Misík, M., and Nosko, A. (2023). Each One for Themselves: Exploring the Energy Security Paradox of the European Union. *Energy Research & Social Science* 99: 103074. https://doi.org/10.1016/j.erss.2023.103074.

Nersisyan, Y., and Wray, L. R. (2021). Can We Afford the Green New Deal? *Journal of Post Keynesian Economics* 44(1): 68–88.

Nguyen, H. H., Nguyen, P. V., and Ngo, V. M. (2024). Energy Security and the Shift to Renewable Resources: The Case of Russia-Ukraine War. *The Extractive Industries and Society* 17: 101442. https://doi.org/10.1016/j.exis.2024.101442.

Panarello, D., and Gatto, A. (2023). Decarbonising Europe—EU Citizens' Perception of Renewable Energy Transition Amidst the European Green Deal. *Energy Policy* 172: 113272.

Pérez, Mata M. de la E., Scholten, D., Stegen K. S. (2019). The multi-speed energy transition in Europe: Opportunities and challenges for EU energy security. *Energy Strategy Reviews* 26:100415. https://doi.org/10.1016/j.esr.2019.100415.

Prisecaru, P. (2022). The War in Ukraine and the Overhaul of EU Energy Security. *Global Economic Observer* 10(1): 16–25.

Reuters. (2023). EU Reaches Deal on Higher Renewable Energy Share by 2030. Accessed on May 15, 2023. https://www.reuters.com/business/sustainable-business/eu-reaches-deal-more-ambitious-renewable-energy-targets-2030-2023-03-30/.

Rodríguez-Fernandez, L., Fernandez-Carvajal, A. B., and Ruiz-Gomez, L. M. (2020). Evolution of European Union's Energy Security in Gas Supply During Russia–Ukraine Gas Crises (2006–2009). *Energy Strategy Reviews* 30: 100518. https://www.sciencedirect.com/science/article/pii/S2211467X20300717?ref=pdf_download&fr=RR-2&rr=7d17b1a31f3da98f, https://doi.org/10.1016/j.esr.2020.100518.

Šćepanović, J. (2024). Still a Great Power? Russia's Status Dilemmas Post-Ukraine War. *Journal of Contemporary European Studies* 32(1): 82–95. https://doi.org/10.1080/14782804.2023.2193878.

Teshome, M. Z. (2023). Ensuring Energy Security through Expanded Access to Nuclear Technology for Peaceful Uses and the Challenge of a Nuclear Taboo. *European Journal of Law and Political Science* 2(2): 20–28. http://dx.doi.org/10.24018/ejpolitics.2023.2.2.76.

Verma, R., and Düben, B. A. (2023). Russia's Invasion of Ukraine: Cementing US Global Preeminence. *Journal of Indo-Pacific Affairs* 6(3): 74–91. https://www.airuniversity.af.edu/JIPA/Display/Article/3371478/russias-invasion-of-ukraine-cementing-us-global-preeminence/.

World Economic Forum. (2023). Can Europe's Rush for Renewables Solve Its Energy Crisis? Accessed on May 15, 2023. https://www.weforum.org/agenda/2023/02/eu-renewables-energy-crisis/.

Żuk, P., and Żuk, P. (2022). National Energy Security or Acceleration of Transition? Energy Policy After the War in Ukraine. *Joule* 6(4): 709–712.

Evaluation of Green Tax Practices and Regulations in the European Union and Turkey

Kendal Deniz and Erdal Eroğlu

INTRODUCTION

In the globalised world, where time and space boundaries are removed in light of the developments in technology and communication, although living standards have improved, intensive production and widespread consumption have caused humanity to face much more serious problems. Ecological problems such as global warming, water, air, and soil pollution, climate change, loss of biodiversity, reduction of water resources, food shortage, drought, desertification, etc. have become the most important agenda of the whole world (Apergis et al., 2021; Hironaka, 2002). Leaving a more liveable world for future generations is the common responsibility of all institutions and organisations at national and international levels. In line with sustainable development goals, the development of public policies that balance economic growth and environmental protection is closely monitored by the European Union. The most important of these policies are environment, ecology, and tax policies characterised as green.

In the neoclassical approach, market failures and externalities constitute the theoretical basis of green taxation and green public policies. An externality can be defined as the positive or negative impact of the economic activities of an individual or firm on other individuals and firms in the market, but in the negative case, the individual or firm does not bear the cost, and in the positive case, the individual or firm does not receive any return (Kargı and Yüksel, 2010). In more general terms, externalities are defined as costs or benefits arising from the production or consumption of goods and services but not reflected in market prices. In theory, economic efficiency in a commodity market is realised when the supply of the good in question is equalised with the demand for that good, and at this level of equality, the marginal private cost is equal to the marginal benefit. In an analysis where environmental costs are included, not only private costs but also total costs should be considered to achieve economic efficiency. In this case, the sum of marginal private cost and marginal external cost should equal the demand for that good (Wallart, 1999, 46). However, external costs are ignored in the market process (Määttä, 2006, 7). Pigou emphasised the role of government intervention to correct market failures caused by externalities through taxes, subsidies, or regulations. With the public intervention called the Pigouvian tax, the activity that creates the negative externality is taxed and the external costs in question are priced. The aim is to adjust the market price to reflect the true social cost and to encourage a more socially optimal level of production or consumption. The amount of tax to be imposed is usually set equal to the marginal external cost of the activity, thus effectively equalising private and social costs. Environmental taxes mainly aim to internalise the costs of environmental degradation, encourage more sustainable behaviour, and support the transition to a greener economy (Ciocirlan and Yandle, 2003). In addition to green taxes, several institutional arrangements, subsidies, fees, pollution permits, and direct controls have also been proposed to internalise negative externalities within the scope of public policies (Kargı and Yüksel, 2010). States are responsible for taking all kinds of financial measures for the protection of the environment, operating audits, control and reporting processes, and encouraging all kinds of ecologically positive activities (Eroğlu, 2021). In these respects, when both tax and expenditure dimensions are carefully evaluated, green public policies are used as an effective tool to combat environmental problems. Ostrom (1990) emphasised the need for communities to develop institutional arrangements to overcome externalities and ensure sustainable resource management. Similarly, Acemoğlu and Robinson (2012) emphasise the importance of inclusive institutions that promote property rights, the rule of law, and economic opportunities to overcome negative externalities.

In terms of the international dimension, the role of the European Union (EU) in environmental issues is very important. The European Union was influenced by the "Stockholm Conference on Environment and Development," the first major meeting on international environmental problems organised by the United Nations in 1972, and started environmental studies in 1973. In this context, many treaties and studies such as the Single European Act (1986), the Maastricht Treaty (1993), the Amsterdam Treaty (1999), the Lisbon Strategy, Environmental Action Programmes (the last of which is the 8th Environmental Action Programme 2021–2030) were enacted. Environmental taxes were seen as a very important issue in the European Union and the idea of charging for energy use and carbon emissions came to the agenda in 1992. Many EU member countries adopted this idea and started to implement environmental taxes in line with tax reforms. In addition, the Union has pioneered the development of important principles and policies for increasing environmental expenditures and has made important legal arrangements for green public procurement. For the European Union, renewable energy, circular economy models, efforts to protect the environment, and transition to sustainable policies in the production and consumption of goods and services are all policies that are emphasised.

When we look at the fiscal policies implemented in Turkey regarding environmental issues, although they do not have a comprehensive framework, many fiscal instruments such as emission fees, user fees, environmental cleaning taxes, user fees paid for travelling on motorways, motor vehicle taxes, special consumption taxes, etc. are used. This study aims to draw conclusions about Turkey based on the practices and regulations implemented in the European Union with regard to green tax and sustainable fiscal policies, which are the responsibility of states for a more sustainable future. In this context, firstly, the environmental taxes and environmental policies implemented by the European Union for the protection of the environment are discussed. In the second part of the study, green tax practices and legal regulations in Turkey are mentioned. In the last part, general conclusions are made about the practices in Turkey in terms of implementation practices.

EUROPEAN UNION IN ENVIRONMENTAL PROTECTION

The environment is affected by the production and consumption activities of people. Countries are constantly trying to increase production to ensure economic growth at the expense of destroying natural resources. At the same time, the increasing population and the desire of consumers to use resources unlimitedly increase the negative effects on the environment day by day. Therefore, behavioural changes affecting labour, product, and capital markets, which involve significant economic costs, are needed to address environmental problems (Eurostat, 2013, 7). Therefore, the necessity of considering the environment in the formulation of economic policies due to climate change, increased pollution, and the destruction of natural resources has become a common concern of policymakers seeking solutions to environmental problems (Remeur, 2020, 2). This situation was first drawn attention to with the United Nations "Human Environment" conference in 1972 and the relationship between global environmental problems and economic activities was explained within the concept of "sustainable development" (Kayhan, 2013, 63; Kuşat, 2013, 4899).

Following the first conference on the environment organised by the United Nations, the need for an environmental policy that supports economic development was emphasised at the 1972 Paris Conference in the European Union and a series of regulations were made in this regard. In the 1987 Single European Act, the "Environment Chapter" was regulated, which provided the first legal basis for the establishment of a common environmental policy to protect environmental quality and human health and to ensure the rational use of natural resources. With the 1993 Maastricht Treaty, the environment became an official EU policy area. With the 1999 Treaty of Amsterdam, "environmental protection" started to be integrated into all EU sectoral policies to support sustainable development. With the Lisbon Treaty in 2009, sustainable development was made a special policy area in relations with countries outside the Union in the fight against climate change (Kurrer and Lipcaneanu, 2023, 1–2). In 2019, the European Green Deal, prepared by the European Commission as the main driving force of the economic growth strategy, placed the "environment" at the centre of the policy-making process in the European Union (Remeur, 2020, 2).

The European Green Deal aims to make Europe the first climate-neutral continent in the world. At the same time, the European Green Deal is a growth strategy that aims to transform the European Union into a fair and prosperous society with a competitive economy that uses resources efficiently, where greenhouse gas emissions are zero by 2050 to combat climate change and environmental degradation, and where an economic growth independent of resource use is achieved (European Commission [EC], 2019, 2).

To achieve these goals, the following objectives are pursued.

- Transforming the economy and society,
- Ensuring sustainable transport for all,
- Pioneering the third industrial revolution,
- Cleaning the energy system,
- Renovating buildings for greener lifestyles,
- Cooperating with nature to protect the planet and our health,
- Strengthening global climate action.

The European green consensus seeks to integrate environmental policies with economic policies to realise the above objectives. In this context, economic instruments are increasingly used in the European Union to implement environmental policies to control environmental pollution and manage natural resources efficiently. Apart from the European Green Deal, the EU 6th Environment Action Programme and the renewed EU Sustainable Development Strategy and Europe 2020 Strategy have also emphasised the importance of economic instruments to ensure resource efficiency and climate protection and encouraged their use (Eurostat, 2013, 8), because economic instruments are the most important tool to help adjust, guide, or change the behaviour of economic agents in protecting the environment and combating climate change (Remeur, 2020, 2).

Among the economic instruments, particular emphasis is given to flexible and cost-effective fiscal instruments that will strengthen the principles of pollution prevention, elimination at source, and "polluter pays" and to achieve environmental policy objectives (Eurostat, 2013, 7). However, as environment and climate have become an integral part of economic and budgetary policies, fiscal instruments should also take a green or environmental dimension in line with the chosen terminology. Fiscal instruments in this direction consist of measures such as environmental taxes, fees, administrative fines, etc. to encourage the transition to more environmentally friendly options, as well as expenditures or subsidies on less polluting, less resource-intensive practices, and technologies, especially in the context of the circular economy (Kurrer and Lipcaneanu, 2023).

ENVIRONMENTAL TAX PRACTICES IN THE EUROPEAN UNION

In line with the European green consensus and environmental action plans, the European Union is transforming its tax policy to be based on the greening of the tax system, green taxes or environmental taxes in the context of environmental policies, and the realisation of the circular economy (Remeur, 2020). The main objective behind the predominant use of green or environmental taxes in tax policy is that green tax arrangements in the European Union and its Member States, as an element of a broad policy mix, can play a key role in solving environmental and climate problems by encouraging a transition to cleaner energy, more sustainable industry, and more environmentally friendly economic activities (European Commission [EC], 2023). The expansion of environmental taxes facilitates the realisation of the basic principles of environmental policy: pollution prevention, elimination at source, and polluter pay (Remeur, 2020, 2–3). Environmental taxes increase the cost of polluting or environmentally damaging activities by adding the relevant social costs known as "negative externalities" to the price by the "polluter pays" principle (Ağcakaya and Kaya, 2022, 516). Conversely, it incentivises environmentally friendly activities by taxing them at a lower rate or excluding them from taxation. Therefore, it obliges producers or consumers to choose between changing their decision-making behaviour or bearing the cost of pollution. This can help reduce waste of resources and damage to the environment (Remeur, 2020, 2–3).

Expanding the scope of green taxation in the European Union and its Member States can also contribute to promoting sustainable growth and transition to a fairer society (EC, 2019, 17). This is because low-income groups are more affected by pollution as they have lower access to green alternatives. In this context, a green tax policy that considers how taxation or market-based instruments are assessed on its citizens will also contribute to ensuring fairness in society (EC, 2023). It is also aimed to reduce the tax burden on labour, which has distorting effects on the market in the European Union and in Member States. To maintain the same level of income, the scope of green taxation is being expanded by shifting the tax burden from labour to pollution (EC, 2019, 17). In this way, it is thought that the "polluter pays" principle will be systematically implemented with the green tax reform (EC, 2023).

In the conceptualisation of environmental tax in the European Union, the definition made by the Organisation for Economic Co-operation and Development (OECD) in the 1990s was adopted and regulated in the EU national accounts system and the regulation on environmental accounts. In this regulation, environmental tax is defined as "a tax defined as a tax in the European system of accounts, where the physical unit of something that has a proven negative impact on the environment constitutes the tax base" (Eurostat, 2013). In line with this definition, the key factor for a tax to be accepted as an environmental tax in the Union is that the elements that make up the tax base have a negative impact on the environment. The name of the tax or the use of the revenue for environmental purposes does not matter. Therefore, the definition of environmental tax in the European Union aims to protect the environment rather than merely generate funds. However, the definition emphasises the tax base from a fiscal point of view, because to classify and analyse the size of environmental taxes, it is necessary to examine the tax base to be objective and make suitable comparisons (Dikmen and Çiçek, 2020, 60). In this context, the Union classifies environmental taxes into four categories as energy, transport, pollution, and natural resources to standardise data on environmental taxes and harmonise the tax systems of member states by taking into account the factors that create pollution such as greenhouse gases, air, water, and soil pollution (Eurostat, 2013; Dikmen and Çiçek, 2020, 66).

Energy Taxes: These are taxes levied on energy production and the use of energy products for transport, fixed purposes, or various purposes. Gasoline, diesel, LPG, fuel oil, natural gas, coal, electricity, biofuel can be given as examples of energy taxes levied for transport purposes, and natural gas, coal, electricity, biofuel can be given as examples of fixed-purpose energy taxes (Cural and Saygı, 2016, 82). In addition, greenhouse gas emissions resulting from the combustion of fossil fuels, or the carbon content of fuels, are also included in energy taxes instead of pollution taxes. The reason for this is to harmonise the classification of environmental taxes for use in member states and international comparisons (Eurostat, 2013, 13).

Transport Taxes: All kinds of taxes levied on the ownership and use of motor vehicles are considered transport taxes. In this context, all kinds of transport vehicles, automobiles, aircraft, helicopters, and railway transport are classified as environmentally friendly, and taxes levied on electric vehicles and taxes levied on the insurance of transport vehicles are included in the scope of environmental taxes. In some countries, instead of basing them on the CO_2 emission amounts of transport vehicles, these taxes are collected in the form of import, registration fee, or annual vehicle tax. In these countries, taxes can be levied on technical specifications such as engine power and weight of vehicles instead of CO_2 emission amounts. Such taxes are included in the scope of transport taxes. Again, in some countries, a fee is charged under the name of the city entrance fee. If this fee is included in the scope of tax in the income classifications of the countries, these fees are also included in transport taxes (Eurostat, 2013,14).

Pollution Taxes: These refer to taxes levied on air, water, soil, noise pollution, and waste. The only exception is that carbon emissions and greenhouse gas emissions are included in energy taxes, not pollution.

Natural Resources Taxes: These are defined as taxes levied on the extraction and utilisation of natural resources. They are levied on activities that reduce or consume natural resources, for example, extraction of raw materials such as oil, gas, minerals, and water; logging; and fishing. Since resource taxes are levied on the use or consumption of resources in the form of a certain rent, they do not increase prices. In addition, taxing the rent obtained from the extraction of natural resources is not within the scope of resource taxes.

In line with the classification of environmental taxes in the European Union, the shares of these taxes in environmental taxes and total taxes are as shown in table 12.1 below.

The largest share of environmental taxes in the European Union belongs to energy taxes. The share of energy taxes in total environmental taxes is around 77 percent on average. After energy taxes, transport taxes follow with an average of 18–19 percent. The lowest share is pollution and natural resources tax, which has an average share of 3.5 percent. Although pollution and natural resources taxes constitute different categories in the classification of environmental taxes in the European Union, they are shown under the same category due to low tax revenues.

In the European Union, the countries with the highest share of environmental taxes in total tax revenues are Greece, Latvia, and Croatia, while those with the lowest shares are France, Germany, Belgium, and Finland.

Table 12.1 Environmental Taxes in the European Union

EU	Total 27 Countries	Energy Tax/Total Environmental Tax	Transport Tax	Pollution and Natural Resources Tax	Green Tax/Total Tax Revenues	Green Tax/GDP
2021	325.837.48	78.4	18.1	3.5	5.52	2.24
2020	300.192.86	77.4	19	3.6	5.57	2.23
2019	329.919.09	77.8	18.9	3.2	5.89	2.35
2018	324.698.77	77.7	19.1	3.3	5.99	2.4
2017	316.579.61	77.7	18.9	3.4	6.06	2.42
2016	310.193.51	77.8	18.8	3.4	6.21	2.47
2015	298.974.85	77.4	19	3.5	6.16	2.45

Source: Eurostat, 2023

Table 12.2   Share of Environmental Taxes in Total Tax Revenues in Some EU Countries

YEAR/EU COUNTRIES	2015	2016	2017	2018	2019	2020	2021
Germany	4.95	4.76	4.61	4.45	4.39	4.26	4.38
Belgium	5.66	6.03	6.02	6.02	6.07	5.8	5.72
Denmark	8.57	8.55	8.02	8.15	7.02	6.71	6
Finland	6.65	7.05	6.9	6.92	6.63	6.51	5.81
France	4.73	4.91	4.98	5.13	5.1	4.78	4.82
Croatia	9.12	9.3	9.41	9.38	9.22	8.92	8.75
Netherlands	8.99	8.73	8.63	8.62	8.64	7.99	7.77
Italy	7.92	8.33	7.99	7.94	7.7	7.14	6.93
Latvia	11.75	11.66	11.23	10.87	9.58	9.81	8.97
Romania	8.79	9.27	7.78	7.59	8.14	7.3	7.43
Slovenia	10.34	10.31	9.84	9.08	8.9	7.85	7.29
Poland	8.17	8.11	7.85	7.7	7.23	7.12	7.84
Portugal	7.03	7.59	7.56	7.41	7.33	6.71	6.63
Greece	10.46	9.82	10.24	9.49	9.79	9.69	9.98

Source: Eurostat, 2023

ENVIRONMENTAL TAX REGULATIONS IN TÜRKİYE

In a period when environmental pollution is increasing day by day due to economic and daily activities, efforts to integrate economic development and environmental policies in the international arena are also followed by Turkey (Ecer et al., 2021, 134). Especially in the EU accession process, Turkey, which is trying to harmonise its policies and legislations with the EU policies and legislations, was not indifferent to the European Green Deal, and the Turkey Green Deal Action Plan was prepared by the Ministry of Trade in 2021. In this action plan, a total of nine targets have been determined and these targets are stated below (Turkey Green Deal Action Plan [YMEP], 2021).

- Carbon Regulations at the Border
- A Green and Circular Economy
- Green Financing
- Clean, Economic, and Secure Energy Supply
- Sustainable Agriculture
- Sustainable Intelligent Transport
- Combating Climate Change
- Diplomacy
- European Green Deal Information and Awareness-Raising Activities

In line with the green consensus, Turkey uses economic instruments to protect the environment and ensure sustainable growth. Among the economic instruments, fiscal instruments are preferred especially because they are cost-effective methods. In the context of realising the circular economy in Turkey, Turkey is trying to transform its tax policy based on environmental taxes within the scope of fiscal instruments and its expenditure policy—which covers the expenditures made for the protection of the environment—into a "green"-oriented structure.

The main objective of the sustainable development strategy is to make economic activities environmentally sensitive. In contrast to the comprehensive policies in the European Union, Turkey does not have a comprehensive green tax policy or regulations for environmental protection and pollution prevention (Toprak, 2006, 157; Ertekin and Dam, 2020, 70). On the contrary, various taxes and fees scattered in various tax laws in Turkey, as well as fees and administrative fines levied according to the Environmental Law, have been implemented at a limited level to protect the environment, prevent pollution, and make polluters pay for pollution (Gülşen, 2021, 39). These regulations consist of Environmental Cleaning Tax (ECT), Value Added Tax (VAT), Special Consumption Tax (SCT), Motor Vehicles Tax (MTV), and recycling participation share, deposit application, environmental labelling, bag fee, and various fees levied in accordance with the Environmental Law. Practices other than the ECT and the fees or administrative fines levied in accordance with the Environmental Law have been introduced to generate revenue by prioritising the possible effects on the environment and the financial purpose instead of directly serving the purpose of protecting the environment (Aydın and Deniz, 2017, 449).

If it is necessary to evaluate the green taxes and fiscal instruments applied in Turkey in terms of their environmental impacts, they are as follows.

Environmental Cleaning Tax: Environmental Cleaning Tax, which is the only green tax levied directly for the protection of the environment in Turkey, is a pollution (waste) tax regulated under Law No. 2464 on Municipal Revenues (MRL). According to this regulation, it is levied on "residential, commercial and other buildings located within municipal boundaries and neighbouring areas and benefiting from environmental cleaning services of municipalities." The taxpayers of the ECT are the users of these buildings.

In terms of its subject matter, ECT consists of two basic taxes: solid waste and wastewater. The tax on solid waste is based on the provision of garbage collection services by the municipality, while the tax on wastewater is based on the provision of sewerage services by the relevant municipalities (Pirler, 1994, 35, 39; Çelikkaya, 2011, 113). Based on the amount of water consumption, the ECT for residential buildings is calculated as 1.50 TL per cubic meter in metropolitan municipalities and 1.10 TL in other municipalities as of 2023. The ECT for workplaces and buildings used for other purposes is calculated based on the monthly tariff determined according to building groups and grades, and this tariff is applied with a 25 percent increase in metropolitan areas (MRL, Repeated Art. 44). The amounts determined for dwellings, workplaces, and buildings used for other purposes are applied with a 50 percent discount for municipalities in priority regions for development and municipalities with a population of less than 5,000, except for those located within the borders of metropolitan municipalities (Art. 5 of the General Communiqué No. 56 of the MRL).

Although ECT is introduced for the purpose of protecting the environment in general and for preventing waste, it is taxed according to the amount of water consumption in residences, and according to building groups and grades in workplaces and other buildings. Therefore, since there is no direct relationship between the tax and the amount of waste, the tax burden does not have any effect on waste generation. As such, since the ECT cannot be associated with the amount of waste and only covers the costs of waste collection and disposal, its environmental effectiveness is limited (Çelikkaya, 2011, 113). In addition to ECT, the Regulation on the Procedures and Principles to be Followed in Determining the Tariffs of Wastewater Infrastructure and Municipal Solid Waste Disposal Facilities in 2010 regulated a fee for wastewater and domestic waste. With this regulation, it has been decided to assess solid waste and wastewater disposal fees in line with the "polluter pays" principle to ensure the disposal, maintenance, and repair of wastewater and domestic wastes. Solid waste and wastewater disposal services are among the services that municipalities are responsible for providing and ECT is paid for these services. In addition, although charging a fee for these services has been criticised on the grounds that it means taxing the same issue twice (Acuner, 2014, 150; Yegen, 2020, 911), it also reflects that the main purpose of taxation is to generate revenue.

Value Added Tax: VAT is a consumption tax levied on all kinds of goods and services included in the law. Therefore, although VAT is not a tax directly introduced for the protection of the environment, the law encourages the use of such goods and services by recognising goods and services that are likely to have a positive impact on the environment as items not included in the tax base or by exempting them from taxation. For example, packaging subject to refunds is excluded from the tax by being counted among the items not included in the tax base according to the VAT law (Şenyüz et al., 2022, 274). It is thought that this article provision will gain more importance, especially as the deposit practice introduced in 2018 with the regulation made in the Environmental Law regarding packaging becomes widespread. At the same time, the exemption of "delivery of metal, plastic, tire, rubber, paper, glass scraps and wastes and garment trimmings" from tax with Article 17/g-4 of the VAT Law is important in terms of encouraging the recycling of such environmentally harmful products (Aydın and Deniz, 2017, 452). In addition, the negative impacts on the environment can be reduced by increasing the prices of environmentally harmful goods and services and reducing their consumption.

Special Consumption Tax: Special Consumption Tax (SCT) is a consumption tax levied on the goods included in the tables annexed to the law. Schedule I of the Law covers petroleum and petroleum products, Schedule II covers motor vehicles, Schedule III covers tobacco products and cola sodas, and Schedule IV covers white goods and luxury consumer goods. Although the purpose of SCT is to tax the consumption of the goods included in these lists, especially the petroleum and petroleum products included in lists I and II, motor vehicles cause negative effects on the environment by emitting wastes such as lead and particulate matter. In SCT, the tax base is determined by considering the sales prices and lump sum tax amounts together with measurements such as kilograms, cubic meters, and kilocalories according to the lists (Article 11 of SCT Law). Therefore, there is no relationship between the tax base and environmental pollution. Although the purpose of SCT is not meant to directly protect the environment, the prices of such products can be increased by increasing the tax burden on them. Thus, by potentially changing the behaviour of users in a way that reduces the consumption of such products, negative effects on the environment can be reduced (Gülşen, 2021, 139).

Motor Vehicle Tax: MTV is a tax levied on motor vehicles included in the tariffs numbered I, II, and IV attached to the law. Motor vehicles may cause negative impacts on the environment by emitting carbon dioxide, greenhouse gases, and carbon emissions. Therefore, to eliminate the effects of motor vehicles on the environment, it is necessary to apply motor vehicles tax in a way that reduces the amount of carbon dioxide emissions, greenhouse gases, and carbon emissions (Gürsoy, 2021, 3; Gürdin, 2017, 42). In Turkey, the base of MTV is determined as fixed or proportional amounts by considering the age, engine volume or electric power, and prices of motor vehicles in tariff I; the type, age, weight, and seat of the motor vehicle and electric power (kW) in electric vehicles in tariff II; and the age and weight of the motor vehicle in tariff IV (MTV Law Art. 5–6). Since MTV does not include emission amount, greenhouse gas, or carbon emissions among the elements that constitute the tax base, it can be said that there is no direct relationship between MTV and environmental protection.

Administrative Fines Pursuant to the Environmental Law: In the Environmental Law, several material and formal obligations are imposed on individuals and institutions regarding the protection of the environment and the elimination of pollution. Failure to comply with these obligations is considered as a misdemeanour under the Environmental Law and administrative fines are imposed. Article 20 of the Environmental Law stipulates administrative fines in different amounts for a wide range of different offenses.

Environmental Pollution Contribution Fee: Environmental pollution contribution fee was introduced to prevent environmental pollution, improve the environment, and support environmental investments with the amendment made to the Environmental Law in 2006 instead of the "environmental pollution prevention fund." For this purpose, environmental pollution contribution is levied at the rate of 1 percent of the Climate Investment Fund (CIF) value of fuels and wastes subject to control and 5 percent of the CIF value of scrap. In addition, 1 percent of the water and wastewater removal fee collected by metropolitan municipalities' water and sewerage administrations is collected as an environmental contribution fee.

Recycling Participation Fee: Plastics are used in many areas of people's daily lives, including clothes, devices, medicines, and food, as they are cheap and elastic. A significant portion of the plastics produced are used in the production of disposable plastic bags, bottles, and containers. Therefore, the use of a significant portion of plastics in the production of disposable products leads to an increase in the number of plastic materials in nature and causes significant harmful effects on the environment (Turna, 2022, 248). Obtaining plastics as a secondary product after the use of petroleum, the fact that bags, unlike other wastes, have a very long period of spontaneous extinction in nature and are broken down into pieces and added to the soil, water, and food chain can have significant harmful consequences for all living things. Therefore, to reduce the use of plastic products and minimise their damage on nature, countries prefer to tax, charge, or ban single-use plastic products (Ertekin and Dam, 2020, 76–77; Şahin, 2020, 112). In this context, in Turkey, with the "Law on Amendments to the Environmental Law and Certain Laws" in 2018, additional article 11 was added to the Environmental Law and the practice of charging plastic products and environmentally harmful products under the name of "recovery participation fee" was introduced to be implemented as of 2019.

Plastic bags, batteries, mineral and vegetable oils, electrical and electronic equipment, pharmaceuticals, and packaging are covered by the recycling participation fee. The recycling contribution fee is to be paid "from the points of sale for plastic bags among the products in the list (1), and from the marketers or importers for other products." Points of sale, marketers, or importers fulfil their obligations by paying a certain amount per unit. These lump sum amounts are applied each year by increasing the previous year's lump sum amount by the revaluation rate. Recycling participation fees are declared to the tax office to which the relevant persons are affiliated in terms of income or corporate tax until the end of the twenty-fourth day of the month following the date the product is placed on the market or imported, and to the tax office to be determined by the Revenue Administration by those who are not liable for income or corporate tax, and paid until the end of the same month

(Environmental Law, additional article. 11). Regarding the recovery contribution fee, those who are found to have failed to pay the recovery contribution fee in violation of the Environmental Law will be imposed an administrative fine of 20 percent of the contribution fee. In addition, those who do not comply with the procedures and principles determined by the ministry are subject to administrative penalties in accordance with the Environmental Law (Art. 20/z of the Environmental Law).

Bag Fee: In addition to charging a fee under the recovery contribution share to those who market plastic bags, to manage resources efficiently and prevent environmental pollution caused by plastic bags, additional article 13 of the Environmental Law requires users who buy plastic bags from points of sale to pay a bag fee. The bag fee has been introduced only for plastic bags among the products covered by the recycling contribution share. It can be concluded that the legislator's inclusion of only plastic bags within the scope of the fee aims to "limit the use of individual plastic bags due to the fact that the harmful effects of plastic wastes on the environment are increasing day by day as people frequently use plastic bags in their daily activities, whether necessary or unnecessary." As a matter of fact, with this regulation, plastic bag sales points can reflect some or all the recovery contribution fees they pay to the consumer. The base fee for plastic bags is determined by the commission to be established by the Ministry of Enviroment, Urbanization, and Climate Change and is updated every year. For 2023, the base fee for plastic bags for users or consumers is set at 25 kurus, while the points of sale of plastic bags in 2023 will pay a recovery participation fee of 38.50 kurus (See Presidential Decree No. 6615). Therefore, while bag sales points will collect 25 kurus of the 38.50 kurus recovery participation fee from consumers or users, they will bear the remaining 13.50 kurus bag cost. In addition, those who sell plastic bags free of charge or produce plastic bags contrary to the standards determined by the Ministry will be subject to administrative fines in accordance with the Environmental Law (Art. 20/z-bb of the Environmental Law).

Deposit: With the regulation introduced by the additional article 12 of the Environmental Law, those who carry out the sales of the products covered by the deposit are obliged to participate in the deposit application collection system for packaging and products to be determined by the Ministry. Producers, importers, and marketers of the products subject to mandatory deposit application and wholesale or retail sales units that offer the products covered by the deposit to consumers/users are obliged to fulfil their administrative, financial, and technical obligations for the establishment, operation, and monitoring of the deposit system. Those who fail to fulfil these obligations are subject to administrative fines in accordance with the Environmental Law (Article 20/z-ee of the Environmental Law).

Table 12.3 Environmental Taxes in Turkey*

	Energy Taxes/ Environmental Taxes	Transport Taxes/ Environmental Taxes	Natural Resource Taxes/ Environmental Taxes	Pollution Taxes/ Environmental Taxes	Total Green Tax/ Total Finalised Tax Revenues
2021	27.1	66.1	6.3	0.4	0.01
2020	51.6	45.4	2.6	0.2	0.01
2019	66.2	30.5	2.6	0.5	0.01
2018	63.3	34.2	2	0.4	0.01
2017	65	33.6	1.1	0.1	0.01
2016	65.2	33.5	1.1	0.1	0.01
2015	65.6	33.2	1	0.1	0.01
2014	68	30.4	1.4	0.1	0.01
2013	70.6	28.1	1.3	0.1	0.02
2012	69.2	29.1	1.4	0.1	0.01
2011	68.9	29.6	1.1	0.3	0.01
2010	73	25.7	0.9	0.3	0.01
2009	75.1	23.6	0.9	0.2	0.02
2008	70.7	27.9	1	0.2	0.02

Source: TÜİK, 2023
*The figures in the table may not give total figures due to rounding.

Environmental Labelling: Environmental labelling is one of the regulations introduced to protect the environment, human, health, climate, and natural life. It refers to the label that shows that the negative effects of a product or service on the environment are reduced throughout the entire life cycle from the raw material procurement process to the disposal of the product or service in line with sustainable environmental goals. In simpler terms, it is the label that shows that the product or service is environmentally friendly (Karaca, 2019, 73). The environmental labelling application aims to raise awareness about environmentally friendly products by providing accurate and scientific-based information to citizens, and by encouraging environmentally friendly enterprises to consider low carbon emissions, waste prevention, energy efficiency, water saving, and harmful chemicals in products and services. Since the application is voluntary and covers product and service groups determined by the Ministry, enterprises are not obliged to use environmental labels (Ministry of Enviroment, Urbanisation, and Climate Change, 2023).

Motor Oils: To eliminate the impact of waste oils on environmental pollution and to ensure the reuse of waste oils, it is obligatory to change motor oil at places authorised by the Ministry of Environment, Urbanisation, and Climate Change or to deliver waste motor oils to these places. Those who do not comply with this obligation are subject to administrative fines in accordance with the Environmental Law (Art. 20/z-dd of the Environmental Law).

When the shares of environmental taxes in Turkey are analysed, it is seen that the portion of green taxes in total tax revenues is quite low (0.01). On the other hand, transport taxes have the largest share of environmental taxes. The share of pollution taxes and natural resource taxes in environmental taxes is at a low level.

CONCLUSIONS

Environmental problems, which have increased with industrial society, now significantly affect daily life with negative consequences such as global warming, climate change, drought, etc. To effectively combat environmental problems, environment-oriented public policies and sustainable economic growth understanding should become the most important issue both at the international and national level. In this respect, it can be said that the international studies organised by the European Union are very important and guiding. As a matter of fact, since the late 1960s, the European Union has been endeavouring to develop a common understanding with its member states in combatting environmental problems. It has organised many international conferences and issued declarations to draw attention to environmental issues. The European Green Deal, prepared especially to combat climate change and environmental degradation, is the most recent of these efforts. Turkey is not indifferent to the European Green Deal and has prepared the Turkey Green Deal Action Plan in 2021, setting sustainable environment-oriented targets.

Environmental taxes are the most important green policy used in combatting environmental problems. The European Union has a wide range of green tax practices. Unlike the Union, Turkey does not have a comprehensive green tax policy. For example, when the environmental taxes implemented in Turkey are analysed, it can be said that there is no environmental tax that is directly based on environmental concerns except the environmental cleaning tax. In various tax laws in Turkey, there are MTV and fuel consumption taxes, as well as fees and administrative fines levied in accordance with the Environmental Law, which are environmentally beneficial taxes although their main purpose is fiscal. In addition, the shares of these revenues remain quite limited in total taxes. Therefore, there is a need for some regulation with regard to environmental taxes in Turkey. In this context, the following conclusions can be drawn for Turkey by considering the practices in the European Union regarding environmental taxes:

In Turkey, there is a tax system that is predominantly based on indirect taxes and consumption taxes within it. In this respect, the scales in both SCT and VAT should be differentiated as environmentally sensitive products (environmental labelling) or non-environmentally sensitive products. By differentiating the rates for the products in these tables, environmentally sensitive products should be taxed at a lower rate, while non-environmentally sensitive products should be taxed at a higher rate, and consumer preferences should be directed towards consumption of environmentally labelled products.

The MTV tariff should be rearranged by considering the emission amounts of vehicles instead of indicators such as price, engine volume, and weight. In addition, MTV tariffs should be rearranged to encourage electric vehicles.

The subject of environmental and cleaning tax should not be limited only to the amount of water consumption. Some regulations should be made for businesses or individuals, especially to ensure the prevention, reuse, and recycling of waste. In addition, although all kinds of waste are included in the scope of the tax, a tax policy consisting of landfill and incineration taxes for the storage and incineration stages of waste should be implemented.

REFERENCES

2464 Numbered Municipalities Revenues Law, Date: 29.05.1981, No: 17354. https://www.mevzuat.gov.tr/mevzuat?MevzuatNo=2464&MevzuatTur=1&MevzuatTertip=5

2872 Numbered Enviromental Law. Date: 11.08.1983, No: 18132. https://www.mev-zuat.gov.tr/mevzuat?MevzuatNo=2872&MevzuatTur=1&MevzuatTertip=5

Acemoğlu, D., and Robinson, J. A. (2012). *Ulusların Düşüşü*. İstanbul: Doğan Kitap.

Acuner, S. (2014). Katı atık ve atık su bedelinin hukuki niteliği ve anayasa mahkemesi kararları ışığında değerlendirilmesi. *Türk İdare Dergisi* 478:131–166.

Ağcakaya, S., and Kaya, I. (2022). Sürdürülebilir kalkınma ve yeşil ekonomi perspektifinden yeşil maliye politikaları uygulamaları. *Çukurova Üniversitesi Sosyal Bilimler Enstitüsü Dergisi* 31(2):514–527.

Apergis, N., Gozgor, G., and Lau, C. K. (2021). Globalization and Environmental Problems in Developing Countries. *Environmental Science and Pollution Research* 28(26):33719–33721.

Aydın, M., and Deniz, K. (2017). Atık Yönetiminde Vergi Politikasının Rolü: Türkiye Değerlendirmesi. *Yönetim Bilimleri Dergisi* 15(30):435–461.

Çelikkaya, A. (2011). Avrupa Birliği üyesi ülkelerde çevre vergisi reformları ve türkiye'deki durumun değerlendirilmesi, *Anadolu Üniversitesi Sosyal Bilimler Dergisi* 11(2):97–120.

Ciocirlan, C. E., and Yandle, B. (2003). The Political Economy of Green Taxation in OECD Countries. *European Journal of Law and Economics* 15:203–218.

Cural, M., and Saygı, H. E. (2016). Avrupa Birliği'nde çevre vergisi uygulamaları ve çevre vergilerinin gelişimi. *Çukurova Üniversitesi Sosyal Bilimler Enstitüsü Dergisi* 25(1):77–92.

Dikmen, S. & Çiçek, H. G. (2020). Avrupa Birliği'nde çevre vergisi gelirlerinin karşılaştırmalı analizi. *Erciyes Üniversitesi İktisadi ve İdari Bilimler Fakültesi Dergisi* 57:57–88.

Dincer, I. (2000). Renewable Energy and Sustainable Development: A Crucial Review. *Renewable and Sustainable Energy Reviews* 4(2):157–175.

Ecer, K., Güner, O., and Çetin, M. (2021). Avrupa yeşil mutabakatı ve Türkiye ekonomisinin uyum politikaları. *İşletme ve İktisat Çalışmaları Dergisi* 9(2):125–144.

Eroğlu, E. (2021). Yeşil kamu alımları uygulaması faydalar ve uygulama sürecinde karşılaşılan zorluklar. *Vergi Raporu* 29(65):156–174.

Ertekin, Ş., and Dam, M. (2020). Türkiye'de çevre vergilerinin çevresel etkileri üzerine bir değerlendirme. Yaşar Üniversitesi E-Dergisi, Special Issue on 3rd International EUREFE Congress, 66–87.

European Commission (EC). (2019). The European Green Deal, https://eurlex.europa.eu/resource.html?uri=cellar:b828d165-1c22-11ea-8c1f-01aa75ed71a1.0002.02/DOC_1&format=PDF

———. (2023). Green Taxation. https://taxation-customs.ec.europa.eu/green-taxation-0_en

Eurostat. (2013). *Environmental Taxes: A Statistical Guide*. 2013 edition. European Commission.

———. (2023). Environmental Tax Revenues. https://ec.europa.eu/eurostat/databrowser/view/ENV_AC_TAX/default/table?lang=en

Gülşen, İ. M. (2021). Çevresel vergi uygulamalarının sınıflandırılması ve seçilmiş ülkelerdeki uygulama örnekleri. *Süreklilikten sürdürülebilirliğe ekonomi* (pp.1–179). Çanakkale: Holistence Publication.

Gürdin, B. (2020). Yeşil pazarlama yaklaşımıyla motorlu taşıtların çevre vergisi kapsamına alınması. *Uluslararası Beşeri ve Sosyal Bilimler İnceleme Dergisi* 1(1):39–49.

Gürsoy, E. D. (2014).Yeşil Vergi. EY, Building a Better Working World. https://www.vergidegundem.com//documents/10156/1659502/ocak2014_makale2.pdf

Hironaka, A. (2002). The Globalization of Environmental Protection: The Case of Environmental Impact Assessment. *International Journal of Comparative Sociology* 43(1):65–78.

Karaca, C. (2019). *Çevre ve Kentleşme Politikası*. Bursa: Ekin Yayınevi.

Kargı, V., and Yüksel, C. (2010). Çevresel dışsallıklarda kamu ekonomisi çözümleri. *Maliye Dergisi* 159:183–202.

Kastrinos, N., and Weber, K. M. (2020). Sustainable Development Goals in the Research and Innovation Policy of the European Union. *Technological Forecasting and Social Change* 157(5):120056.

Kayhan, A. K. (2013). Birleşmiş Milletler çevre programı üzerine bir inceleme. *Public and Private International Law Review* 33(1):61–90.

Kurrer, C., and Lipcaneanu, N. (2023). *Environment Policy: General Principles and Basic Framework*. Fact Sheets on the European Union. https://www.europarl.europa.eu/factsheets/en/sheet/71/environment-policy-general-principles-and-basic-framework

Kuşat, N. (2013). Yeşil sürdürülebilirlik için yeşil ekonomi: avantaj ve dezavantajları— Türkiye incelemesi. *Journal of Yasar University* 29(8):4896–4916.

Määttä, K. (2006). *Environmental Taxes: An Introductory Analysis*. Edward Elgar Publishing.

Monteiro, N. B. R., da Silva, E. A., and Neto, J. M. M. (2019). Sustainable Development Goals in Mining. *Journal of Cleaner Production* 228:509–520.

Ostrom, E. (1990). *Governing the Commons: The Evolution of Institutions for Collective Action*. Cambridge University Press.

Pirler, O. (1994). Belediyelerde çevre temizlik vergisinin uygulanması. *Çağdaş Yerel Yönetimler Dergisi* 3(2):33–44.

Remeur, C. (2020). *Understanding Environmental Taxation*. European Parliament Briefing EU Policies—Insights. https://www.europarl.europa.eu/RegData/etudes/BRIE/2020/646124/EPRS_BRI(2020)646124_EN.pdf

Resmi Gazete. 2023 Yılında Uygulanacak Çevre Temizlik Vergisi Tutarları, 56 Seri No.lu Belediye Gelirleri Kanunu Genel Tebliği, Tarih: 30.12.2022, Sayı: 32059.

Resmi Gazete. 6615 Cumhurbaşkanı Kararı. Tarih: 28.12.2022, Sayı: 32057.

Şahin, M. (2020). Sürdürülebilir çevre dinamikleri için yeni bir enstrüman: plastik poşet vergisi. *Vergi Raporu Dergisi* 246:107–121.

Şenyüz, D., Yüce, M., and Gerçek A. (2022). *Türk Vergi Sistemi*. Bursa: Ekin Yayınevi.

T.C. Ministry of Enviroment, Urbanisation, and Climate Change (2023). Enviroment Labelling. https://cevreetiketi.csb.gov.tr/en/enviromental-label-i-111610.

T.C. Ticaret Bakanlığı. (2021). Yeşil mutabakat eylem planı. https://ticaret.gov.tr/data/60f1200013b876eb28421b23/MUTABAKAT%20YE%C5%9E%C4%B0L.pdf

Toprak, D. (2006). Sürdürülebilir kalkınma çerçevesinde çevre politikaları ve mali araçlar. *Süleyman Demirel Üniversitesi Sosyal Bilimler Enstitüsü Dergisi* 2(4):156–169.

Turna, F. (2022). Plastik poşet vergisi: gerçekten etkili mi? In İpek, S., Kılıç, C., and Tan, S. S. (Eds.), *Sosyal Bilimlerde Güncel Araştırmalar II* (pp. 248–262). Bursa: Ekin Yayınevi.

TÜİK (2023). Çevre İstatistikleri. https://data.tuik.gov.tr/Kategori/GetKategori?p =Cevre-ve-Enerji-103.

Wallart, N. (1999). The Political Economy of Environmental Taxes," Books, Edward Elgar Publishing, No: 1876.

Yegen, B. (2020). Atık su bedel ve tarifelerinde yaşanan uyuşmazlıkların örnek yargı kararları eşliğinde incelenmesi. *Malî Hukuk Dergisi* 16(84):899–918.

13

Evaluations of the Possible Impact of Turkey's Efforts to Transition to a Green and Circular Economy on Turkey-EU Relations in the Framework of Harmonisation with the European Green Consensus

Omca Altın

INTRODUCTION

The European Union (EU), which is committed to being a global leader in the fight against climate change, published the "European Green Deal" on December 11, 2019, and introduced a new growth method based on the climate and environmental protection. Within the scope of this Deal, the European Union aims to reach its goal of net-zero greenhouse gas emissions by 2050 with the regulations in many areas and be the first continent to achieve this. This goal also closely concerns the countries that have commercial relations with the Union. One of these countries is Turkey. In addition to the fact that Turkey's largest export market is the European Union, due to the Customs Union Agreement and its ongoing EU candidate country position, Turkey is involved in an effort to adapt to the new EU regulations and directives as well as acquis communautaire. Within the framework of the EU harmonisation process, Turkey is taking the necessary steps to have a green and circular economy in line with the European Green Deal. Particularly, public authorities in Turkey have published a strategy paper on green transformation, action plans related to the European Green Deal, and also included what needs to be done for green transformation in the Medium Term Programme (MTP).

Within the scope of the EU harmonisation process, achieving the transition to a green and circular economy in line with the European Green Deal will enable Turkey to maintain its position as an entry point to the Union market. Therefore, green transformation will provide important advantages to Turkish companies, which can adapt and realise this transformation to make them much more competitive in the international arena. At the same time, during this transformation and harmonisation with the Union rules, various stakeholders will further increase their contacts with EU institutions and will further revive relations between Turkey and the European Union. However, it should not be forgotten that although the green transformation process will have a positive effect on Turkey-EU relations and provide some advantages, it will also bring some additional costs and the process will be difficult and painful. Even if many problems are solved, the fact that the Customs Union has not been updated will especially increase the difficulty of the process. Furthermore, green transition in line with the European Green Deal will have a limited contribution to Turkey's EU membership process, as in the Customs Union process.

In this direction and within the scope of harmonisation with the European Green Deal, the steps taken by Turkey for the transition to a green and circular economy—in other words, the works it has carried out and how this situation will affect Turkey-EU relations—will be evaluated in this study. Concordantly, first of all, the European Green Deal is discussed, then the efforts to transition from a linear economy towards a circular economy within the framework of the European Green Deal and the European Circular Economy Action Plan are examined, and finally Turkey's efforts to transition towards a circular economy within the scope of the European Green Deal are discussed and the effects of this on Turkey-EU relations are evaluated.

THE EUROPEAN GREEN DEAL

Climate change driven by global warming is recognised as a worldwide threat, and various policies have been developed across the world to implement the necessary measures to cope with it. The European Union, in particular, is among those that has set the problem of climate change as a priority target and shows the most serious efforts in the global arena to combat this issue (Keser and Ceyhun, 2023, 58; Karakaya, 2020). One of the steps taken in this regard is the European Green Deal. On December 11, 2019, the European Commission published the "European Green Deal," also known as the "European Green Deal Document," which is considered a roadmap for the EU climate agenda and also as the Union's new economic growth strategy, covering a series of strategies and legislative proposals for the twenty-seven

EU Member States to achieve the goal of making the European Union and even the entire European continent climate neutral (zero emissions) by 2050, as well as to be the first continent to achieve this. The European Green Deal is also described as the new EU transformational economic change plan to tackle climate change. With this plan, the Union aims to reduce carbon emissions by transitioning to adopt a new green order and at the same time turn this transformation into an opportunity for employment and growth. The European Union, therefore, aims to be a pioneer in the circular economy, clean technologies, and decarbonised energy-intensive industries. In this sense, the European Green Deal is an economic transformation model that can be used as a guide to achieve these goals (Diriöz, 2021, 110–111; European Commission, n.d.; Siddi, 2020, 4; Üstün, 2021, 333). Conservation and restoration of natural ecosystems, protection of human health from environmental impacts, and energy systems network, circular economy, and sustainable buildings in this framework are among the crucial components of the document (Üstün, 2021, 333). Hence, in the fight against climate change and environmental degradation, a severe threat to both Europe and the world, the European Green Deal will help the Union become a resource-efficient and competitive economy, and will seek to ensure that net greenhouse gas emissions are eliminated by 2050 (European Commission, 2020).

The European Green Deal is also a complement to the United Nations' 2030 Agenda and Sustainable Development Goals. In this respect, the European Green Deal makes an essential contribution to the global effort to keep the global temperature rise below 2ζC compared to the pre-industrialisation period, and additionally below 1.5°C, in line with the Paris Agreement, which has been internationally recognised as the most important source of climate protection targets since 2015. The European Union has put an equal effort into the Paris Agreement as it did for the implementation of the Kyoto Protocol on controlling climate change and has considered it an urgent task to ensure the implementation of this agreement (Talu 2019, 26, 27; Talu and Kocaman, 2019, 13; Üstün, 2021, 334). The legal order and instruments envisaged by the European Green Deal clearly and bindingly express the measures that member states should take to achieve the 1.5°C target (Üstün, 2021, 334). In its blueprint for action to increase the efficient use of resources, recover biodiversity, and reduce pollution by transitioning to a clean, circular economy, the European Green Deal outlines the investments needed and financing instruments available and outlines how to achieve a fair and comprehensive transition. Furthermore, the European Union has proposed "a European Climate Act" to turn the commitment to make it and even the entire EU continent climate-neutral (zero emissions) by 2050 into a legal obligation. It has been emphasised that all industries of the EU economy should be mobilised to achieve this goal. To this end, it is crucial to invest in clean technologies; support the industrial sector to innovate; promote much cleaner, cheaper, and healthier forms of private and public transport; and ensure that buildings are much more energy efficient (European Commission, 2021). In addition, the fact that the Union had already made various legal arrangements and put forward action plans on issues such as climate change prevention and transition to a green economy, renewable energy, energy efficiency, and carbon trading before the European Green Deal was an indicator of the Union's determination in the fight against climate change (Üstün, 2021, 334). Nonetheless, the European Green Deal has taken EU policies towards green transformation one step further and has brought and continues to bring about significant changes in the Union's policies and legal order (Sikora, 2021, 684; Krämer, 2021, 268). The Deal envisages policy changes in many areas and covers almost all fields of activity of the Union and its Member States, such as energy, agriculture, climate, industry, environment and oceans, finance, transportation, regional development, and research and innovation (Üstün, 2021, 337). This is an indication that within the framework of the aims and objectives of the European Green Deal, it will affect all economic industries, inter-country policies, and even social life (Keser and Ceyhun, 2023, 57).

In addition to all these, "the Just Transition Mechanism" has been established to provide financial support to the sectors and individuals that might be affected by the transformation for the economic and social problems that may occur during the transition to the green order (Üstün, 2021, 333). In other words, the Just Transition Mechanism, which is a part of the European Green Deal Investment Plan, has been created to focus on the social as well as economic costs of transition in the most affected regions and to provide financial support to projects ranging from the creation of new workplaces, financial support to companies, job searches, and ensuring that those who are looking for new employment due to transition acquire new skills ([the Foreign Economic Relations Board of Türkiye] DEİK, 2022, 16).

In line with the targets determined on the basis of the European Green Deal, there are eight key policy areas. These are "raising the EU's climate related targets for 2030 and 2050," "providing clean, cheap and secure energy," "mobilizing industry to deliver a clean and circular economy," "building and renovating by using energy and resources efficiently," "accelerating the transition to sustainable and smart mobility," "farm to fork: Designing a fair . . . healthy and environmentally friendly food system," "protecting and restoring ecosystems and biodiversity," "zero pollution for a non-toxic environment" (Üstün, 2021, 333–341).

The European Green Deal envisages the Union's transition from a growth dependent on carbon emissions to a decarbonised economic growth strategy based on energy efficiency and the circular economy. This new growth strategy aims not only to protect people, animals, and nature by reducing pollution but also to achieve a much more efficient economic system that is inclusive for all. Within the scope of raising the EU climate targets for 2030 and 2050 with the European Green Deal, the Union has committed to further increase the level of emission reductions it had already planned for 2030, committing to 50%–55% below levels of 1990, while committing to 100% reduction in 2050. Accordingly, it has been decided to review the EU emissions trading system, increase the number of sectors covered by the emissions trading system, and introduce amendments to "the Energy Taxation Directive." It has been also stated that certain changes would be introduced regarding land use and forests (Üstün, 2021, 337–338).

It is emphasised that further decarbonisation of the energy system is important to achieve the 2030, 2050 climate targets set in the European Green Deal. In particular, energy production and use across all sectors of the economy accounts for more than 75 percent of the Union's greenhouse gas emissions. For this reason, creating an energy sector based on renewable resources and ensuring that the Union's energy supply is reliable and affordable for consumers as well as businesses are among the priority objectives within the framework of the Deal (Keser and Ceyhun, 2023, 60).

Within the framework of mobilising industry to transition to a clean and circular economy, the significance of fully mobilising industry to achieve climate neutrality and a circular economy has been emphasised. In the circular economy action plan, identifying policies for sustainable products has been prioritised. In this respect, it has been decided to promote different business alternatives and to identify the needs necessary to prevent products that will pollute the environment from being placed on the Union market. Moreover, the key role of digital technologies in achieving sustainability goals has been emphasised. In particular, digital technologies such as 5G, cloud computing, and the Internet of Things create different alternatives for monitoring and optimising water and air pollution (Keser and Ceyhun, 2023, 60–61).

Within the scope of the policy area of building and renovating by using energy and resources efficiently, which was determined in the European Green Deal, the focus was on the renovation of public and private buildings in terms of energy efficiency (Üstün, 2021, 339).

For sustainable and smart mobility, the Union has set a target to reduce transport emissions by 90 percent by 2050. This reduction target includes road, waterway, and rail transportation. A significant part of the 75 percent of inland freight transported by road will instead be transferred to rail and inland waterways. It is stated that "the Single European Sky for Aviation" is to be relaunched, which would lead to a significant reduction in emissions from airlines. In addition, it has been emphasised that the environmental and health impact of traffic will be taken into account when setting the price of transportation. In other words, it has been stated that through taxation, attempts to ensure that people prefer clean means of transportation would be made (Üstün, 2021, 340).

Farm to fork: Within the framework of designing a fair, healthy, and environmentally friendly food system, the aim is to reduce the environmental damage of the food processing and retail sectors through measures to be taken for transportation, storage, packaging, and food waste. By promoting sustainable food consumption, it is also intended to support healthy food that is affordable for everyone. In this respect, plans include implementation of measures such as preventing imported foods that do not meet EU environmental standards from entering the EU market, minimising food waste, and sharing information such as nutritional values and ecological footprint of foods with consumers (Keser and Ceyhun, 2023, 61).

Within the scope of protecting ecosystems and biodiversity and restoring them to their previous state, the Union presented "the Biodiversity Strategy Plan" as of 2020, stating that new measures will be taken to expand the scope of land and marine areas with biodiversity, protect forests and further increase forest areas, and protect oceans and seas (Üstün, 2021, 341).

As part of zero pollution for a toxic-free environment, the Commission stated that the "Zero Pollution Action Plan" for air, sea, and soil would be put into practice in 2021, and within this framework, measures will be taken to purify water from microplastics and chemicals, ensure regular monitoring of air quality, and reduce pollution caused by large industrial facilities (Üstün, 2021, 341).

Considering all policy changes and targets, it is clear that the Union has set these taking into account climate change and sustainability. Moreover, it is envisaged that the changes and transformations to be realised within the framework of the determined policy areas will affect EU member countries in political, economic, and cultural-social terms, as well as the countries that have relations with these countries (İHKİB, 2021, 8).

EFFORTS TO TRANSITION FROM LINEAR TO CIRCULAR ECONOMY AND EUROPEAN CIRCULAR ECONOMY ACTION PLAN

The linear economy is defined as the conversion of natural resources to waste through production. The take-make-use-dispose linear economy model began with the industrial revolution and the global economy was shaped within the frame of this model. This one-way structure, in which natural resources convert into waste through production, is based on the assumption that natural resources are available, sufficient, cheap to waste, and end up as waste, and at the same time that this problem-free. Instead, this type of waste generation has caused environmental degradation in two ways: through natural capital depletion and through natural capital depreciation due to waste pollution. Increasing population, inequality, and consumption, as well as demographic change and an ever-increasing demand for resources, has rendered this model unsustainable. Particularly in recent years, the pandemic crisis, climate change, and rapid decrease of world resources have led humanity to a crossroads at the ecological boundaries of the planet, and it has been concluded that today's economic system can no longer meet the needs of societies nor can it produce solutions to crises (Murray et al., 2017, 371; Veral, 2021, 7–8). In this direction, the linear economy model, which is based on the assumption that there is an unlimited supply of natural resources and that the environment has an unlimited capacity to absorb wastes and pollution, has begun to be questioned, and the circular economy model has emerged. It has been observed that many countries have turned to green transformation and circular economy in order to reach a "net-zero" target to increase resilience to climate change and reduce its effects (Cooper, 1999, 10; Sayın and Utkulu, 2023, 188; Veral, 2021, 7).

Despite the fact that there are different definitions of the circular economy model, it is generally described as a model that has a holistic process, enables the reuse of products and raw materials, recycles waste, uses energy and all resources efficiently, and incorporates clean production in a way that produces almost no waste, and is an important tool in terms of sustainability. Making efforts to transition to circular economy model necessitates a basic transition and transformation process in society. Such a process requires simultaneous changes in some subsystems, not only on a regional or national scale but also on a global scale. The circular economy—which is based on the "cradle to cradle" approach, aiming at an industry that operates without waste and harming the environment, and on biomimetics, where the structure and function of natural systems provides information to industrial processes, as well as industrial ecology—aims to reduce waste and to make resources more long-lasting in the economy (Murray et al., 2017, 373; Sayın and Utkulu, 2023, 190; Veral, 2021, 8).

In December 2015, the European Commission adopted the Circular Economy Package, which includes the Circular Economy Action Plan and its annexes, in order to accelerate the transition of the European region to the circular economy. The main objective of the Circular Economy Package is expressed as closing production life cycles with more recycling and reuse, and bringing common benefits to both the environment and the economy. At the same time, this economic model will increase the Union's competitiveness by protecting businesses against resource scarcity and volatility, enabling the creation of alternative job opportunities, and developing innovative and much more efficient production and consumption methods (European Commission, 2015, 2; Veral, 2018, 465).

The European Commission has taken a number of steps to support not only the transition to the circular economy in the European region but also on a global scale. Particularly, it has proposed the "Global Alliance on Circular Economy" to identify information and management deficiencies in the transition process towards a circular economy on a global scale and to develop partnership initiatives including large economies. Moreover, it tries to ensure that Free Trade Agreements reflect the main objectives of the circular economy, further accelerate its aid activities according to the principles of European Green Deal and Circular Economy, and make efforts to establish coordination with the Union member states for the transition to a global circular economy (European Commission, 2020, 18).

Action areas of the Circular Economy Package consist of production, consumption, waste management, and secondary raw materials, while innovation, investment, and monitoring include the whole cycle. Biomass, bio-based products, plastics, construction and demolition, critical raw materials, and food waste have been considered as priority sectors (Veral and Yiğitbaşıoğlu, 2018, 16). In this direction, objectives within the scope of production have been determined to provide incentives that support circular product design and create innovative and efficient production processes. Main action plan topics include the eco-design directive, durability, reparability and recycling of products through extended producer responsibility, best practices for waste management and resource efficiency in industrial sectors, and industrial symbiosis. In order to prevent valuable material loss, since it is extremely difficult to recover, it has been indicated in the eco-design directive that the essential elements would be determined within the framework of increasing the durability, repairability, and recycling of products, and that the Commission would primarily propose some rules for electronic displays. It has been stated that the Commission will prepare BREFs (Best Available Techniques [BAT] Reference Documents) for various industrial sectors in order to reduce resource use and waste generation in production processes, and finalise the rules on by-products and end-of-waste criteria to support industrial symbiosis. It has been indicated that these initiatives for more resource-efficient and innovative industrial processes will be supported within the framework of Horizon 2020 and Cohesion Fund (Veral, 2018, 467).

The choices made by millions of consumers have an important role in supporting or preventing the circular economy. These choices are determined by the information available to consumers, the types of products, prices, and regulatory framework (European Commission, 2015, 6). Hence, the objectives within the scope of consumption have been stated as providing reliable information to consumers regarding the repair and reuse of products. In this direction, main action plan topics consist of better labelling, EU eco-label, environmental footprint, new forms of consumption, sharing economy, digital platforms, actions and guarantees for misleading green/environmental claims, independent test programs assessing planned obsolescence, circular economy criteria to be applied in green public procurement (Veral and Yiğitbaşıoğlu, 2018, 17).

Waste management objectives have been stated as to improve waste management in accordance with the waste hierarchy of the Union, to meet the gaps in practice, to provide a long-term vision and target for guiding investments. Within this scope, main actions consist of improvement of waste management, new investments for recycling capacity, prevention of excess capacity in incineration and during mechanical-biological processes, consistency in waste-related investments within the framework of EU Harmonization policy and waste hierarchy, as well as waste-related objectives (Veral and Yiğitbaşıoğlu, 2018, 18).

The objectives included in the secondary raw material market title have been determined as increasing the use of secondary raw materials, increasing the use of recycled food and water, safe management of chemicals, and increasing knowledge on material flows. The main action titles include EU Regulation on fertilizers, legal proposal for minimum requirements for reused water, quality standards for secondary raw materials, analysis of the interface between chemicals, product and waste legislation, and development of an electronic system throughout the Union in order to monitor the transport of waste across borders (Veral and Yiğitbaşıoğlu, 2018, 18).

In line with all these, it has been envisaged that the EU Circular Economy Package would create 170,000 direct jobs within the Union as of 2035; prevent 600 million tons of CO_2 emissions between 2015 and 2030; increase the competitiveness of the Union waste management, recycling, and manufacturing sectors; reduce the Union's dependence on raw material imports; and decrease administrative costs (Veral, 2018, 470).

While the European Union struggles with climate change, it also aims to have a circular economy. The circular economy approach, which represents the economic side of the European Green Deal, has first found a place in the Union with the adoption of the Circular Economy Package, which includes the Action Plan for the Circular Economy and its annexes, in December 2015, as stated before. Following the adoption of the European Green Deal, "the New Circular Action Plan" was adopted on March 11, 2020, which is based on the circular economy actions of the European Commission implemented since 2015 and which will accelerate the transformational change required by the European Green Deal (Ecer et al., 2021, 131–132; European Commission, 2020, 2–3). With the New Circular Economy Action Plan, it is aimed to make sustainable products a norm for the Union; to focus on resource-intensive industries such as textiles, food, packaging, plastics, and construction with high potential for circular actions; to generate less waste; to become a pioneer in the circular economy; and to ensure that circularity works for regions, people, and cities (İHKİB, 2021, 10). With the New Circular Economy Action Plan, which is in line with the European Green Deal, it is also aimed to achieve climate neutrality until 2050, to achieve economic growth by preventing overuse of resources, and not to harm the competitiveness of the European Union while doing all these. In the New Circular Economy Action Plan, it is envisaged that the application of circular economy principles across the EU economy will create approximately 700,000 new jobs, increasing EU GDP by 0.5% by 2030 (European Commission, 2020, 2).

As all this suggests, the transition to a circular economy will be profound in the Union and elsewhere. Nonetheless, it is a fact that the process of transforming the linear economy approach that follows a take-make-use-dispose model into a cyclical one will not be easy and some challenges will arise. Thus, overcoming these challenges will require cohesion and cooperation at all levels: EU, national, regional, local, and international. Therefore, the Commission invites EU institutions and bodies to approve and actively contribute to the implementation of this Action Plan, and encourages member states to adopt and update their national circular economy plans in line with their objectives (Ecer et al., 2021, 132; European Commission, 2020, 19).

TURKEY'S EFFORTS TO TRANSITION TO A CIRCULAR ECONOMY WITHIN THE FRAMEWORK OF HARMONISATION WITH THE EUROPEAN GREEN DEAL AND ITS POTENTIAL IMPACT ON TURKEY-EU RELATIONS

Turkey strives to harmonise with new EU regulations, directives, and acquis mainly driven by the Customs Union Agreement and its ongoing status as a candidate for EU accession, as well as the fact that its largest export market is the EU market. In this respect, Turkey has not been indifferent to the efforts of the European Union, its largest trading partner, to address the climate crisis; it has taken steps to ensure the necessary adaptation in line with the objective of creating a circular economy, in other words, a green economic development, which is highly significant in terms of decoupling economic development from resource use, using limited resources much more efficiently, creating a sustainable growth and employment environment, achieving climate change targets, and preventing biodiversity loss. Especially in Turkey, public authorities have published a strategy document on green transformation, action plans related to the European Green Deal, and also included what needs to be realised for green transformation in the Medium Term Plan (Diriöz, 2021, 111; Güney, 2022, 90; T. C. Ticaret Bakanlığı, 2022, 20).

In the "2023 Industry and Technology Strategy" published in 2019, the Ministry of Industry and Technology emphasised that the determining role of the green production approach in industrial policies and practices is to be increased, and in this regard, the technology-oriented modernisation of infrastructure and enterprises in organised industrial zones and new investments based on clean production are to continue to be supported. It was also stated that "the Industrial Registry Information System" is to be developed to establish an "Economically Valuable Waste Monitoring System" within the framework of the circular economy (T. C. Sanayi ve Teknoloji Bakanlığı, 2019, 49).

With Presidential Circular No. 2021/15, the "Green Deal Action Plan" was published by the Ministry of Trade in the Official Gazette dated July 16, 2021. This action plan assesses the direction of Turkey's transition to a green economy and circular economy within the framework of harmonisation with the European Green Deal (Güney, 2022, 90; T. C. Ticaret Bakanlığı, 2022, 6–7). Accordingly, the action plan aims to ensure sustainable growth and development in Turkey inclusively, to support the green transformation of the Turkish economy and industry, to maintain competitiveness in trade relations with third countries, primarily with the European Union, and to ensure integration into transforming global value chains (T. C. Ticaret Bakanlığı, 2022, 7). Furthermore, within the framework of Presidential Circular No. 2021/15, the "Green Deal Working Group" was established to follow up the implementation of the Green Deal Action Plan, to direct the work by taking into account the needs of global policy, to further develop the framework of the Action Plan, and to coordinate the work to ensure that it is more effective by the relevant Deputy Minister of the Ministry of Trade with the participation of the Vice Presidents of the Presidential Strategy and Budget Presidency and the Digital Transformation Office; Deputy Ministers of Labor and Social Security, Environment, Urbanization and Climate Change, Foreign Affairs, Interior, Energy and Natural Resources, Treasury and Finance, National Education, Industry and Technology, Agriculture and Forestry, Transport and Infrastructure; and private industry representative organisations (T. C. Ticaret Bakanlığı, n.d.; T. C. Ticaret Bakanlığı, 2022, 7).

The Green Deal Action Plan includes nine headings, namely carbon border adjustments, green and circular economy, green financing, clean economic and secure energy supply, sustainable agriculture, sustainable smart mobility, combating climate change, European Green Deal information, and awareness-raising activities, and eighty-one actions to be carried out to achieve the thirty-two targets set under these headings. Moreover, in addition to horizontal areas such as energy, finance, and technology, Specialized

Working Groups were also established for industrial areas such as textiles, construction, cement and steel, in addition to horizontal areas such as energy, finance, and technology, in order to assist the Green Deal Working Group, to create thematic/sectoral roadmaps and/or policy recommendations by analysing the Green Deal requirements, current situation, and demands and risks for the work areas, and to report to the Green Deal Working Group. Specialized Working Groups have also been established to work on fair transition policies and the relevance of education during the green and digital transformation, which are not directly included in the action plan, based on cross-cutting sectoral as well as horizontal requirements ([Republic of Turkey Ministry of Trade] Ticaret Bakanlığı, 2022, 7, 9).

The green and circular economy section of the Green Deal Action Plan focuses on the following issues: Identifying priority sectors, determining their needs, and developing a national circular action plan; updating consumer protection legislation in line with green transformation and sustainable development goals; initiating the necessary work for the creation of green organised industrial zones and green industrial zones; developing an R&D and innovation-based approach to the development of green technology; establishing a national life cycle database; implementing regulations for the textile and leather sectors in order to prevent water pollution; and preparing sustainable production and consumption action plans. Additional efforts will concentrate on spreading green transformation to all regions in Turkey to ensure that it becomes an essential part of the development process; establishing the national environmental labelling system on a widespread basis; preparing an action plan for the widespread reuse of treated wastewater; communicating the importance of using international financing sources and IPA funds for activities and projects that contribute to green and circular production and emission reduction in industry; reducing the use of harmful chemicals, which is crucial for a green economy; taking action on the management of industrial emissions, including implementation of both sustainable consumption and production and integrated pollution prevention and control; and making life cycle assessment studies widespread in Turkey (Güney, 2022, 91; T.C. Ticaret Bakanlığı, 2022, 20–35).

Furthermore, in the 2022–2024 Medium Term Plan published in 2021, it was stated that green transformation in industry and economy is necessary in line with the new policies to be implemented by countries, especially the European Union, which is Turkey's main export market; that necessary supports will be provided for the transition to the circular economy model in the fields of industry, trade, transportation, energy, and environment to realise the green transformation; that R&D activities will be supported to accelerate the green transformation; that the green organised industrial zone and green industrial zone certification system will be completed; that the regulatory framework of the financial sector will be improved in order to realise the green transformation of industry; that investments in environmentally friendly production will be supported; and that zero-waste implementation will be made widespread to include households (T. C. Cumhurbaşkanlığı Strateji ve Bütçe Başkanlığı, n.d.).

The European Union has a critical role, both in Turkey's international relations and its domestic reform processes. This importance has become much more evident with the EU-Turkey Customs Union Agreement that entered into force in 1995, and with Turkey's becoming a candidate country for accession to the Union in 1999 (DEİK, 2022, 47). Therefore, alignment with the European Green Deal, and hence the transition to a circular economy within the scope of the Deal, is of utmost importance for Turkey within the framework of the Customs Union and the EU harmonisation process owing to its ongoing candidate status. It is also closely related to many different areas, ranging from trade to the electricity market, from the creation of a carbon emission market to logistics, industry, and production, and it is also of great significance as it affects the trade with the Union and its future investments (Diriöz, 2021, 113).

A similar process of harmonisation with the European Union took place during the process with the EU Customs Union. At the time of the 1995 EU-Turkey Customs Union, the number of member states of the Union had increased from twelve to fifteen, which meant that it was not as large an economic area as it is today. Reviewing the similarities with the process at that time, it is seen that producers, exporters, and service providers who can adapt to this transformation and the Union standards have an advantage. Even if it is an agreement that needs updating today, it can be said that it was highly crucial for the international competitiveness of Turkish industry and enterprises at that time. In a case where Turkey realises a green transformation, it will maintain its position as an entry point to the Union market; therefore, significant advantages are likely for those Turkish companies that are able to adapt and realise a green transformation, making them more competitive internationally, which means investing in the future commercially, economically, and environmentally. During this transformation and harmonisation phase with the Union rules, various stakeholders will further increase their links with EU institutions, further revitalising Turkey-EU relations. Nonetheless, it should be kept in mind that while the green transformation process would positively impact Turkey-EU relations and provide some advantages, it would also bring additional costs, challenges, and disadvantages. In particular, even if many problems were overcome, the issues related to nonrenewal of the Customs Union would persist. With the emergence of new barriers related to the Green Deal in addition to an unrenewed Customs Union, the process might be viewed as if new nontariff barriers were being put in place.

An unrenewed Customs Union could further increase the difficulties of the process and, thus, would require mutual sensitivity to protect the advantages and interests of the Customs Union between Turkey and the European Union, especially with regard to free trade agreements signed with other countries and regions (Diriöz, 2021, 114–115, 118, 120–121, 124).

While a green transformation in line with the European Green Deal is considered positive, it is unlikely to be reflected positively in Turkey's accession process, as was the case in the Customs Union process. Since Turkey joined the Customs Union in 1995, even the accession process of Turkey has been complicated, and Turkey is still a candidate country today. Despite the Customs Union, no significant progress has been made in this regard. Hence, as with the Customs Union, the European Green Deal and the process of harmonisation to the circular economy within this framework may not lead to membership. In other words, the European Green Deal and the process of harmonisation to the circular economy within this framework will have a limited contribution to Turkey's EU accession process (Diriöz, 2021, 107, 109, 121).

CONCLUSION

The European Union, which is committed to being a pioneer in the fight against climate change, published the "European Green Deal" on December 11, 2019, and introduced a new growth model based on climate and the environmental protection. Within the scope of the European Green Deal, the Union aims to reach its goal of net-zero greenhouse gas emissions by 2050 with the changes and regulations it will implement and to be the first continent to achieve this. This goal also closely concerns the countries that have commercial relations with the European Union. One of these countries is Turkey. In addition to the fact that Turkey's largest export market is the European Union, due to the Customs Union Agreement and its ongoing EU candidate country position, Turkey is trying to adapt to the new EU regulations, directives, and acquis communautaire. Within the scope of the EU harmonisation process, Turkey is taking the necessary steps for the transition to a green and circular economy in line with the European Green Deal. Particularly, public authorities in Turkey have published a strategy paper on green transformation and action plans related to the European Green Deal, including what needs to be done for green transformation in the Medium Term Programme.

Within the framework of the EU harmonisation process, Turkey's ability to achieve the transition to a green and circular economy in line with the European Green Deal will allow it to maintain its feature of being the entry point to the Union market. Besides, the green transformation will provide important advantages to Turkish companies which can adapt and realise this transformation, which will make them much more competitive in the international arena. At the same time, during this transformation and harmonisation with the Union rules, various stakeholders will further increase their contacts with EU institutions and will further revive the relations between Turkey and the European Union. However, it should not be forgotten that, despite the fact that the green transformation process will have a positive effect on Turkey-EU relations and provide some advantages, it will also bring additional costs, and the process will be difficult and painful as well. In particular, even if many problems are solved, the fact that the Customs Union has not been updated will remain. With the emergence of new obstacles to the Green Deal in addition to an unrenewed Customs Union, it will be possible to evaluate the process as if new nontariff barriers have been introduced; an updated Customs Union may further increase the difficulties of the process. In this case, mutual protection of the advantages and benefits related to the Customs Union between Turkey and the European Union, especially the free trade agreements signed with other countries and regions, will be essential in the process.

Additionally, the green transition in line with the European Green Deal will have a limited contribution to Turkey's EU membership process, as it was in the Customs Union process. In particular, despite the Customs Union, Turkey has not made any significant progress in the EU membership stage and is still a candidate country. Therefore, the EU Green Deal harmonisation process may not lead to a membership either. Hence, harmonisation with the Green Deal can be considered as an investment in the future in terms of trade, economy, and environment.

REFERENCES

Cooper, Tim. (1999). Creating and Economic Infrastructure for Sustainable Product Design. *Journal of Sustainable Product Design* 8. Accessed June 14, 2023. https://cfsd.org.uk/journal/archive/99jspd8.pdf#page=7.

DEİK. (2022). Sanayide Yeşil Dönüşümün Desteklenmesi Projesi: AB'nin Yeni Büyüme Stratejisi "Yeşil Mutabakat" ve Türkiye için Önemi. Erişim 15 Haziran, 2023. https://www.deik.org.tr/contents-fileaction-28960.

Diriöz, Oğuz Ali. (2021). AB Yeşil Mutabakat Kapsamında Yeşil Ekonomiye Dönüşüm Süreci, Türkiye-AB İlişkilerine Olası Etkilerinin Değerlendirilmesi. *Uluslararası Suçlar ve Tarih Dergisi* 22:107–130.

Ecer, Kübra, Güner, Oğuz, ve Çetin, Murat. (2021). Avrupa Yeşil Mutabakatı ve Türkiye Ekonomisinin Uyum Politikaları. *İşletme ve İktisat Çalışmaları Dergisi* 9(2):125–144.

European Commission. (n.d.). Delivering the European Green Deal. Accessed April 04, 2023. https://commission.europa.eu/strategy-and-policy/priorities-2019-2024/european-green-deal/delivering-european-green-deal_en#documents.

———. (2015). Communication from the Commission to the European Parliament, the Council, the European Economic and the Social Committee and the Committee of the Regions: Closing the Loop—An EU Action Plan for the Circular Economy. Accessed May 27, 2023. https://eur-lex.europa.eu/legal-content/EN/TXT/?uri =CELEX:52015DC0614.

———. (2020). Communication from the Commission to the European Parliament, the Council, the European Economic and Social Committee and the Committee of the Regions: A New Circular Economy Action Plan for a Cleaner and More Competitive Europe. Accessed June 04, 2023. https://eur-lex.europa.eu/resource .html?uri=cellar:9903b325-6388-11ea-b735-01aa75ed71a1.0017.02/DOC_1&for-mat=PDF.

Güney, Gül. (2022). Yeşil Endüstri Kapsamında Avrupa Yeşil Mutabakatının Türkiye'deki Sektörlere Olası Etkisi ve İzlenecek Politikaların Değerlendirilmesi. *Dünden Bugüne İktisadi ve Finansal Konular Üzerine Tartışmalar*, Eds. Ahmet Arif Eren, Emre Günerşer Bozdağ (pp. 83–95). Ankara: Gazi Kitabevi.

İstanbul Hazır Giyim ve Konfeksiyon İhracatçıları Birliği (İHKİB). (2021). Avrupa Yeşil Mutabakatı'nın Türk Hazır Giyim ve Konfeksiyon Sektörüne Etkisi. Erişim 15 Haziran, 2023. https://www.ihkib.org.tr/fp-icerik/ia/d/2021/07/29/ avrupa-yesil-mutabakati-nin-turk-hazirgiyim-ve-konfeksiyon-sektorune-etkisi -202107291209430840-FF26B.pdf.

Karakaya, Ethem. (2020). Sorun "Karbon Sınır Düzenlemesi" Değil, Siz Daha Anlamadınız mı? *İklim Haber*. Erişim 17 Haziran, 2023. https://www.iklimhaber .org/sorun-karbon-sinir-duzenlemesi-degil-siz-daha-anlamadiniz-mi/.

Keser Yıldırır, Hilal, ve Ceyhun, Çiçek Gökçe. (2023). Avrupa Yeşil Mutabakatı'nın Denizyolu Taşımacılığı Kökenli Hava Kirliliği Yönünden İncelenmesi. *TESAM Akademi Dergisi* 10(1):53–72. https://doi.org/10.30626/tesamakademi.1245662.

Krämer, Ludwig. (2020). Planning for Climate and Environment: The EU Green Deal. *Journal for European Environment & Planning Law* 17:267–306. https:// doi:10.1163/18760104-01703003

Murray, Alan, Skene, Keith, and Haynes, Kathyrn. (2017). The Circular Economy: An Interdisciplinary Exploration of the Concept and Application in a Global Context. *Journal of Business Ethics* 140:369–380. https://doi.org/10.1007/s10551-015 -2693-2

Sayın, Ferhan, ve Utkulu, Utku. (2023). Türkiye'nin Döngüsellik Performansı: Avrupa Birliği Ülkeleri ile Karşılaştırmalı Bir Araştırma. *Verimlilik Dergisi, Döngüsel Ekonomi ve Sürdürülebilirlik Özel Sayısı* 187–202. https://doi.org/10 .51551/verimlilik.1110168

Siddi, Marco. (2020). The European Green Deal: Assessing Its Current State and Future Implementation. Finnish Institute of International Affairs Working Paper 114. Accessed June 18, 2023. https://www.fiia.fi/wp-content/uploads/2020/05/ wp114_european-green-deal.pdf.

Sikora, Alicja. (2021). European Green Deal—Legal and Financial Challenges of the Climate Change. *ERA Forum* 21:681–697. https://doi.org/10.1007/s12027-020 -00637-3.

Talu, Nuran. (2019). Avrupa Birliği İklim Politikaları, İklim Değişikliği Eğitim Modülleri Serisi 3. Erişim 10 Nisan, 2023. https://www.iklimin.org/moduller/abpolitikalari.pdf.

Talu, Nuran, ve Kocaman, Habip. (2019). Türkiye'de İklim Değişikliği ile Mücadelede Politikalar, Yasal ve Kurumsal Yapı, İklim Değişikliği Eğitim Modülleri Serisi 4. Erişim 10 Nisan, 2023 https://www.iklimin.org/wp-content/uploads/egitimler/seri_04.pdf.

T. C. Cumhurbaşkanlığı Strateji ve Bütçe Başkanlığı. (n.d.). Orta Vadeli Program (2022–2024). Erişim 14 Haziran, 2023. https://www.sbb.gov.tr/wp-content/uploads/2021/09/Orta-Vadeli-Program-2022-2024.pdf.

T. C. Sanayi ve Teknoloji Bakanlığı. (2019). 2023 Sanayi ve Teknoloji Stratejisi. Erişim 11 Haziran, 2023. https://www.sanayi.gov.tr/assets/pdf/SanayiStratejiBelgesi2023.pdf.

T. C. Ticaret Bakanlığı. (n.d.). Yeşil Mutabakat Eylem Planı ve Çalışma Grubu. Erişim 13 Haziran, 2023. https://ticaret.gov.tr/dis-iliskiler/yesil-mutabakat/yesil-mutabakat-eylem-plani-ve-calisma-grubu.

———. (2022). Yeşil Mutabakat Çalışma Grubu, Yıllık Faaliyet Raporu. Erişim 14 Haziran, 2023. https://ticaret.gov.tr/data/643ffd6a13b8767b208ca8e4/YMEP%202022%20Faaliyet%20Raporu.pdf.

Üstün Türkoğlu, Kamil. (2021). Yeni Bir Dönemin Başlangıcı: Avrupa Yeşil Mutabakatı ve Türk Çevre Hukuku ve Politikalarına Etkileri. *Memleket Siyaset Yönetimi* 16(36):329–366.

Veral Sapmaz, Evren. (2021). Döngüsel Ekonomi: Engeller, Stratejiler ve İş Modelleri. *Ankara Üniversitesi Çevrebilimleri Dergisi* 8(1):7–18.

———. (2018). Döngüsel Ekonomiye Geçiş Doğrultusunda Yeni Tedbirler ve AB Üye Ülkelerinin Stratejileri. *Ankara Avrupa Çalışmaları Dergisi* 17(2):463–488. https://doi.org/10.32450/aacd.511998

Veral Sapmaz, Evren, ve Yiğitbaşıoğlu, Hakan. (2018). Avrupa Birliği Atık Politikasında Atık Yönetiminden Kaynak Yönetim Yaklaşımına Geçiş Yönelimleri ve Döngüsel Ekonomi Modeli. *Ankara Üniversitesi Çevrebilimleri Dergisi* 6(1):1–19. https://doi.org/10.1501/Csaum_0000000082

14

European Union Investment Bank and Its Role in Green Economy and Finance in the World

Didem Öztürk Günar

INTRODUCTION

The European Union Investment Bank (EIB) has played an essential role in the economic development and infrastructure construction of the members from the early days of the European integration process. The European Union (EU) adopted development strategies in the 2000s and tried to adapt itself to the conditions of the period in terms of economic, political, and energy competence in the context of these strategies. The Lisbon Strategy, the first of the EU efforts to adapt itself, was unsuccessful due to the 2008 crisis and the political crises the European Union faced. Another strategy plan, the EU 2020 development strategy, was prosperous compared to the Lisbon Strategy but failed to realise the desired transformation in economic terms. The fact that the European Union has long wanted to change its economic structure is concretely demonstrated in the relevant strategy plans. The last step taken in this direction was the adoption of the Green Deal. With the Green Deal, the Union has embarked on a significant transformation process by envisaging a new industrial revolution in the political and energy fields, especially in its economic model.

The Green Deal strategy envisages a radical green transition. Achieving the targets set by the European Union for 2030 and 2050 in the context of combatting climate change, achieving carbon-zero production, and reducing use of fossil resources reveals a severe need for financing. As a matter of fact, the European Investment Bank (EIB), which is a financial body of the European Union, is involved in the process in this sense. The EIB's goal of becoming a "climate bank" for the green transition process and its roadmap for this goal can be considered a globally unique initiative.

The study consists of two parts. In the first, the current situation of the EIB in the green transition process and the green transition processes will be discussed. In the second part, the EIB's achievement of the "climate bank" goal in the green transition process, the instruments related to green financing, and the financial support provided for the realisation of the Green Deal targets will be presented.

EUROPEAN UNION INVESTMENT BANK AND GREEN TRANSITION

The EIB is an EU body established by the Treaty of Rome in 1957. It is worth noting that the EIB can be described as an "invisible hero" of the European Union, which has been in the background for a long time but has supported many EU investments, particularly during the 2008 crisis. Over the years, its financial activities in international markets have given the EIB an essential position in EU integration. As stated in the Treaty of Rome, the EIB acts as a pillar for financial investment in the integration process. An analysis of the EIB's activities today shows that it is rapidly supporting investments in the environment, in sustainability, and in realising the European Union's green goals. If the last ten years are taken into account, it is clear that the EIB has acted as a climate bank, has taken concrete steps to realise this goal, and has agreed to cut financial support for fossil-based projects. Today, the EIB has become the Union's main force and engine for investment and financing to achieve EU climate change green transition and other sustainability goals. Research by the EU Commission estimated that completing the green growth and achieving zero-carbon emissions by 2050 would cost an additional €175 to €290 billion Euro, while research by EIB and the EU Commission in 2021 found that the cost of not taking action to address climate change and other environmental challenges is much higher, reaching approximately €350 billion per year (Mertens and Thiemann, 2023, 68).

The EIB stands out as a global financier on climate change and environmental issues. While the climate and environmental activities carried out by the European Union are globally recognised as standard, the Union is a global follower/rule-setter in this field. In particular, the "Green Deal Document" adopted by the EU Commission has attracted worldwide attention and designed an inclusive green transition process for the Union and a radical economic transformation. At this point, EIB has a vital role to play. EIB is central to the realisation of the Paris Agreement on climate change and environmental protection and the Sustainable Development Goals to be realised by the European Union, and it provides the financing needed by actors globally. The figures for 2022 show that EIB has increased its investments in the context of green transformation to €36.5 billion for climate change mitigation, sustainability, and environmental projects. EIB's financing is growing by more than 50 percent (European Investment Bank, May 2023).

EIB's interest in the environment and climate change is not new. In 2007, EIB created "Climate Awareness Bonds" to raise climate awareness. With the design of the first planet-financial instrument, awareness of sustainable energy and more efficient use of energy has been raised and energy-related projects have been funded with the bonds. Following the climate awareness funds, the "Environmental and Social Handbook" adopted by the EIB listed the environmental concerns of the EIB and served as a guide. After this development in 2010, the "Emission Performance Standards" adopted in 2013 enabled EIB to establish a relationship between investments and emission rates and to track fossil-based projects that passed the emission rate threshold from the investments it funded, and these standards became a climate investment standard for EIB. In terms of climate and green transition, 2015 was a turning point. EIB adopted its first climate strategy and a comprehensive EIB climate approach was established. "Sustainability Awareness Funds" were created by the Bank in 2018, aiming at a more sustainable access to finance and financing health and education projects, in particular water-related projects. The approach of the Union and the Bank began to change in 2019 and initiatives were launched to establish a climate bank. In this context, a lending approach for energy projects was adopted by the EIB to provide financing for energy transition. The most striking point in this respect is that the EIB has decided to stop financing or lending to fossil-fuel energy projects. By 2021, it was decided to gradually stop lending to projects with fossil resources, an important step towards the establishment of the EIB's climate bank against climate change. The EU members approved the EIB's plan for the establishment of the climate bank, which includes a comprehensive outline of how the EIB will support the achievement of the targets in the Green Deal and how it will support sustainability in 2021–2030, a critical period for countries outside the European Union. In 2022, the EIB took an important step towards the creation of a climate bank by adopting the "Environmental and Social Sustainability Framework" program (European Investment Bank, May 2023).

In the context of the Global Transition project initiated by the Union, the European Commission and EIB cooperated and created an investment plan of 18 billion Euros, primarily in the fields of climate action and energy; EU and partner countries, in cooperation, aim to overcome or alleviate the financial difficulties of members that do not have sufficient funds for climate change actions (European Commission, 2023).

One of the most important green transition actions taken by EIB has been the concrete steps taken towards the establishment of the "Climate Bank." By 2020, the Bank had prepared a very serious plan to comply with the Paris

Climate Agreement and prepared a transformation plan for 2021–2025 to quickly transform into a Climate Bank. After becoming a Climate Bank, EIB is expected to provide the world's leading climate change and green transition project support. By 2030, a total of €1 trillion Euro is planned to be allocated to climate action, sustainability, and green projects, and by 2025, EIB has agreed to allocate almost half of its expenditures to green actions. The EIB's role in the so-called green transition is built on a number of programs to comply with the Paris Climate Agreement. The first one is the "Leave No One Behind" program, inspired by the "Just EU Transition" program. EIB has thus gone beyond climate action and more inclusively included environmental sustainability issues in its support. The EIB has radically changed its approach and role towards the green transition. In addition to increasing adaptation efforts, supporting the creation of new business models that will facilitate the green transition, minimising costs through green technologies in infrastructure, and ensuring that investments are replicable and used at scale are the four pillars of the new green transition approach promoted by the EIB (Griffith-Jones and Carreras, 2021, 6–7).

EIB continues its activities in support of most of the programs implemented by the European Union in the context of climate change. The EU climate action programs such as "EU Emissions Trading System," "Commission Action Plan on Financing Sustainable Growth," "EU Adaptation Strategy," "2030 Climate and Energy Package" are integrated with EIB financial instruments. In particular, the climate targets that the Union aims to achieve by 2050 are guiding in terms of providing the necessary financing (European Investment Bank, 2020).

The European Union's climate and global environmental awareness goes back to the 1990s. However, the last twenty years have witnessed the emergence of a serious awareness and radical decisions towards climate change. In this context, the most important step taken by the Union was the initiation of the process known as the "Green Deal," which it defined as the green transition. The Green Deal aims to transform the European Union into a more economically and environmentally competitive and resource-efficient economy. The European Commission provides policy advice to EU member states in the green transition process and provides support on how to design green policies and how to achieve the goals and objectives set by the member states. Significant investment support is needed to realise the economic transformation of the European Union and its Member States during the green transition (European Commission, n.d.).

Since the beginning of the European integration process, EIB has been the engine of investment for the European Union and has provided significant financial support to the countries involved in the integration. The support provided by the Bank between 1958 and 1967 was concentrated in the energy, telecommunications, and transportation sectors. This situation, which can be considered reasonable at the beginning of the integration process considering the effects of the Second World War, continued until the 2000s and there was no radical change in the sectors that received financial support. Between 1958 and 1967, EIB provided support to EU member states in the fields of energy and transportation, and between 1968 and 1977, the support provided in the field of energy ranked first in all member states with a rapid increase. Similarly, energy continued to be the main area of financial support between 1978 and 1987. Between 1988 and 1995, investment in energy started to give way to transport and transport became the main area supported by the EIB. Starting in 1958, the EIB provided significant funding to EU Member States over a period of ten years. In the first 10-year period (1958–1967) the total support provided by the EIB was €5,393.69 million, in the second 10-year period (1968–1977) €30,956.8 million, in the third 10-year period (1978–1987) €100,726.9 million and in the fourth 10-year period (1988–1995) €200,301.1 million (Clifton, Díaz-Fuentes, and Gómez, 2017, 6–7).

The EIB's lending policy changed according to the changes in the international conjuncture and after the mid-1980s, the EIB shifted from its previous role as an investment bank to that of a "market maker." In these years of the end of the international monetary system and the oil crisis, the EIB adopted a new lending policy. At the same time, the developments in the global markets and the acceleration of the globalisation process with the technological and communication revolution accelerated the deregulation process in the financial markets and led to a monetarist economic climate in which market liberalisation and privatisation policies increased. These policies, implemented in the context of the Washington Consensus, were encouraged and supported globally by the World Bank and the International Monetary Fund. These developments also led to a change in global lending policy. The model of broad financial support normally provided by international institutions in times of cash shortages has led to a change in global lending policy and the model of EIB's lending policy has had to change as a result of the privatisation of public services, privatisation and financial deregulation, and financial globalisation. Public services have started to be financed by financial deregulation and globalisation. These global developments started to manifest themselves in the European Union and Jacques Delors, the then President of the Commission, started initiatives for the enlargement of the EU single market. Since the Commission did not have a monopoly on privatisation in the Union, the result was a deepening of economic integration. In this context, a liberalisation process started in the European Union, including basic services such as gas, electricity, transport, and telecommunications as well as other areas. As financial liberalisation gained momentum, the EIB's main priority was to support liberalisation in the member states (Clifton, Díaz-Fuentes, and Gómez, 2014, 6).

A significant decline in global investments in renewable energy was observed due to the 2008 global economic and financial crisis. At the same time, the uncertain demand for green energy led to a decline in green investments during this period. This was offset by the support provided by the European Bank for Reconstruction and Development, the German Development Bank, and the World Bank, in particular EIB. In such a situation, the importance of banks that provide such financing emerges and the task of normal banks is taken over by EIB and banks similar to EIB. Indeed, the financing provided globally by the EIB and similar banks has enabled the realisation of many of the green projects globally (Eyraud et al., 2013, 855).

The European Investment Bank's Supporting Role in Green Transition and Financing

The most concrete step taken by EIB to support the green transition was the transformation of the bank into a "Climate Bank." With this change agreed upon by EIB and the Union, EIB is planned to be the investment powerhouse for EU green financing and for achieving the 2050 green transition targets. Although the effectiveness of EIB's activities and policies towards green transition and climate action has emerged recently, it can be seen that they date back to 1960. A review of EIB's recent investments clearly shows that the projects and activities supported are concentrated in the energy and transportation sectors. In addition to the role of the "climate priorities" that the European Union aims to achieve by 2050, it is claimed that members such as Germany, Italy, and France stand out as the countries that have benefitted the most from the relevant sectors within the Union and have benefitted from the supports. When the green investments made between 1960 and 2020 are analysed, 2,100 of the 4,375 investments in total are concentrated in the energy and transportation sector and among the EU developed member states. Since the 2000s, EIB's financial support for green investments has steadily increased and the share of green investments in EIB investments reached 25 percent in 2015 (Ebeling, 2022, 1–2).

With the announcement of the EIB's transformation into a "Climate Bank" in 2019, there will be a significant change in the EU governance system. It can be argued that the EIB has completely changed its mandate in the EU integration process and has centralised the EIB to overcome the problems/challenges that the Union will face in the realisation of the Green Deal goals and climate priorities in the process of climate change and green transition. After planning by the EIB for the support to green transition and projects globally, especially in the European Union and its member states, the EIB can play a driving role in the green transition through various instruments (Kavvadia, 2021, 185).

For green projects, there is a long evaluation phase in the process of granting support by EIB. The reason for the long period of evaluation is to demonstrate full compliance with the EIB's environmental, economic, and technical conditions for support. The EIB uses a cost-benefit analysis to determine the support to be granted, as well as a very precise set of economic assessments that take into account other criteria such as internal rate of return, net present rate of return, economic rate of return (Clintworth et al., 2017, 30).

A review of the EIB's "Climate Bank" strategy for 2021–2025 shows that the EIB has fully prioritised the green transition. In this context, in order to support the EU "Green Deal," the Bank supports twelve priority areas of the Green Deal. Ten determinants of the EIB's support to the Union are direct and correspond to the targets set by the EU "Green Deal." The green transition supports policies established by the EIB group to reinforce the Bank's role as a global climate bank outside the European Union. The EU "Green Deal" has eleven areas of central policy focus that can be summarised as climate legislation, smart transportation and the use of sustainable resources, developing green industries, preventing pollution, involving all parties in the deal, supporting green projects, and leading the green transition globally. EIB has fully aligned itself with the EU policy structure in order to realise these policy focuses. This alignment is crucial in order to utilise the EU budget and to initiate dialogue processes with EU members on investment opportunities and possibilities. It is a necessity for the EIB to act with the Commission in order to provide support for investment programs such as "Recovery and Resilience Plans," "2030 National Energy and Climate Plans," "National Adaptation Strategies and Plans," "Territorial Just Transition Plans," and "National Long-Term Strategies," especially in the medium and long term. The EIB also provides funding to support members' own programs and projects outside the Union in the context of the United Nations Sustainable Development Goals (European Investment Bank Group, 2022, 12–13).

EIB's lending policy for green transition projects has certain preconditions. The conditions for lending are determined by the Bank on a four-yearly basis. EIB's lending priority is primarily assessed under the principle defined as "Energy Efficiency First." In the context of the relevant principle, EIB makes an assessment around four themes for the investment it will support. In this regard, the Bank examines the contribution of the investment to energy efficiency, takes into account the use of carbon-free sources in energy supply, and within the scope of the lending policy, the extent to which the investment includes innovative technologies and the new energy infrastructure it uses, and how it makes this structure secure. In addition to that, EIB's lending policy is based on these four main themes. The European Union has set a target of 32.5 percent energy efficiency by 2030. Likewise, the United Nations wants to realise the goal of doubling energy efficiency globally in the context of sustainable development goals. In this context, EIB has an important role to play, both for the European Union and to support global investments. The main objective of energy efficiency can be defined as minimising the need for energy and achieving high efficiency. Particularly for high-energy industries, investment becomes dependent on how much a project saves compared to the amount of energy it needs. The financial support provided by the EIB is up to 75 percent of the total cost, inside and outside the European Union (European Investment Bank, May 2023, 18–19).

Moreover, the EIB set the condition of decarbonisation of energy supply within its lending policy, taking into account the decarbonisation standards adopted by the European Union. By 2030, the Union wants to reduce its carbon emission rate by 40 percent from 1990 levels. In order to achieve the stated target, it has revised the regulation of carbon emissions as the "Emissions Trading System" and energy-intensive power and heat generation sectors have been included in the scope. EIB wants to increase the amount of renewable energy in total energy consumption to a minimum of 32 percent by 2030. In 2030, 30 percent of the total energy in the European Union will come from solar and wind and 60 percent from renewable energy. To reach these EU targets, the amount of renewable energy needs to be doubled or tripled. At this point, the EIB has adopted an investment policy to support 75 percent of investments to reach the 2030 targets. In order to combat climate change and support the green transition, the Paris Agreement emphasises the need for radical and game-changer innovations, especially in end consumer products. For this reason, EIB supports the Union to realise innovations that enable low-carbon production. Most energy transition technologies are still in the research and development phase. At the EU level, there is a "Strategic Energy Technology Plan" and an "Implementation Plan" that member states have to utilise. EIB continues to support the Union under the "Strategic Energy Technology Plan." Finally, EIB is committed to the integration of renewable energy transportation in Europe and globally. In this context, the Bank supports the secure distribution of energy and financing for the establishment of decentralised distribution infrastructures. The EIB also supports projects for the implementation of autonomous and smart technologies for the secure storage and distribution of renewable energy generation and other integration issues (European Investment Bank, 2023, 19, 21, 23, 25).

The projects supported by the EIB are very sectorally diverse. Apart from the sectors related to tobacco and gambling, EIB provides financing support in a wide range of areas. The EIB does not have a single evaluation methodology for projects, and when analysed sectorally, it requires the use of different calculation tools depending on the type of projects (European Investment Bank, March 2023, 3).

The green transition is realised through the Green Deal adopted by the EU Commission. In this context, EIB undertakes the financing pillar, which automatically makes EIB an integral part of the Green Deal. As already mentioned, EIB's involvement in green projects and financing is not new. Since 2012, the EIB has supported major green projects such as combatting climate change and protecting the environment, with a budget of 170 billion Euro dedicated exclusively to climate challenges in 2019. EIB's support for the EU green transition can be realised through traditional financial instruments as well as through new financial instruments newly developed by the Bank. The project to be financially supported by the EIB is subject to evaluation according to the institutions or persons involved, the efficiency and character of the project, and the type of investment. In general, projects with large resource requirements involving large public institutions and firms/companies are supported by direct loans. Smaller companies or smaller scales of organisations requesting financial support are supported by secondary financing instruments. While loans are important for the implementation of a climate policy or industrial climate policy, EIB has the right to apply green transformation criteria in the financing of projects. In addition, concessional resources can be mobilised by the EIB (Griffith-Jones and Carreras, 2021, 17).

In addition to the traditionally used supports, in recent years the Bank has been providing support using innovative financial instruments. Innovative financial instruments are preferred especially when the project or investment is profitable. The most important reason why innovative financial instruments are preferred is that the need for financing will be required for a long period of time in the process considered as the green transition. By using innovative financial instruments and obtaining more funds, it is aimed to create new sources of support for future projects. As a matter of fact, "Venture Debt," which is a financial instrument that attracts attention in this respect, is quite remarkable. With venture debt, a new type of support instrument has been created by sharing the risk among project partners and combining positive returns with risk. Considering the previous uses of venture debt, it is clear that it was not designed for green transition or green projects. While EIB is the largest lender of venture debt in the European Union, the venture debt instrument is being adapted for green transition projects and green financing to realise the EU Green Deal (Griffith-Jones and Carreras, 2021, 17).

The financial instrument referred to as venture debt was introduced in the United States in the 1970s. The use of this instrument in Europe took place ten years later. Venture debt stands out as a financial instrument that combines the characteristics of venture capital and debt. In terms of its structure, it is an instrument designed to provide financing to new and medium-sized companies. When venture debt is utilised, a portion of the equity is taken as collateral and the support has a grace period of one year. This instrument stands out as a type of financial support that is obtained with funds created in the context of venture capital and allocated to newly established or growing firms or enterprises. In recent years, this loan, which is received by insolvent and newly established companies, has been mostly used for green transition. Venture financing has also become a rapidly growing market in Europe. Looking at 2018 figures, the utilisation rate of the venture debt instrument in Europe remained low compared to that in the United States and amounted to EUR 1.05 billion. In terms of venture financing, the USA is well ahead of Europe. While the total use of venture financing in the form of debt and equity in the United States reached EUR 102 billion, this ratio remained at 21 billion Euro in the European Union. Among EU member states, Germany and France are the biggest beneficiaries of venture financing. These two countries use more than half of the financial instrument. Italy, Finland, and Sweden receive more support than these two countries. However, the main issue in venture financing is whether the emphasis on green transition can be increased when the areas of support are analysed (Griffith-Jones and Carreras, 2021, 17–18, 22–23).

At the centre of the green transition process is the Green Deal prepared by the European Union. The targets set out in the Green Deal are ambitious, and EIB is the most important financing institution in the process to realise the goals set out in this document, and above all, it is in the process of becoming a climate bank. At the same time, EIB's compliance with the Paris Climate Agreement means that by the end of 2025, it has committed to transfer more than half of its activities to the green transition process and to provide a total of 1 trillion Euros of financial support by 2030. At the same time, the EIB has included its support for transport in the green transition process, but more ambitious targets need to be set to achieve the levels targeted for carbon-neutral transport. However, the EIB needs to prioritise investment areas and focus on cleaner and larger alternatives. It needs to align its investments towards the introduction of electric rail or cleaner alternative modes of transport and mobility before electric cars become widespread. While EIB currently has no such investment plans, the Bank should quickly consider electric transport as part of its investment plans and channel resources to expand the use of hydrogen. To maximise its role in the green transition, EIB should also increase the level of investment in technologies and innovations related to climate, environment, and energy use. As a matter of fact, making EIB and the European Investment Fund effective in the context of climate and environmental actions and monitoring them will strengthen the green transition process in the European Union. The role of EIB's effectiveness and support in the green transition process cannot be underestimated. However, in order to achieve the targets set by the Union, the EIB needs to encourage versatility in its investments. In order to act in an incentivising way, the EIB must move beyond being a passive agency, not only receiving project requests but also becoming a project implementing agency and having a voice in emerging substitute sectors. If the EIB dominates the creation of new energy sectors, its role in the green transition will be greater than ever. The targets set out in the Green Deal are ambitious but achievable. However, in order to strengthen the EIB's role in achieving them, increased capital contributions from EU Member States to the EIB, additional guarantees, and more risk-taking financial instruments with the support of the European Commission will contribute to the realisation of the objectives of the Green Deal and will contribute to raising capital for the investments needed in the green transition (Griffith-Jones and Carreras, 2021, 26–27).

The war between Ukraine and Russia has revealed the European Union's energy dependence. It has taken significant steps to break its energy dependence for many years but without success. The green transition or transformation process in energy, politics, and economy to be achieved through the Green Deal has become a necessity for the Union to establish a stable economy and peace in Europe. Therefore, the EIB's role as the EU investment and financing powerhouse in the process is very prominent. Considering the 2023–2025 investment plan, the EIB's main priorities are to concretely end Europe's energy dependence on Russia and to support the green and digital transition processes. At the same time, the Bank has made plans to assist Ukraine in all areas to address urgent needs and rebuild the country. The transformation of EIB into the Climate Bank by 2020, the fact that EIB has allocated approximately 30 billion Euros of financing in five years to achieve zero emissions and reduce dependence on fossil fuels, and the fact that EIB has allocated 8.5 billion Euros of support outside the European Union to meet global demands make the Bank a central capital power in the green transition process (European Investment Bank, n.d.).

CONCLUSION

The most critical problem in the green transition process is financial support. Although the costs of projects aimed at creating a climate change, environment and nature-friendly economy, and production system are high, the European Union can achieve the targets set in the green transition process by providing the necessary financial support. At this point, a step that can be recognised as a globally unique initiative has been taken by EIB, and it is planned that the Bank will become a "climate bank" by 2025. With EIB becoming a climate bank, it is thought that shifting more than 50 percent of its investments to green investments and projects and creating new green financing instruments will facilitate the realisation of the Green Deal targets for the

European Union, as well as overcoming problems such as the energy crisis that arises in the green transition process. Above all, the idea of a "climate bank" is a unique and highly entrepreneurial approach that has only been put forward by the European Union.

REFERENCES

Antoine, E. (2022). *European Investment Bank Loan Appraisal, the EU Climate Bank?* Working Papers of BETA 2022-10. Bureau d'Economie Théorique et Appliquée, UDS, Strasbourg.

Clifton, J., Díaz-Fuentes, D., and Gómez, A. L. (2017). The European Investment Bank: Development, Integration, Investment? *JCMS: Journal of Common Market Studies* 56(4):733–750. https://doi.org/10.1111/jcms.12614

Clifton, J., Díaz-Fuentes, D., and Revuelta, J. (2014). Financing Utilities: How the Role of the European Investment Bank Shifted from Regional Development to Making Markets. *Utilities Policy* 29:63–71. https://doi.org/10.1016/j.jup.2013.10.004

Clintworth, M., Boulougouris, E., and Lee, B. S. (2017). Combining Multicriteria Decision Analysis and Cost–Benefit Analysis in Assessing Maritime Projects Financed by the European Investment Bank. *Maritime Economics & Logistics* 20(1):29–47. https://doi.org/10.1057/s41278-017-0072-x

European Investment Bank. (2020). *EIB Climate Strategy.* European Union. https://www.eib.org/attachments/strategies/eib_climate_strategy_en.pdf

———. (2023, March). *The Economic Appraisal of Investment Projects at the EIB.* European Union. https://www.eib.org/attachments/lucalli/20220169_economic_appraisal_of_investment_projects_en.pdf

———. (2023, May). *EIB Energy Lending Policy Supporting the Energy Transformation.* European Union. https://www.eib.org/attachments/lucalli/20230164_eib_energy_lending_policy_en.pdf

———. (n.d.). *EIB Group—Operational Plan 2023–2025.* European Union. Retrieved from https://www.europarl.europa.eu/cmsdata/274060/EIB%20Group%20Operational%20Plan%202023-2025%20(Summary).pdf

European Investment Bank Group. (2020). *EIB Group Climate Bank Roadmap 2021–2025.* European Union. Retrieved from https://www.eib.org/attachments/thematic/eib_group_climate_bank_roadmap_en.pdf

European Union. (n.d.). *Climate and environmental sustainability.* European Investment Bank. Retrieved from https://www.eib.org/en/about/priorities/climate-action/index.htm

European Commission. (n.d.). *Green Transition.* European Union. https://reform-support.ec.europa.eu/what-we-do/green-transition_en

———. (2023, April 27). Press Release: Global Gateway: Commission and EIB Announce Funds Worth €18 Billion to Boost Investments in Climate Action and Sustainable Economies. European Union. New York. https://ec.europa.eu/commission/presscorner/detail/en/ip_23_2463

Eyraud, L., Clements, B., and Wane, A. (2013). Green Investment: Trends and Determinants. *Energy Policy* 60:852–865. https://doi.org/10.1016/j.enpol.2013.04.039

Griffith-Jones, S., and Carreras, M. (2021). The Role of the EIB in the Green Transformation: Policy Study. Foundation for European Progressive Studies.

Kavvadia, H. (2021). The European Investment Bank's "Quantum Leap" to Become the World's First International Climate Bank. *Politics and Governance* 9(2):185–195.

Mertens, D., and Thiemann, M. (2023). The European Investment Bank: The EU's Climate Bank? In Rayner, T., Szulecki, K., Jordan, A. and Oberthür, S. (Eds.), *Handbook on European Union Climate Change Policy and Politics* (pp. 68–82). Edward Elgar.

A Disaster in the Context of Global Warming, Climate Change, and Drought

Forest Fires

Nahit Bek

INTRODUCTION

Under normal conditions, ecological cycles function tremendously, enabling the continuous movement of essential gasses, water, and other substances within a specific system, crucial for the continuity of life. These movements are highly significant for the existence of terrestrial and aquatic ecosystems. Disruptions occurring in ecological cycles due to human activities threaten the presence of a sustainable environment. Forests, which are part of terrestrial ecosystems, play a vital role in biodiversity due to their diversity. Approximately 31 percent of the world's terrestrial areas are covered by forests, with over one-third of these forest areas classified as primary forests[1] (FAO, 2020b, 2). Furthermore, more than half (54%) of the forested areas in the world are located within the borders of five countries: the Russian Federation, Brazil, Canada, the United States (US), and the People's Republic of China (FAO, 2020b). Forests are dynamic systems, comprising living and nonliving things. As dynamic ecosystems are crucial for the sustainability of life, forests face various hazards. Forests, one of the most important components of biological diversity, confront diverse dangers such as uncontrolled logging, excessive consumption, the invasion of harmful species, and wildfires[2] (Bek, 2022, 1). Among these hazards, wildfires, exacerbated by the loss of moisture caused by global warming, are on the rise. Scientific evidence supports the fact that temperature increases resulting from climate change lead to wildfires. Therefore, wildfires emerge as a prominent threat among the dangers faced by forests. The consequences of the increasing wildfires, influenced by global warming, make them global disasters that affect not only the country where they occur but also the entire world.

GLOBAL WARMING, CLIMATE CHANGE, AND DROUGHT

Global warming, in its simplest definition, is the long-term heating of the Earth's surface due to human activities, primarily the increase in greenhouse gas levels caused by fossil fuel usage, which traps heat in the Earth's atmosphere. In a more straightforward expression, global warming refers to the increase in Earth's surface temperature that affects the world and its living beings. Although global warming and climate change are sometimes used interchangeably, they represent different phenomena (NASA, 2020). While both terms are occasionally used with similar meanings, they are distinct concepts. Global warming refers to the temperature rise that can lead to climate change, whereas climate change encompasses the overall seasonal variations in temperature, precipitation, and humidity in a specific region (Yamanoğlu, 2006, 139). Due to disruptions in precipitation patterns within climate change, unexpected floods occur in unforeseen places and times, while unexpected droughts are observed in other regions.

Water stands at the forefront of the essential resources required for the continuity of life. The decrease in water resources due to the impact of climate change and global warming has turned water into a strategically important resource. From the transition to settled life to the industrial revolution, the primary function of water was for drinking and agricultural irrigation. However, in today's world, water is needed in many sectors. After agricultural irrigation, the industrial sector stands as the second-largest consumer of water (İZKA, 2020). Considering the necessity of water for the continuity of living beings and agricultural production, the reduction of water resources due to climate change and global warming highlights the significance of the issue. Among the problems related to water resources, drought emerges as a primary concern. Drought is a natural occurrence observed when certain regions on the Earth experience insufficient rainfall due to disruptions in the water cycle. However, describing it as a natural event is insufficient, as human activities significantly disrupt the ecological water cycle, making its restoration challenging. Excessive use of water resources, interference with riverbeds, and disruptions caused by global warming and climate change permanently amplify the effects of natural events like droughts and floods (Şahin and Kurnaz, 2014, 9). In addition to the adverse impact on water resources, drought affects various sectors such as agriculture, industry, the use of freshwater sources for drinking, and energy production from rivers, leading to social and economic consequences (Mishra and Singh, 2010, 203). Based on the decrease in overall rainfall in a particular area, it is possible to define drought. Accordingly, drought, which is expected to be a temporary condition, is also used in place of terms like desertification and aridification, which signify permanent situations (Şahin and Kurnaz, 2014, 11). While the notion that human activities exacerbate drought was once disregarded, contemporary viewpoints have begun to emphasise the connection between human-induced global warming and its consequences (Giannini et al., 2008, 127). According to the Intergovernmental Panel on Climate Change's (2022) sixth assessment report, climate change exerts pressure on living beings, human health, and livelihoods by causing extreme weather events such as heavy rains, droughts, and associated forest fires (Pörtner et al., 2022, 18). It is a scientific fact that trees convert carbon dioxide in the atmosphere into oxygen and that forests provide raw materials for many industries. Even these two well-known benefits of forests underscore the importance of maintaining a sustainable forest presence. Hence, taking measures against wildfires, which threaten forest existence, and the climatological events causing them is of utmost importance.

In this context, the awareness of global warming and the climate crisis, which has become a topic of global debate, dates back to the late nineteenth century. Arrhenius first brought the issue to the agenda with his report titled "Climate Change and Its Risks" published in 1894. In this report, he emphasised that changes in the proportion of gasses in the air would directly affect the moisture and temperature on Earth, discussing the greenhouse effect (1896, 240–254). In the 1930s, there were discussions about the impact of greenhouse gases on the climate in the United States. By the 1960s, studies in the United States and Canada revealed an increase in greenhouse gas levels (Şanlı and Özekicioğlu, 2007, 462). In 1972, the United Nations Human Environment Conference (Stockholm Conference)[3] was held in Stockholm. The increasing recognition of environmental issues and their impact on the international agenda played a significant role in the organisation of this conference. Environmental issues began to be intensely debated on a global scale in the 1970s, and sustainability became a crucial topic in these discussions. Development-oriented policies started to give way to the concept of sustainable development (Bozlağan, 2005, 1015–1017). The severity of global warming was expressed at the 1979 World Climate Conference[4] in front of 53 countries and 24 international organisations by 350 experts from fields such as agriculture, water resources, environment, energy, fisheries, medicine, economy, and ecology (public.wmo.int). In the following years (1985, 1987, and 1988)[5] the policies developed to combat climate change were reviewed, and alternative policies were formulated (Şanlı and Özekicioğlu, 2007, 463). The Rio Declaration on Environment and Development, which has the characteristics of a final declaration, was published at the Rio Conference (1992), where the "Convention on Biological Diversity" and the "Framework Convention on Climate Change" were opened for signature (Alada et al., 1993, 96). Following this conference, sustainable development became an actively adopted international policy. Additionally, Agenda 21, an action plan that sets principles for coping with environmental issues and achieving a balance between the environment and the economy in the twenty-first century, is also one of the outcomes of the Rio Conference. The "Berlin Meeting" held in 1995, the "Kyoto Protocol" aiming to keep greenhouse gasses at a certain level in 1997, the "Intergovernmental Panel on Climate Change" established in 2001, the "Climate Change Conference"[6] held in Canada in 2005, and the United Nations World Climate Council meetings in 2007 took place in three stages. In the meetings held in Paris, Brussels, and Bangkok, discussions were held on scientific data related to global warming, its impacts, and ways to combat global warming without harming economic growth (Şanlı and Özekicioğlu, 2007, 463–468). The Paris Agreement signed in 2015 in Paris is also an international initiative aimed at reducing greenhouse gas emissions on a global scale, and all countries that ratified the Agreement committed to reducing their greenhouse gas emissions (mfa.gov.tr). Those mentioned here are among the main international meetings/agreements held to address the climate crisis.

Research indicates that the world is becoming an increasingly warming planet. Global warming, which has been discussed since the late nineteenth century, is now showing its effects more prominently. Despite numerous conferences and meetings organised to prevent or mitigate the effects of global warming and the climate crisis, this crisis continues to threaten the world in all its reality. The negative effects of global warming, which were not of this magnitude in the early years of its discussion, are increasing day by day. Global warming, caused by human activities that lead directly or indirectly to many problems such as changing seasons, decreasing water resources, droughts, and forest fires, persists relentlessly despite numerous decisions taken. Disagreements among developed countries and the reluctance of developing countries to bear equal costs with developed countries have resulted in all efforts yielding no significant results. For instance, disputes between the European Union and the United States at a meeting held in Bali in 2007 prolonged the meeting and prevented a full consensus (Ünver, 2008, 99). Despite all the meetings and agreements held from the Stockholm Conference to the present day, the impact of the climate crisis is increasingly being felt. Seasonal changes, droughts, and the increasing occurrences of forest fires pose threats to living beings as reflections of this situation.

THE RELATIONSHIP BETWEEN FOREST FIRES AND CLIMATE CHANGE

Atmospheric events that occur or are observed anywhere on Earth at any given time are referred to as weather. Climate, on the other hand, is defined as the combination of average values of weather events observed over many years in any given location, as well as the frequencies of occurrence and the intensity of severe natural events (Türkeş, 2001, 188). Based on these definitions, climate change can be expressed as meaningful changes in the statistical state of climatic data (Türkeş, 2008, 27). The effects of climate change are increasingly being felt worldwide. The United Nations (UN) states that greenhouse gas emissions must be reduced to combat climate change and stop/slow down global warming (UNEP, October 2022). The need to prevent global warming and its adverse effects on climates were emphasised at the Rio Conference on Environment and Development organised under the United Nations in 1992. Reducing greenhouse gas emissions, which is still a subject of debate today, was also among the issues highlighted during the same meeting (unfccc.int). Moreover, greenhouse gas emissions resulting from human activities contribute to climate change by intensifying the greenhouse effect. One of the main activities causing this effect is the emission of carbon dioxide from the use of fossil fuels. The energy demand, which is one of humanity's basic needs, is one of the main reasons driving the increased use of fossil resources. The energy demand has rapidly increased since the Industrial Revolution, and this trend continues today. Fossil fuels are the primary sources used to meet energy demands.[7] Nonrenewable fossil fuels such as coal, oil, and natural gas emit more pollutants and greenhouse gasses into the environment. This situation puts pressure on the environment and affects climate change (Erdoğan, 2020, 278). The pollution caused by the use of fossil fuels leads to global warming and climate change.[8]

Increasing temperatures and the extension of the dry season are associated with climate change. In this context, the question arises of what impact climate change has on forest fires. At this point, the existence of a chain of events is crucial; changes in atmospheric gas ratios resulting from human activities lead to global warming, and global warming disrupts the ecological cycle, which in turn puts pressure on climates. As a result of this pressure on climates, climate change occurs. Nature events that reflect climate change include an increase in sudden and intense rainfall, heat waves, and prolonged droughts. With the prolongation of droughts and rising temperatures, the pressure of fires on forests increases. Regions experiencing prolonged drought periods with reduced soil moisture are at an increased risk of forest fires (Dabanlı, 2021, 28). According to a report published by the United Nations Environment Programme, forest fires are predicted to increase by 14 percent by 2030, 30 percent by 2050, and 50 percent by the end of the twenty-first century. In the current century, the year 2021 marked the highest loss of forests due to fires. In 2021, a total of 9.3 million hectares of forested areas were destroyed worldwide. Heatwaves have increased fivefold compared to 150 years ago and are expected to become even more frequent as global warming continues. Therefore, the increasing frequency of heatwaves and the reduction of humidity due to climate change negatively affect fires (MacCarthy et al., 2022).

According to the findings of the Intergovernmental Panel on Climate Change (IPCC), a globally discussed topic has emerged surrounding the impacts of global warming and the climate crisis. This issue, which has been under discussion since the late nineteenth century, is now showing its effects in an increasingly alarming manner in today's world. The IPCC's *Climate Change 2023: Synthesis Report* emphasises that if global warming continues at its current pace, the effects of climate change will intensify and worsen (UNEP, February 2022). The rising temperatures, changing rainfall patterns, and various other alterations caused by global warming are said to be contributing to the more frequent and severe occurrence of forest fires compared to the past (Borunda, 2020). Moreover, the IPCC's sixth assessment report underscores the significance of heat waves, droughts, and forest fires when discussing the far-reaching effects of climate change. It is also noteworthy that the melting of permafrost,[9] the ecosystem response to increasing temperatures, and the release of greenhouse gasses from forest fires will further elevate atmospheric carbon dioxide concentration, making the challenge of combatting global warming even more daunting (IPCC, 2023, 36–53).

Another effect of climate change on fires is the lengthening and variability of fire seasons. For instance, in Australia, fires typically occur in mid-January, but in 2020, the "mega-fire"[10] occurred in September. A global effort to combat global warming will also benefit in preventing forest fires. According to the European Space Agency, fires affect an area of four million square kilometres every year, which is nearly half the size of India or four times the size of Nigeria's land area (Al Jazeera, 2021).

METHOD

With the escalation of environmental issues to a transboundary scale, it has become evident that they pose a threat to the entire world. Environmental problems felt on a global level have become a collective concern for humanity. Among the ongoing and escalating challenges of today, forest fires hold a significant place. This study focuses on the relationship between environmental issues, namely global warming, the climate crisis, and drought, and their connection to forest fires. To elucidate this relationship, previous studies and reports from international organisations have been utilised. Therefore, the study incorporates literature review and document analysis techniques. Document analysis, the process of examining materials containing information about the researched topic, contributes to diversifying the data and enhancing its validity (Yıldırım and Şimşek, 2016, 190).

FINDINGS

Global warming has been scientifically proven to significantly alter climates, disrupt precipitation patterns, and lead to prolonged periods of drought. Reports from reputable international organisations, such as the United Nations, also substantiate the undeniable existence of this pressing problem. Efforts to find solutions to the issues caused by global warming continue on a global scale. The problems caused by global warming, climate change, and drought are among the fundamental issues that threaten living beings. As a direct consequence of prolonged droughts, an observable surge in wildfires has been witnessed across various regions. While it is acknowledged that drought may not singularly cause wildfires, it certainly acts as a pivotal trigger, facilitating their rapid spread and intensification. The decrease in relative humidity in forested areas due to drought heightens the susceptibility to ignition and creates an environment where wildfires can thrive unabated. Countries situated in regions classified as the Mediterranean climate zone experience the most pronounced impacts of climate change. Within this zone, these countries are the most affected by forest fires. Despite the existence of international cooperation in firefighting efforts, it is evident that it remains insufficient on a global scale.

CONCLUSION

The continuity of living beings is directly related to the flawless functioning of the ecosystem. Within a specific system, ongoing ecological cycles experience disruptions due to human interventions. These disruptions adversely affect many aspects of life, from industrial production to agriculture. As a result of global warming, an increase in temperatures leads to drought. One of the fundamental characteristics of forest ecosystems is the decrease in soil moisture during drought. At this point, the dry layer on the forest floor, which plays a significant role in the initiation and spread of fires, becomes more prone to ignition and rapid spread. Therefore, drought plays a crucial role in the spread of forest fires and their impact on broader areas. The threat of forest fires confronts forests in various parts of the world. This globally felt threat puts the functioning of the ecosystem at risk. Evaluating the findings of the research, it is observed that one of the most effective ways to combat forest fires lies in addressing the factors that contribute to their ignition.

Thus, combatting global warming becomes essential to break the negative impact of the climate crisis on forests. The most effective fight against global warming, which affects the entire world, can only be achieved through synchronised global action. To implement this struggle, mechanisms established on a global scale should primarily focus on human activities that cause the climate crisis. International organisations have been engaging in such efforts for over fifty years. However, despite these endeavours, it is considered that the actions taken on an international level have some missing aspects, as the pressure on the climate continues to increase. Identifying and eliminating the causes of this situation will be a significant development to enable global governance in the fight against the climate crisis. In this context, a final evaluation suggests that implementing global sanctions against countries engaged in activities that contribute to the climate crisis and monitoring these activities would not only reduce global pressure but also contribute to a decrease in the climatic factors that cause forest fires.

NOTES

1. Primary Forest (Virgin Forest): It is defined as forests where clear indicators of human activity are not visibly present, and ecological processes are significantly undisturbed, allowing native tree species to naturally regenerate.

2. Of the wildfires, 3% are caused by lightning strikes, 12% are intentionally set (arson, land clearing, etc.), 38% result from negligence and lack of precaution, while 47% originate from unknown causes. Considering these ratios, it can be observed that 50% of forest fires are human-induced (Korkmaz, 2002, 104). With an assumption that the unknown causes are also human-related, this percentage goes beyond 90%.

3. In memory of this conference, every year on June 5th, World Environment Day is celebrated worldwide.

4. In the literature, it is generally referred to as the "First World Climate Conference."

5. For example, in the "Changing Atmosphere" themed conference held in Canada (in the city of Toronto) in 1988, it was determined as a global target that carbon dioxide emissions should be reduced by 20% worldwide by the year 2005 (Taylor, 2014:27).

6. In this conference where the decisions of the Kyoto Protocol were formalised, the greenhouse gas emission targets of 190 countries were set, aiming to achieve these targets by the year 2012 (dw.com, 2005).

7. Approximately 80% of the world's energy needs are met by fossil fuels (eesi .org).

8. While being a major topic of debate, ensuring a sustainable environment and, indirectly, preserving the environment necessitates a transition to renewable energy sources.

9. Permafrost is the permanently frozen layer of soil beneath the Earth's surface (education.nationalgeographic.org). It constitutes approximately one-fourth of the soil in the Northern Hemisphere. With global warming, the permanence of permafrost is weakening, and the risk of thawing arises. Researchers predict that if global warming and climate change continue at the current pace, about two-thirds of the near-surface permafrost in the Arctic will thaw. This thawing process carries the potential to release ancient viruses and bacteria that have been isolated for thousands of years.

10. In this fire, an area of eight million hectares was affected, and it resulted in the loss of twenty-five human lives and the lives of millions of animals (bbc.com).

REFERENCES

Al Jazeera. (2021). Mapping Wildfires around the World. Accessed June 3, 2023. https://www.aljazeera.com/news/2021/8/19/mapping-wildfires-around-the-world-interactive

Alada, A., Gürpınar, E., and Budak, S. (1993). Rio Konferansı Üzerine Düşünceler. İstanbul *Üniversitesi Siyasal Bilgiler Fakültesi Dergisi* 3-4-5.

Arrhenius, S. (1896, April). On the Influence of Carbonic Acid in the Air upon the Temperature of the Ground. *Philosophical Magazine and Journal of Science* 5(41):237–276.

BBC News. (2020). Avustralya'da "Mega Yangın" Endişesi. https://www.bbc.com/turkce/haberler-dunya-51018798

Bek, N. (2022). Yapay Zekanın Orman Yangınlarıyla Mücadelede Kullanımı: Tarım ve Orman Bakanlığı Uygulamaları Üzerine Bir Araştırma. In *Siyaset, Kamu Yönetimi ve Uluslararası İlişkiler Bağlamında Yapay Zeka Tartışmaları*, edited by M. H. Korkusuz and E. Kutluk (pp. 189–215). Ekin Yayıncılık, Bursa.

Borunda, A. (2020). The Science Connecting Wildfires to Climate Change. *National Geographic.* https://www.nationalgeographic.com/science/article/climate-change-increases-risk-fires-western-us

Bozlağan, R. (2005). Sürdürülebilir Gelişme Düşüncesinin Tarihsel Arka Planı. *Journal of Social Policy Conferences* 50:1011–1028.

Dabanlı, İ. (2021). İklim Değişikliği ve Artan Orman Yangınları İlişkisi. *Orman Yangınları, Kitapiçi bölüm*, Ed. Taşkın Kavzoğlu. Türkiye Bilimler Akademisi

Deutsche Welle (DW). (2005). Kyoto Protokolü Yürürlükte, https://www.dw.com/tr/kyotoprotokol%C3%BCy%C3%BCr%C3%BCrl%C3%BCkte/a-2525334

Environmental and Energy Study Institute (EESI). (2021). Fossil Fuels. https://www.eesi.org/topics/fossil-fuels

Erdoğan, S. (2020). Enerji, çevre ve sera gazları. *Çankırı Karatekin Üniversitesi İİBF Dergisi* 10(1):277–303. https://doi.org/10.18074/ckuiibfd.670673

FAO. (2020a). Global Forest Resources Assessment 2020: Main Report. Food and Agriculture Organization of the United Nations. UNEP: Rome. https://www.fao.org/documents/card/en/c/ca9825en

FAO. (2020b). The State of the World's Forests 2020. Food and Agriculture Organization of the United Nations. UN Environment Programme (UNEP). Accessed
June 2, 2023. https://www.fao.org/3/ca8642en/online/ca8642en.html

Giannini, A., Biasutti M., and Verstraete, M. M. (2008). A Climate Model-Based
Review of Drought in The Sahel: Desertification, the Re-Greening and Climate
Change. *Global and Planetary Change* 64:119–128.

İklim Konferansında Uzlaşma Sağlandı. (2005). Accessed June 4, 2023. https://
www.dw.com/tr/i%CC%87klim-konferans%C4%B1nda-uzla%C5%9Fma-sa%C4
%9Fland%C4%B1/a-2522939

IPCC. (2023). *Climate Change 2023 Synthesis Report.* Contribution of Working
Groups I, II and III to the Sixth Assessment Report of the Intergovernmental Panel
on Climate Change (IPCC). Geneva, Switzerland. Accessed June 9, 2023. https://
www.ipcc.ch/report/ar6/syr/downloads/report/IPCC_AR6_SYR_LongerReport
.pdf

İzmir Kalkınma Ajansı (İZKA). (2020). Türkiye'de Sanayi Sektöründe Su Kullanımı.
Accessed May 5, 2023. https://kalkinmaguncesi.izka.org.tr/index.php/2020/08/06/
turkiyede-sanayi-sektorunde-su-kullanimi/

Korkmaz, M. (2002), Ormanlık Alanlar ve Orman Varlığı Üzerine Bir Değerlendirme,
Dumlupınar Üniversitesi Fen Bilimleri Dergisi, 99–106.

MacCarthy, J., Tyukavina, S., Weisse, M., and Harris, N. (2022). New Data Confirms: Forest Fires are Getting Worse. World Resources Institute. UNDRR (United
Nations Office for Disaster Risk Reduction).

Mishra, A. K., and Singh, V. P. (2010). A Review of Drought Concepts. *Journal of
Hydrology* 391(1–2):202–216.

NASA. (2020). What's in a Name? Global Warming vs. Climate Change. https://gpm
.nasa.gov/education/articles/whats-name-global-warming-vs-climate-change

National Geographic. (n.d.). Encyclopedic Entry: Permafrost. Accessed June 8, 2023.
https://education.nationalgeographic.org/resource/permafrost/

Pörtner, H.-O., Roberts, D. C., Tignor, M. M. B., and Poloczanska, E. (2022). *Climate
Change 2022: Impacts, Adaptation and Vulnerability.* Working Group II Contribution to the Sixth Assessment Report of the Intergovernmental Panel on Climate
Change (IPCC). Cambridge University Press. https://www.ipcc.ch/report/sixth
-assessment-report-working-group-ii/

Şahin, Ü., and Kurnaz, L. (2014). *İklim Değişikliği ve Kuraklık.* İstanbul Politikalar
Merkezi. Sabancı Üniversitesi, İstanbul.

Şanlı Gülbahar, F., and Özekicioğlu, H. (2007). Küresel Isınmayı Önlemeye Yönelik
Çabalar ve Türkiye. *Karamanoğlu Mehmetbey Üniversitesi Sosyal ve Ekonomik
Araştırmalar Dergisi* 7:456–48.

Taylor, M., (2014). *Global Warming and Climate Change What Australia Knew
and Buried.* https://library.oapen.org/bitstream/id/a5df4d22-5c9f-42df-b922-
e9321274c0b4/515850.pdf

Türkeş, M. (2001). Hava, iklim, şiddetli hava olayları ve küresel ısınma. Devlet
Meteoroloji İşleri Genel Müdürlüğü 2000 Yılı Seminerleri. Teknik Sunumlar,
Seminerler Dizisi 1:187–205. Ankara.

————. (2008). Küresel İklim Değişikliği Nedir? Temel Kavramlar, Nedenleri, Gözlenen ve Öngörülen Değişiklikler. *İklim Değişikliği ve Çevre* 1:26–37.

Türkiye Cumhuriyeti Dışişleri Bakanlığı. (n.d.). Paris Anlaşması. Accessed June 22, 2023. https://www.mfa.gov.tr/paris-anlasmasi.tr.mfa

UNEP. (2022, October 27). Emissions GAP Report 2022. https://www.unep.org/resources/emissions-gap-report-2022

————. (2022, February 23). Number of Wildfires to Rise by 50% by 2100 and Governments Are Not Prepared, Experts Warn. Accessed May 3, 2023. https://www.unep.org/news-and-stories/press-release/number-wildfires-rise-50-2100-and-governments-are-not-prepared

United Nations Climate Change. (1992). The Rio Conventions: The Interconnected Challenges of Climate Change, Desertification and Biodiversity Loss. Accessed May 3, 2023. https://unfccc.int/process-and-meetings/the-rio-conventions

United Nations Digital Library. (1988). Proceedings, World Conference, Toronto, Canada June 27–30, 1988: The Changing Atmosphere: Implications For Global Security = Actes, Conférence mondiale, Toronto, Canada, 27–30 juin 1988: l'atmosphère en évolution: implications pour la sécurité du globe.

Ünver, İ. (2008). Barış Ödülünün Üzerinde İlkim Değişikliği Gölgesi. *Mülkiye Dergisi* 32(259):83–100.

Yamanoğlu, G. Ç. (2006). Türkiye'de Küresel Isınmaya Yol Açan Sera Gazı Emisyonlarındaki Artış ile Mücadelede İktisadi Araçların Rolü (Y. Lisans Tezi), A. Ü., SBE, Ankara.

Yıldırım, A., and Şimşek, H. (2016). Sosyal Bilimlerde Nitel Araştırma Yöntemleri. Seçkin Yayıncılık, 10. Baskı, Ankara.

Zillman, J. W. (2009). A History of Climate Activities. *World Meteorological Organization* 58(3). Accessed June 3, 2023. https://public.wmo.int/en/bulletin/history-climate-activities

Index

About the Contributors

Altuğ GÜNAR is Associate Professor of European Union Politics and International Relations in Bandirma Onyedi Eylül University at Faculty of Economics and Administrative Sciences. He has a large number of works, including articles, book chapters, books, and book editorials in the field of the European Union. His main research areas are the European Union, International Relations and Economics, and Schumpeterian Economics. Today, he is Director of the Mediterranean Policy Applications and Research Center, and Lecturer in the Department of International Relations. His most recent books are *Creative Destruction, Crisis and European Union: The 2008 Crisis within the Framework of the Schumpeterian Approach European Union and Globalization, Future of The European Union Integration: A Failure or A Success? Future Expectations,* and *The European Union in the Twenty-First Century: Major Political, Economic and Security Policy Trends.*

Çağatay BAŞARIR is Associate Professor of Finance in Bandırma Onyedi Eylül University, at faculty of Application Sciences on International Trade and Logistics Department. He received his undergraduate degree (B.A.) in Business Administration from the Ege University in 2003. He earned his M.A. in 2006 and his Ph.D. is in Business Administration in 2016 from Balıkesir University. He has studies on financial markets, stock exchange markets, commodity markets, and precious metals in the field of time series analyses, multi criteria decision analysis, and performance measurement. He instructs financial management, financial analysis, financial markets, international finance, and portfolio management lessons, both in graduate and undergraduate degree programs. He is the editor of *Bandırma Onyedi Eylül University Social Sciences Research Journal.* In addition to many published articles, book chapters, and reviews, he is the editor of five international books.

Samet ZENGİNOĞLU completed his bachelor's degree in International Relations at Kocaeli University, his master's degree in the Department of International Relations at Akdeniz University, and his doctorate in the European Union Studies program at Süleyman Demirel University. Samet Zenginoğlu is still working at Adıyaman University. His main research areas of the European Union constitute the Turkey-European Union Relations and European history.

Ferhat APAYDIN graduated from Hitit University, Department of Economics in 2011. He is doing his Ph.D. in economics at Çukurova University. He is still working as a lecturer in the Department of Economics, Faculty of Economics and Administrative Sciences at Adıyaman University. He teaches "Introduction to Economics, Microeconomics, International Economics and Turkish Economy." His fields of study are Economic Theory, Economic Development, Industrialisation-Deindustrialisation, and Political Economy.

Didem ÖZTÜRK GÜNAR, who got a master's degree by defending her thesis titled "The Effects of Changes in the Global Economy on the Customs Union Process" in the Department of European Union Economics at Marmara University European Union Institute in 2016, completed her doctoral studies at the Department of European Union at Istanbul University in 2023 and received her Ph.D. degree. Although European Union, European Union Economics, and Economics are her main fields of study, Dr. Didem ÖZTÜRK GÜNAR has studied in the field of European Union economics.

Omca ALTIN graduated from the Department of International Relations and European Union at İzmir University of Economics. She completed her master's and doctorate studies at the Department of European Union at Istanbul University. She is currently an assistant professor at the Department of International Relations, Faculty of Economics and Administrative Sciences, at Kastamonu University. She is also the Head of the Department of European Union Law and the Deputy Dean of the Faculty of Economics and Administrative Sciences. Altin teaches numerous courses for undergraduate and postgraduate students, including: European Integration Process, EU Law, Introduction to Political Science, History of Political Thought, EU-Turkey Relations, EU Foreign Policy, International Energy Policies, and Regional Policies: The Balkans, Political Developments in the Balkans, Nationalism, and Minorities. She has conducted various academic studies and projects about the European Union. Her research focuses on the European Union,

EU-Turkey Relations, Europe and Regional Efforts, EU History, EU Law, and EU Foreign Policy.

Kaan ÇELİKOK received a B.A. in Labor Economics and Industrial Relations from Istanbul University in 2012, and an M.A. in Economic Policy from Istanbul University in 2014. He completed the Postgraduate Program Master of European Studies at University of Vienna in 2014, where he was an award holder of Jean Monnet Scholarship. He received his Ph.D. in European Union in Institute of Graduate Studies in Social Sciences from Istanbul University. During his doctoral studies, he was a doctoral fellow at the Institute of Political Science at Heidelberg University, Germany, in 2017, where he was awarded a scholarship by the DAAD (German Academic Exchange Service). He works as an assistant professor at the Department of Foreign Trade, Bandırma Onyedi Eylül University, Bandırma Vocational School, since 2020. His academic fields of interests include industrial economy, competition policy, and transport economy.

Nahit BEK graduated from Çanakkale Onsekiz Mart University, Faculty of Economics and Administrative Sciences, Department of Public Administration. In 2013, he completed his master's degree at Çanakkale Onsekiz Mart University, Department of Public Administration. In 2018, he completed his doctorate at the Department of Public Administration, Institute of Social Sciences, at the same university. Initially employed by various private sector and public institutions, Dr. Bek has been a faculty member at Çanakkale Onsekiz Mart University since 2020. His work focuses on examining the scope of environmental problems, urbanisation, and local governments.

Arzu ALVAN earned a bachelor's degree in business administration. Her master's and doctoral studies were in economics. An analysis of the relationship between monetary policy and inflation in Turkey after 1980 is the subject of her master's thesis. She was advised on her doctoral dissertation topic by Dr. Glenn Paul Jenkins, professor at Queens University and Eastern Mediterranean University. The topic of her doctoral dissertation is "Sources of Growth at Turkish Manufacturing Industry: A Two-Deflator Growth Accounting Approach." This is the first time that the two-deflator growth accounting method has been applied in Turkey. Several international publishing houses have printed her master's and doctoral theses as books. She specialises in economic growth and development, world economy and finance, political economy, and innovation and transformation economics. In these fields, Dr. Alvan has written on various academic subjects, most recently contributing a chapter included in the book, *Blockchain Driven Supply Chain Management (BCSCM): A Multidimensional Perspective*, published by Springer in 2023.

She is still a faculty member in the Department of Business Administration at Cyprus Science University. She is also Vice Dean of the Faculty of Economics, Administrative and Social Sciences, and Assistant Director of the Graduate Education and Research Institute.

Sina KISACIK is Assistant Professor at the International Relations Department of Cyprus Science University in Ozanköy-Kyrenia (Girne) in Turkish Republic of Northern Cyprus since October 2021. Before that, he worked as a lecturer in the Energy Law Programme of Department of Public Law at the Social Sciences Institute of Özyeğin University, İstanbul Sabahattin Zaim University, and İstanbul Gelişim University. Dr. Kısacık has co-authored four books and has authored/co-authored several book chapters and papers in various academic national and international journals in English and Turkish. His research interests include: Energy Geopolitics and Security, Turkish Foreign Policy, Russian Foreign Policy, Caucasia, Central Asia, Eurasia, and European Union. Sina Kısacık holds a Ph.D. in Political Science and International Relations from Yeditepe University, İstanbul, Türkiye; an M.A. in European Union Studies from Galatasaray University; and B.A. in International Relations from Bilgi University, İstanbul, Türkiye. He speaks English.

Pınar KOÇ is Associate Professor in the Department of Economics at Amasya University. She received her undergraduate degree in economics from Sakarya University-Turkey in 2010 and her Ph.D. degree in economics from Sakarya University-Turkey with a thesis titled "The Cost of Illness: Example of Cancer in Turkey" in 2017. Her fields are health economics, environmental economics, macroeconomics, and econometrics. She works on the effect of economic development on environmental degradation, cost of illness, labor markets, and energy markets, especially focusing on advanced economies and Turkey. Her articles and book chapters have been published both nationally and internationally. She has also presented her findings at international scientific meetings and proceedings.

İbrahim Tanju AKYOL is Associate Professor, Çanakkale Onsekiz Mart University, Çanakkale Vocational School of Social Sciences, Department of Local Governments, ibrahimakyol@comu.edu.tr. In 2009, he graduated from Gaziosmanpaşa University, Faculty of Economics and Administrative Sciences, Department of Public Administration. In 2012, he completed his master's degree at Gaziosmanpaşa University, Department of Public Administration. In 2012, he began work as a research assistant in Çanakkale Onsekiz Mart University Public Administration Department, Department of Urbanization and Environmental Problems. In 2018, he completed his doctorate at the Department of Public Administration, Institute of Social Sciences, at the same university. Dr. Akyol's primary fields of study are local governments, rural development, and governance.

Seher SULUK graduated from Zealand Business College in Denmark and continued her education in Turkey. After completing her bachelor's degree in economics at Hitit University, Suluk finished her master's degree; she then earned her Ph.D. at Nevşehir Hacı Bektaş Veli University in 2021. During this period, she also worked part-time in the Project Coordination Unit at Hitit University. Suluk focuses on macroeconomics, development, environmental issues, sustainability, etc. Danish is her native language and she speaks English at an advanced level.

Serdar ÖZTÜRK graduated from Ankara University Faculty of Political Sciences and completed his master's degree at Istanbul University in the Department of Economic Theory. In 2002, he earned his Ph.D. in the Department of Economics, also at Istanbul University. Öztürk is Head of the Department of Economics at the Faculty of Economics and Administrative Sciences at Nevşehir Hacı Bektaş Veli University.

Salih Ziya KUTLU completed his undergraduate degree at Dokuz Eylül University, Department of Public Administration. He earned his master's and his doctorate degrees at Çanakkale Onsekiz Mart University, Graduate School of Social Sciences, Public Administration Programme. He is an assistant professor at Çanakkale Onsekiz Mart University, Biga Faculty of Economics and Administrative Sciences, Department of Urbanization and Environmental Problems. Dr. Kutlu is interested in the fields of governance, urbanisation, and development agencies.

Tahir Anıl GÜNGÖRDÜ graduated from İzmir Dokuz Eylül University, Department of Public Administration, in 2017. He obtained his master's degree in 2020 from the same department. The subject of his master's thesis was the common arguments of the liberal opposition in the late Ottoman and early Turkish Republic periods. In this context, the family tree of the opposition in Turkey between 1918–1950 was also examined. He is currently a student at Dokuz Eylül University Public Administration Ph.D. Program, and has also been working as a research assistant at Çanakkale Onsekiz Mart University, Department of Public Administration, since 2018. His research interests include Turkish political life, election studies, party politics, and populism. The doctoral thesis he is working on focuses on populism in Turkey; however, he also has publications on topics such as climate change and the history of the Turkish revolution.

M. İnanç ÖZEKMEKÇİ is Associate Professor in Political Science and Public Administration Department, Erciyes University. Following his graduation from Istanbul University, Faculty of Politics, International Relations Program (B.A.), and from Boğaziçi University, Institute of Modern Turkish Politics, he received his Ph.D. in Political Science and International Relations at Istanbul University, Institute of Social Sciences. His research fields are Turkish politics, immigration and politics, oral history.

Alper ÇAKMAK is Professor and Lecturer in Foreign Languages Department, Preparatory English Program (ACUPEP), at Acıbadem University. He is a graduate of Boğaziçi University, completing degrees in Western Languages and Literatures Department, English Language and Literature Program (B.A.), and European Studies Program (M.A.). He received his Ph.D. in 2019 from Istanbul University, Institute of Social Sciences. Dr. Çakmak is the author of the monograph, *History, Discourse and Policy in Modern Turkey*, published by John Benjamins Company. He has also published several articles with a focus on critical discourse analysis and the storytelling techniques of authoritarian leaders.

Kendal DENİZ is a research assistant in the Department of Fiscal Law in the Department of Finance, Çanakkale Onsekiz Mart University. Primarily involved in the field of tax law and public procurement law in the digitalisation process, he also works as the relations coordinator of Public Institutions at the Financial Research Association. Deniz is an editor of the *Journal of Management Science*. Some of his key competencies are in the areas of discipline, teamwork, management skills, and law and finance.

Erdal EROĞLU works at the Public Administration Department, Çanakkale Onsekiz Mart University, Çanakkale, Turkey, and is also an associate professor in its Finance Department. He received his undergraduate education at Hacettepe University, Faculty of Economics and Administrative Sciences Department of Finance (2001–2007); he earned his master's degree at Ankara University, Political Sciences Faculty Finance Department (2007–2009), and Bursa Uludağ University, Faculty of Economics and Administrative Sciences, Department of Finance (2009–2020). He completed his doctorate at Bursa Uludağ University, Faculty of Economics and Administrative Sciences, Department of Finance. He started his academic career as a research assistant at Bursa Uludağ University, Faculty of Economics and Administrative Sciences Department of Finance, in 2009, and has worked at Çanakkale Onsekiz Mart University since 2018. Dr. Eroğlu has written articles on budget, financial planning, local governments, governance, green economy, and participation. In addition, he has many scientific projects on active participation, budget literacy, and sustainable green campus supported by ÇOMÜ Scientific Research Projects Unit and TÜBİTAK (1001; 1002; 2209). He continues his academic studies in the fields of active participation in local governments, green public procurement, and green economy.

İhsan Erdem KAYRAL graduated from the Department of Economics at Hacettepe University as the top student of the faculty and department. He received his M.Sc. and Ph.D. degrees in the field of Finance in the Department of Business Administration at the same university. Completing his studies, Associate Professor İhsan Erdem Kayral started to work in TÜBİTAK (Scientific and Technological Research Council of Turkey) as a Chief Expert in 2010 and he served there for over eight years. He worked in the Department of Economics and Department of International Trade and Business Administration at Konya Food and Agriculture University for approximately four years. Currently, Dr. Kayral works as a faculty member in the Department of International Trade and Finance at OSTIM Technical University. He has written several papers and book chapters about finance. Associate Professor Kayral has many awards in various fields. He also receives a National Tubitak Master's Degree Scholarship and Turkish Economics Association Achievement Grant at Bachelor's Degree Level.

Baki Riza BALCI obtained his undergraduate degree from Marmara University in 1990, majoring in English Business Administration. Subsequently, he pursued a master's program in English Accounting-Finance at the same university. His professional journey commenced as a research assistant at Sakarya University, where he actively contributed to the academic environment. Concurrently, he played a pivotal role in overseeing the Internship Center of the Sakarya Chamber of Certified Public Accountants. He gained experience as an accounting and finance manager across diverse sectors. His international exposure was acquired through his role as an accounting/finance manager for a Turkish company based in the United Arab Emirates. After his international work experience, he reentered the field of education, making valuable contributions by serving as an academician in the founding of private universities in Turkey, Kuwait, and Bahrain for an extended period. In 2007, he successfully completed his doctoral studies and achieved the rank of professor in 2023. Furthermore, he became a registered member of the İzmir Chamber of Certified Public Accountants in 2009. He possesses a strong proficiency in English and has intermediate-level knowledge of the German language.

Gülden POYRAZ received a B.A. in Economics in 2008 and an M.A. in Economic Theory in 2012, both from Atatürk University. She received her

Ph.D. in Economics from the Institute of Graduate Studies in Social Sciences at Istanbul University in 2019. During her doctoral studies, she worked as a research assistant at the Department of Economics, Faculty of Economics, Istanbul University between 2013–2019. She has worked as an assistant professor at the Department of Foreign Trade, Bandırma Onyedi Eylül University, Bandırma Vocational School, since 2019. Dr. Poyraz's academic fields of interest include macroeconomics, international finance, and monetary policy.